Exploding
THE
Myths
of

School Reform

David Hopkins

ACER Press and
Open University Press

First published 2013

Published in Australia and New Zealand by ACER Press, an imprint of
Australian Council *for* Educational Research Ltd
19 Prospect Hill Road, Camberwell, Victoria, 3124, Australia
www.acerpress.com.au
sales@acer.edu.au
ISBN: 9781742860985

Published in the United Kingdom by Open University Press
McGraw-Hill Education
McGraw-Hill House
Shoppenhangers Road, Maidenhead
Berkshire, England, SL6 2QL
www.openup.co.uk
enquiries@openup.co.uk
and Two Penn Plaza, New York, NY 10121-2289, USA
ISBN-13: 9780335263141
ISBN-10: 0335263143
eISBN: 9780335263158

Edited by Elisa Webb
Cover design, text design and typesetting by ACER Project Publishing
Indexed by Russell Brooks
Printed in Australia by BPA Print Group

Every effort has been made to acknowledge and contact copyright owners. However, should
any infringement have occurred, ACER tenders its apology and invites copyright owners to
contact ACER.

National Library of Australia Cataloguing-in-Publication data:
Author: Hopkins, David, 1949–
Title: Exploding the myths of school reform / David Hopkins.
ISBN: 9781742860985 (pbk.)
Notes: Includes bibliographical references and index.
Subjects: Education—Australia
                Educational change—Australia
                Educational innovations—Australia
                Education and state—Australia
Dewey Number: 370.994

A catalogue record of this book is available from the British Library

Library of Congress Cataloging-in-Publication Data
CIP data applied for

Exploding
THE
Myths
of
School Reform

This book is dedicated to Trish

Contents

List of figures

List of tables

About the author

David Hopkins is Professor Emeritus at the Institute of Education, University of London where until recently he held the inaugural HSBC iNet Chair in International Leadership. He is Director of Education for the Bright Tribe Trust, chairs the Board of the new charity 'Adventure Learning Schools', is a Trustee of Outward Bound and consults internationally on school reform.

David holds visiting professorships at the Catholic University of Santiago, the Chinese University of Hong Kong and the Universities of Cumbria, Edinburgh, Melbourne and Wales. Between 2002 and 2005 he served three Secretaries of State at the Department for Education and Skills in the United Kingdom as the Chief Adviser on school standards.

Previously, he was Chair of the Leicester City Partnership Board and Dean of the Faculty of Education at the University of Nottingham. Before that, he was a tutor at the University of Cambridge Institute of Education, a secondary school teacher and Outward Bound instructor.

David is also an International Mountain Guide who still climbs regularly in the Alps and Himalayas. His recent books include *Every school a great school*, *System leadership in practice* and *Powerful learning: a strategy for system reform*.

Acknowledgements

As I have noted on numerous occasions, I have been particularly blessed by having wonderful colleagues in the global invisible college who continue to sustain, enrich, educate and care for me. Among those who have been particularly helpful during the period covered by this book are: Marianne Alwyn, Sir Michael Barber, Jose Joaquin Brunner, Phil Butterfield, George Carter, Chris Chapman, Paul Clarke, Cristian Cox, Chris Day, Simon Day, Francoise Delannoy, Mike Dwan, David Egan, Dave Elliot (The Office Bar, Argentière, Mont Blanc), Neil Fisher, Kevin Flint, Sir Paul Grant, Jos Hagens, Rob Higham, Ben Levin, the late Steve Marshall, Sir Alasdair Macdonald, Peter Matthews, Barry McGaw, Tony McKay, Allan Moss, John Munro, Dave Reynolds, Parsi Sahlsberg, Pam Sammons, Andreas Schleicher, Iain Sedgman, John Stone, Sam Stringfield, Dahle Suggett, Mike Treadaway, Alan Walker and Vic Zbar.

I also owe a great debt of gratitude to my old teachers and mentors—Richard Elmore, Michael Fullan, David Hargreaves, Bruce Joyce and Matthew Miles—who I still continue to learn from, and to some newer ones such as John Hattie and Fenton Whelan.

I remain indebted and in awe of the work of those thousands of heads, principals and teachers with whom I have been privileged to work with in recent years. You are too many to name, but your work has inspired me and is reflected in the pages that follow.

Whatever their differences in background, I am certain that all of these colleagues would agree that although school and system reform is a serious business driven by moral purpose, it can also be fun and that we should retain a sense of whimsy. So I would suspect that they would agree with Frank Turner when he sings in *I still believe*:

> *I still believe that everyone*
> *Can find a song for every time they've lost, and every time they've won*
> *So just remember folks we're not just saving lives, we're saving souls and we're having fun.*[1]

Finally I would never have got to the starting point of this book, nor many other things, if it had not been for the personal and professional love and support of, to me, six very special people.

▸ My children, Jeroen, Jessica and Dylan, now all well into or beyond their university education, tell me that they think that they eventually understand what their father does! They do, however, remain bemused at my writing yet another book, when I could be out skiing, climbing or 'having fun'. Their gentle encouragement and affection means so much to me.
▸ Karen Carter, an old friend from the early days in the National College for School Leadership in England has taken on the unenviable job of preparing the manuscript for this book. Her experience, drafting and editing skills and attention to detail and deadlines have improved immeasurably the quality of what is here. My admiration and gratitude are boundless.
▸ Wayne Craig, Regional Director of the Northern Metropolitan Region, Victoria has been a brother-in-arms over the past five

years. Wayne is one of Australia's great educational leaders and the transformation (I do not use that word lightly) of the life chances of the young people in Melbourne's Northern Region is due to him. It has been a real privilege to work with and learn from him in generating many of the perspectives and approaches related to our *Powerful learning* reform strategy.

▶ It was Trish Franey, however, who has created the conditions to enable me to write this book. An outstanding educator and leader in her own right, she has provided an exemplary example of how the 'committed individual' lives a personal and professional life to the benefit of both. By so doing she has expanded my own vision of what is possible both personally and professionally—for that I am eternally grateful. This book is dedicated to her.

---

1   'I still Believe'. Words and music by Francis Edward Turner.
    © Universal Music Publishing Ltd.
    All rights reserved. International copyright secured. Reprinted with
    permission.

Introduction

'Plato demanded rhythm and harmony in education because ... they will inculcate 'the instinct of relationship' ... Experience stabilised and made definite by reflection, ever widening concepts, relationships and associations perceived, these are the old ideas from which, mainly, the new may be formed.'

AF Alington (1961, p. 3)

The title of this book—*Exploding the myths of school reform*—is deliberately provocative. It is underpinned by a conviction that the failure of so many educational reform efforts to impact on the learning and performance of students is due to misguided action based on a number of myths that remain prevalent in education to the present day. It is instructive here to be reminded of the danger of living by myths, as Jonathan Powell (2010, p. 5) did for me in this quotation from Machiavelli's *The Prince* that he cited in his recent book, *The new Machiavelli: how to wield power in the modern world*:

> *But since it is my object to write what shall be useful to whosoever understands it, it seems to me better to follow the real truth of*

things than an imaginary view of them. For many republics and princedoms have been imagined that were never known to exist in reality.

Powell's point is that too often in politics a conventional wisdom emerges that satisfies a particular group's version of the truth and quite rapidly enters the zeitgeist but, at best, it is a myth, a parody of the truth. If the myths are then acted on, the subsequent actions will fail. Sadly, myths abound in education; think for example of the debates around class size, teaching quality and the influence of external accountability. Education also seems to have developed its own mythical language that is open to individual nuance and interpretation, such as when Humpty Dumpty said in *Through the looking glass*, 'When *I* use a word ... it means just what I choose it to mean—neither more nor less' (Carroll 1998, p. 186). Sadly, in education, even that degree of individual certainty is not always apparent, but that is another matter. This book is about myth busting and introducing a heavy dose of truth and realism!

In light of this, the intention here is to present a comprehensive, accessible and strategic overview of what is currently known about school and system reform in the early 21st century. It reflects on the knowledge that we have acquired from research, policy and practice over the past three decades and presents it in a way that provides frameworks for action and practical strategies that educators can use to improve the life chances of the young people they are fortunate enough to serve.

Inevitably, having been active in this field for over 30 years, this book will draw on ideas and strategies developed previously. On reflection, this is no bad thing. During the writing of this book I visited David Hockney's latest exhibition—*A bigger picture*—at the Royal Academy of Arts, London. It was one of those life-changing events; I will never look at landscape in the same way again. As I pause from writing and look out from my window, I see either the gritstone edges of the Peak District or the Aiguilles of the Chamonix Valley. Now however, I see them in a deeper, more analytic and romantic way than ever before. I do hope that I will continue to do so. Hockney's imagination, boldness and energy have challenged me to re-imagine my world and understand it better. After viewing the exhibition, I read Martin Gayford's book *A bigger message: conversations with David Hockney* (2011). Hockney's concept of 'layering' as described by Gayford (2011, p. 143) gave me the courage to keep on re-visiting themes that I began writing about many years ago.

> *As these conversations continued, I began to grasp the point of Hockney's insistence on that word 'layers'. A painter is not simply adding more and more paint to a canvas or piece of paper; fresh thoughts and observations are going on, each adjusting the one that came before. The process of writing—reflecting on the subject, editing and adding to what we have written before—is essentially similar. Much human experience, when one comes to think about it, is a matter of layering. We understand the present by comparing it with the past—layer on layer—then we think about it afterwards, adding more and more layers. As we do, our angle of vision changes.*

This book completes my trilogy on school improvement, following on from *School improvement for real* published in 2001 and *Every school a great school* in 2007. It is also published as a companion volume to *Powerful learning* (Hopkins, Munro & Craig 2011). In keeping with the principle of layering, this book is different from these previous publications in four substantive ways.

First, the notion of the 'myth' immediately engages the attention of the reader and provides a clear structure around which the narrative of the book is developed. In identifying the myths and then exploding them, the book is able to present a realistic and increasingly precise and aligned approach to school reform that can enhance not just the academic achievement, but also the learning capability of all students.

Second, it contains reference to my more recent work in system level change in Australia, Wales and Bermuda; my engagement in international benchmarking studies and policy analysis through involvement with PISA; the development of system leadership and the connection with regional capacity building; the creation of whole-school designs as with Adventure Learning Schools; and a deeper focus on teaching and learning, particularly through the 'theory of action' and 'models of teaching' approaches.

Third, the book has a much stronger emphasis on implementation. As I note later, there is not much new in education. The problem of the past has not been a paucity of knowledge, but rather not utilising what we know, or not implementing it to a level of practice that influences student learning. This is a continuing theme. Sam Stringfield (pers. comm.) recently reminded me of Matthew Miles' edict, 'Pick an innovation and go at it HARD'. Implement with precision and energy, then study the effort, reflect on it, re-energise and refine. It seems to me as I look back at my time as a policy maker that we abandoned good initiatives such as Education Action Zones and Beacon Schools on the basis of political whim and as a consequence they were never fully implemented.

Fourth, the book is designed to provide a practical guide to action based on the best evidence and knowledge currently available. Although this has been a feature of much of my previous work, the effort to translate theory into action is taken to a deeper level here. The book does not, however, present a blueprint for successful school reform; rather, it presents a series of action frameworks and guidelines that both internal and external change agents can use to diagnose and design interventions appropriate for their own particular situations.

These heuristics are designed to help practitioners think strategically, rather than telling them what to do.

In the words of Plato cited above, I hope this book will distinctively present new ideas and ever-widening concepts on school reform, rooted in the current evidence base, and informed by the benefit of reflection and analysis of the lived experience of those actively involved in school improvement efforts. It is written for all those involved in school development and leadership roles and those in the wider community who are interested in finding ways to meet the current challenges of school and system reform. It has four principal audiences in mind:

1. **Education professionals such as teachers, principals, network leaders and regional directors** who are looking for an action framework to guide their work. The book contains a strategic framework for in-school and system reform based on an interpretation of the best research and thinking, but framed in a way that leads directly to intelligent and informed action. This knowledge will be equally helpful for both school improvement teams working directly within schools and system leaders who work both within and between schools in order to build local capacity.

2. **Policy makers** who are seeking a sustained argument for an approach to policy-making based on improved attainment and learning for all students, irrespective of their socioeconomic backgrounds. This embraces values such as social equity and a commitment to creating the conditions whereby all students can reach their potential; strategies that enhance the quality of teaching and leadership; and an approach that integrates all levels within the system.

3. **Students and researchers** who require a comprehensive review of current research and thinking about school improvement and

practical examples of educational reform within an action-oriented framework.

4. **Parents and members of the wider community** may also find the book useful. Particularly those who are interested in the key features of an effective school and who wish to understand it better, either to support their own children or to support the education system more generally.

In response to the varying interests of each of these audiences and in order to aid accessibility, each chapter is succinct, follows a clear pattern and is relatively short. I do not know whether I have managed to emulate Henry's advice in Tom Stoppard's play *The real thing*, when he talks in Act 2 about writing cricket bats, 'so that when we throw up an idea and give it a little knock, it might ... travel'. I may not have succeeded, but at least I have tried.

David Hopkins
Hope Valley, Peak District and Argentière, Mont Blanc
April 2012

READER GUIDE

'We must not be hampered by yesterday's myths in concentrating on today's needs.'

Harold S Geneen (1997)

By exploring and exploding the myths of school reform for the 21st century over the course of the next ten chapters, this book aims to enable readers to engage with perspectives from research, policy and practice. This is in order to examine emerging ideas about effective school and system improvement for the success of all learners. The book poses challenges and presents practical examples to support progress towards systemic solutions. In so doing, it aims to contribute to the current debate about the direction of school reform and the possibilities this presents for the future.

To achieve these purposes, the book has been conceived with a strong narrative drive enhanced by the concept of the 'myth'. The idea of narrative as an energiser of school and system reform recurs most prominently in the ten myths of school reform, providing the structure around which the argument of the book is developed. Each chapter addresses a different confusion that besets education policy and practice.

In identifying each of the myths and then exploding them, the book intends to provocatively engage the attention of the reader, while at the same time presenting a realistic and increasingly precise and aligned approach to school reform that can enhance not just the academic achievement, but also the learning capability of all students. To this end, the argument for school and system reform is outlined in cameo in the first chapter and then elaborated in a cumulative way in subsequent chapters. In each chapter you will find:

▶ an introduction that identifies the relevant myth, connects its particular themes with the broader argument of the book and outlines the key elements of the chapter
▶ four sections that articulate the essential themes that constitute the overall substance of the chapter—these themes are presented as frameworks or conceptual tools that provide the essential toolbox for the educational change agent
▶ case studies or exemplification of the practical application of the key ideas of the chapter within an Australian, United Kingdom and international school context
▶ guidelines for internal change agents and school improvement teams and external change agents such as system leaders and policy makers
▶ a concluding coda that summarises the argument exploding the myth introduced in the chapter and then makes a link to the following chapter.

Chapter 1

Moral purpose and system reform

The myth that achievement cannot be realised at scale for all students

In beginning to explode the myth that achievement cannot be realised at scale for all students, we go way back to the 1970s at the very start of the effective schools movement. It was then that the renowned educator Ron Edmonds, who became known as the movement's initial leader in the United States, posed the following challenge by way of three declarative statements (1979, p. 23):

1. *We can, whenever and wherever we choose, successfully teach all children whose schooling is of interest to us.*
2. *We already know more than we need to do that.*
3. *Whether or not we do it must finally depend on how we feel about the fact that we haven't so far.*

Although these declarations are now more than 30 years old, in several respects Edmonds' assertions ring true in underlining the aspiration that student achievement *can* be realised at scale if it is underpinned by a strong sense of moral purpose and will. A recent review of the research on school and system improvement (Hopkins, Harris et al. 2011), however, suggests that Edmonds was both right and wrong.

Edmonds' passion for school effectiveness and social justice was certainly right, as was his aspiration for the realisation of potential for all students. He was also correct when he intimated that this passion was not being realised in the current context. Where he was almost certainly wrong was his contention that enough was known back then to improve all schools 'whenever and wherever we choose'. As will be argued on the pages that follow, it is only now, in the light of sufficient contextually specific knowledge, that we are learning enough to be helpful to most professional educators in meeting the challenge of improvement posed by school reform in the 21st century.

Despite this, there are many examples in this book that disprove the myth and support Edmond's original aspiration. Here, briefly, are three that serve to make the point and will be described in more detail later:

▶ The *Twelve outstanding secondary schools* (Ofsted 2009a) that despite serving some of the most economically disadvantaged communities in England consistently have 80% of their 16-year-old students achieving five or more good passes at the GCSE examinations as compared with the national average of about 65%.
▶ The *National literacy strategy* in England that between 1997 and 2001 raised the performance of 11-year-olds from 63% reading at expected levels in 1997, to 75% in 2000.
▶ Evidence from the OECD international benchmarking study, PISA, that tracks the dramatic educational improvement of 15-year-old students in countries such as Canada, Norway, Poland and Switzerland. This is in terms both of excellence in student

performance and equity (i.e. reducing the variation within the whole student population).

Although this evidence is sufficient to disprove the myth, it should not make us feel complacent. This is because we have not as yet uniformly realised the desire that Edmonds expressed in the opening paragraph, despite having enough evidence from around the world to suggest that the aspiration is realisable, particularly in local contexts. The field of school and system improvement needs ever more applied research. The operational work of improving schools requires educators who understand and implement the results of that research and in so doing contribute to future research. Crucially, they must be able to contextualise the evidence base on successful school improvement and customise it to their own context for the benefit of all learners.

Not only do strategies need to be contextually specific and address the meanings that those involved in change give to them, they also need to be cast in the form of a narrative that connects a real and lived past to a desired, better and achievable future. The idea of narrative as the energiser of school and system reform recurs in different forms throughout this book. For as Mark Turner (1996, p. 12) says: 'Story, projection and parable do work for us; they make everyday life possible; they are the root of human thought'.

In light of this stated intent, the chapter that follows begins the story of exploding the myths of school reform for the 21st century by:

▶   reflecting on and defining the nature of moral purpose
▶   reviewing the knowledge base on school effectiveness and school improvement
▶   discussing current understandings around system improvement
▶   offering an initial framework for linking school and system reform efforts.

The nature of moral purpose

Moral purpose may be at the heart of successful school and system improvement, but we will not be able to realise this purpose without powerful and increasingly specified strategies and tools to allow us to deal with the challenges presented by globalisation, as well as the increasingly turbulent and complex communities we serve. This is perhaps the key message of the book—that moral purpose and strategic action are opposite sides of the same coin. Neither is sufficient by itself: we realise our moral purpose through strategic action. As much of this book is about action, it is worth spending a little time at the outset in reflecting on the nature of moral purpose.

As we see in the words of Plato and Aristotle below, the concern for moral purpose has a long and honourable tradition, both in terms of education and more broadly in considering aspirations for society as a whole:

> *The direction in which education starts a man will determine his future in life ... If a man neglects education he walks lame to the end of his life ... No man should bring children into the world that is unwilling to persevere to the end in their nature and education. (Plato)*

> *Moral excellence comes about as a result of habit ... We become just by doing just acts, temperate by doing temperate acts, brave by doing brave acts ... The moral virtues, then, are produced in us neither by nature nor against nature. Nature, indeed, prepares in us the ground for their reception, but their complete formation is the product of habit. (Aristotle)*

A more contemporary perspective on the nature of moral purpose and its meaning for school leaders in the 21st century is given by education practitioners Andy Brown and Darren Holmes (2004, p. 22):

> *The notion of moral purpose has become part of our leadership lexicon. We all recognise that it is a central element of who we are and what we stand for as school leaders. We say it drives our work and gets us through the dark days when things look vulnerable and outcomes are uncertain. But moral purpose is not value free and ultimately it goes back to the fundamental aims of what we want to achieve through our work.*

It is well established that any authentic approach to school improvement is based on a clear and consistent set of values. Virtually every high-performing school has a moral purpose that they express in different ways—this often reflects values such as the following.

▶ Every student has the right to be helped to reach his or her potential.

▶ Intelligence is not a finite concept—the harder you work the smarter you get.

▶ Knowledge, learning skills and aptitudes, especially curiosity, are equally important and these are what we should teach in our schools.

▶ Teachers and schools can and do make a difference—all schools can and should be good, and most should be on a journey to greatness.

▶ Students can and do learn from each other; that is why are schools are open to all, inclusive and celebrate diversity.

▶ Poverty is no excuse for school failure, only an argument for additional support.

It was Michael Fullan (2005, p. 4) who has recently popularised the concept of moral purpose in school reform and defined it as follows:

1. A commitment to raising the bar and closing the gap of student achievement.
2. Treating people with respect—which is not to say low expectations.
3. An orientation to improving the environment, including other schools in the local authority.

It is worth elaborating a little of this definition, particularly Fullan's first and third points. In terms of student achievement, we stress that the essence of moral purpose is enabling students to reach their potential—whatever that may be. But even this aspiration is too abstract: there is a need to be as concrete and as operational as possible when defining moral purpose. For example, we found in government that it was far better to express aspirations for performance not as percentages but in actual numbers of students. Half a million students had their life chances positively changed during the early years of the literacy strategy in England. Similarly, but at the other end of the spectrum, Glenn Proctor, Principal of Hume Central Secondary College in Melbourne, whom we shall meet later in this book, expresses his moral purpose as 'two in one'. What he means by this is that because his students come into the school so far behind state expectations, he and his staff have to create a learning environment whereby all students can make two years progress in one. I visited Hume Central just before reading the proofs of this book and Glenn told me that recently, for the first time, student progress had reached the 2 in 1! Glenn's is a robust moral purpose both compelling and simply communicated.

In relation to the third point, Fullan has also argued that for the moral imperative in education to be fit-for-purpose for the 21st century, it needs to transcend the boundaries of the individual school and become both an organisational and a systemic necessity. He comments (Fullan 2003, p. 47) that:

the moral imperative will never amount to much unless school leaders take it on the road ... Sticking to one's neck of the woods guarantees that the moral imperative will never exist in more than a very small percentage of schools.

One could go even further than that. Recently, many nations, both developing and developed, have engaged in massive reform efforts to better their education systems and practices. Generally speaking, all these efforts are intended to ensure that schooling is more effective and efficient in preparing and educating all citizens for the rapidly emerging global economy (Hopkins 2008, p. 4).

It is the pervasiveness of the commitment to globalisation that provides a common language and purpose for educational reform. In short, this is the moral purpose of ensuring that every student, irrespective of their background, has the opportunity and is actively encouraged to reach their potential and to understand the world in which they live and are helping to create (Hopkins 2008, p. 5).

Bringing the discussion of globalisation down to the level of the individual is critical. Moral purpose in education is not just about achieving academic success. It is also about the underlying skills, dispositions and confidence that result in such success and sustain it. In our recent work with the Adventure Learning Schools charity in the UK (Hopkins 2012), we have been using the term 'life script' to describe this broader aspiration of moral purpose. We all have life scripts; some of us choose to develop them and others are forced to do so. Life scripts evolve as the individual confronts direct experience and adapts and assimilates it with their self. As Mahatma Gandhi said, 'You must be the change you wish to see in the world'.

Stewart and Joines (1987, p. 100) define the life script in a similar way:

A [life] script is a life plan, directed to a reward. It is decisional and responsive. It is decided upon in childhood in response to perceptions of the world and as a means of living with and making sense of the world. A script is reinforced by parents or other influential people and/or experiences and is for the most part, outside awareness. It is how we navigate and what we look for.

With its roots in psychology, the concept of the life script is credited to the forefather of transactional analysis theory, Eric Berne (1961, 1964). In his seminal work—*What do you say after you say hello? The psychology of human destiny* (1973)—Berne's contention was that in early childhood each person writes the script that will govern the general course of their lives. It is similar to what the humanistic psychologist Carl Rogers (1977) called 'personal power'. Despite the fact that psychologists suggest that one's life script is mostly complete by the ages of five, six or seven—'Fortunately, scripts can be changed, since they are not inborn, but learned' (Dusay 1976, p. 311). As early enthusiasts of script analysis have claimed, 'most people with a loser's script can change to a winner's script' (Abell 1977, p. 99), although recent practitioners suggest that this is much more often 'a matter of learning to exercise new choices' (Stewart & Joines 1987, p. 269).

Almost by definition we would expect professional educators to have positive life scripts, otherwise they would not have developed the skills and personal competencies to become educators in the first place. Sadly, for whatever reason, not all the students who enter our schools, or indeed their parents or carers, have such positive life scripts, and on occasion not all of our members of staff do either.

It is an expression of moral purpose at a deep level when teachers and school leaders acknowledge the influence they can exert in formulating, challenging and changing the life scripts of the young people in their care. Life scripts evolve as the individual confronts direct experiences, enjoys consequent success and adapts and assimilates such behaviours into their 'self', creating a positive cycle of development. As we shall see in Chapters Three, Four and Five there are whole-school designs, as well as specific approaches to learning and teaching, that have the ability to develop life scripts in the most immediate way. We will also see in the discussion on leadership for learning in Chapter Eight that one aspect of the contemporary role is to create situations where others can develop their own life scripts.

It should be clear by now that moral purpose, in the sense that the term is being used here, has great depth to it. Although it is fundamentally about enabling our students to reach their potential, it is not just about academic success and exam results. It is also about acquiring those skills and dispositions that enable individuals to become effective global citizens and this, in turn, is sustained and underpinned by nurturing a positive life script. On reflection, perhaps the use of the word 'enabling' is too imprecise. What we do as educators is to create reliable conditions and practices in schools, whereby the realisation of moral purpose becomes the norm. The beginnings of this story are unfolded in the subsequent sections of this chapter.

School improvement

In the summer of 1979, I read a book that changed the course of my professional life. Prior to then—and remember, this was the year that Ron Edmonds issued his challenge—the ability of schools to make a difference to student learning was widely doubted. Michael Rutter and his colleagues (1979), however, with the publication of *Fifteen thousand hours*, demonstrated unequivocally that schools with similar intakes had widely contrasting effects on student performance. More importantly, the factors that accounted for that difference were largely internal and open to modification by the school staff themselves. So at last, research evidence was emerging on the differential effectiveness of schools that gave an impetus and direction to those who, like myself, were beginning to work in the field of school improvement.

We now know far more about what constitutes an effective school than we did 30 years ago and there is now a vast amount of evidence to support the common-sense notion that individual schools can make a significant difference to student progress. The school effects research, besides articulating the characteristics of effective schools, has without doubt demonstrated that given the right conditions *all* students can learn. The research knowledge about the characteristics of those schools and classrooms, as Peter Mortimore (1991, p. 216) said, 'whose pupils progress further than might be expected from considerations of intake', is among the most robust there is in the quest for educational reform.

Even as late as the 1960s and 1970s, however, well-known studies and 'blue-riband' reports, many of which influenced national policy, looked to factors other than the school as predictors of a student's academic performance. The family, in particular, was regarded as being far more important. The Coleman (1966) study in the United States of America and the Plowden (1967) report in Britain were highly influential both publicly and politically, and both strongly maintained that the home influence outweighed that of the school (Hopkins 2001). Other more controversial views were also advanced. A few reasserted the claim that hereditary influences were pre-eminent, while some claimed that educational inequalities were rooted in the basic subcultures and social biases of our economy. The one thing that these widely divergent views had in common was that they all vastly underestimated the influence of the school on pupil progress.

By the late 1970s though, the prevailing view began to change in the face of an emerging consensus that schools *do* make a difference. The effective schools described in *Fifteen thousand hours* were characterised by factors as varied as 'the degree of academic emphasis, teacher actions in lessons, the availability of incentives and rewards, good conditions for pupils, and the extent to which children are able to take responsibility' (p. 178). It was this constellation of factors that Rutter and his colleagues later referred to as the school's 'ethos'. They further claimed (Rutter et al. 1979, p. 179) that:

> *the cumulative effect of these various social factors was considerably greater than the effect of any of the individual factors on their own. The implication is that the individual actions or measures may combine to create a particular ethos, or set of values, attitudes and behaviours which will become characteristic of the school as a whole.*

By and large, subsequent research supported these findings. There is broad agreement (see, for example, Purkey & Smith 1983) that the following eight criteria are representative of the 'organisational factors' that characterise effective schools:

1. curriculum-focused school leadership
2. supportive climate within the school
3. emphasis on curriculum and teaching
4. clear goals and high expectations for students
5. a system for monitoring performance and achievement
6. ongoing staff development and in-service
7. parental involvement and support
8. local authority and external support.

As expressed in previous work (Hopkins 1990), these factors do not, however, address the dynamics of schools as organisations. There appear to be four additional factors that infuse some meaning and life into the process of improvement within the school. These so-called 'process factors' provide the means of achieving the organisational factors; they lubricate the system and 'fuel the dynamics of interaction', described by Fullan (1985, p. 400) as follows:

1. *A feel for the process of leadership; this is difficult to characterize because the complexity of factors involved tends to deny rational planning. A useful analogy would be that schools are to be sailed rather than driven.*
2. *A guiding value system; this refers to a consensus on high expectations, explicit goals, clear rules, and a genuine caring about individuals, etc.*
3. *Intense interaction and communication; this refers to simultaneous support and pressure at both horizontal and vertical levels within the school.*
4. *Collaborative planning and implementation; this needs to occur both within the school and externally, particularly in the local education authority.*

One should not get too excited, however, over the outcomes of the school effects research, even those as authoritative as the review by Teddlie and Reynolds (2000)—the reason being that descriptions of the characteristics of effective schools are only one half of the story. It is vitally important to know the 'what', but without knowing the 'how', that knowledge is merely academic and practically redundant. During the 1980s, while the research knowledge on school effectiveness was being refined, more attention was being given to the development of strategies for school improvement that were designed to enhance the effectiveness of schools.

In 2001, David Reynolds and I (Hopkins & Reynolds 2001) suggested that during its relatively short history, school improvement as an approach to educational change had passed through 'three ages'.

▶ Many of the 'first age' of school improvement initiatives during the 1980s focused on individual strategies such as school self-evaluation and leadership training that were loosely connected to student learning and struggled to impact upon classroom practice.

▶ The catalyst for a 'second age' was the merger of the two traditions of school effectiveness research and school improvement practice. This resulted in the development of tools such as 'value added' measures of school performance and approaches to staff development based on partnership teaching that are directly applicable in the emerging new policy contexts (Joyce & Showers 2002).

▶ The key characteristic of 'third age' approaches to school improvement is the dual focus on 'how to accelerate the progress and achievement of students, as well as establishing effective management practices within the school' (Hopkins 2000, p. 149).

As we shall see in Chapter Three, we now have increasing numbers of examples of what are described above as 'third age' approaches to school improvement, whereby schools have broken the association between poverty and achievement. The experience of these third age approaches laid the foundations of an 'integrated model of school improvement' that provides a guide to strategic action (Hopkins 2001). As shown in Figure 1.1, the model 'expresses the context and process of school improvement through the image of a series of concentric rings' (Department of Education and Early Childhood Development [DEECD] 2011, p. 8). Although described briefly here, the model and its constituent elements are further developed and described, as well as being applied to different contexts, in subsequent

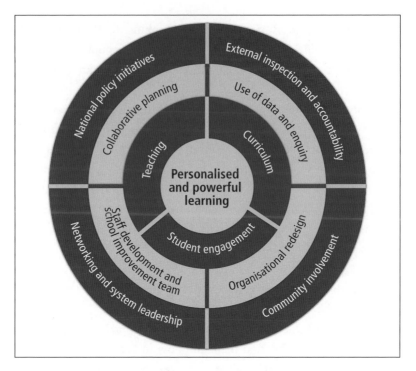

Figure 1.1 An integrated school improvement model

chapters. By way of introduction, however, it is important to note that neither the model nor the integrated approaches suggested within it should be followed slavishly; they are presented as action frameworks to help education practitioners and school leaders to think strategically about school improvement.

At the centre of the model, *personalised and powerful learning* is recognised as being at the heart of the school's moral purpose. This represents the goal that every student will reach their potential and that they acquire a range of knowledge, skills and dispositions that will equip them, not just to meet the challenges of the 21st century, but to help shape it. The next ring is comprised of those essential ingredients of effective *classroom practice* that focus on the instructional core so necessary for personalised learning. This is the teacher's repertoire of teaching and learning strategies, the organisation of curriculum in terms of frameworks and standards and the ways in which students are involved in their learning (NMR 2009). Such classroom practice is found in schools that have *organisational capacity* supportive of high levels of teaching and learning—these key elements are found in the next ring (DEECD 2011). In today's educational systems it is recognised that 'no school is an island'. Schools exist within a broader *systemic context*, represented in the outer ring of the diagram.

This model of school improvement is more than the sum of its parts. There are four implications for viewing the process of school improvement in this way:

1. The first is that 'when all the circles are pulling in the same direction, then the aspirations of school improvement have much more chance of success. All need to exist in a reciprocal relationship if student attainment is to be enhanced' (DEECD 2011, p. 11).

2. The second is that this way of working places great demands on school leadership. It requires the courage to collaborate; the abandonment of activities that do not best serve student achievement; the creation of a culture of mutual interdependence and trust; and being open to evidence of what works in school reform.

3. The third is that schools need to develop a deep appreciation of their current performance along with their particular strengths and weaknesses (with external assistance as required) to determine where in the model to focus their energies and hence where their improvement journey needs to start.

4. The fourth relates to the crucial issue of where the initiative for improvement comes from. Most school reform assumes that change comes from the 'outside–in'. In those schools that have made the jump from 'good to great' the linear logic of policy implementation has been inverted—they start from the centre of

the circle and move outwards; they survey the range of policy initiatives confronting the school to see which they can most usefully mould to their own improvement plans. Paradoxically, it is these schools that appear to be the most effective at interpreting the centralised reform agenda. This is what we call later working from the 'inside–out' (DEECD 2011).

As we shall see in the following section, however, successful reform is neither singularly system-led nor led by individual schools—it is best achieved by one supporting the other in an actively interdependent, mutually beneficial relationship.

System improvement
Before describing the interaction between school and system reform it is instructive to look, albeit briefly, at what we know about the early attempts at system reform.

> *In his recent chapter in* Change wars, *Sir Michael Barber (2009) reminds us that it was the school effectiveness research in the 1980s that gave [us] increasingly well-defined portraits of the effective school that led in the 1990s to increasing knowledge of school improvement (i.e. how to achieve effectiveness). In the same way, we have in the last decade begun to learn far more about the features of an effective educational system, but are now only beginning to understand the dynamics of improvement at system level. (DEECD 2011, p. 2)*

What is needed is a 'grand theory' of system change in education that results in relatively predictable increases in student learning and achievement over time—this book is a modest contribution to that worthwhile and necessary goal.

The equivalent of the school effectiveness research at the system level has been provided during the last decade or so by the advent of international benchmarking studies. Probably the best known and most influential of these is the Organisation for Economic Co-operation and Development's (OECD) Programme for International Student Assessment (PISA). Since 2000 when the OECD launched PISA, they have been monitoring learning outcomes in the principal industrialised countries on a regular basis. (DEECD 2011, p. 2)

As Andreas Schleicher (2009, p. 100) who leads PISA for the OECD recently said, 'In the dark, all institutions and education systems look the same. It is comparative benchmarking that sheds light on the differences on which reform efforts can then capitalize.' As Schleicher admits, although international benchmarks alone cannot identify cause and effect relationships between inputs, processes and educational outcomes, they can highlight those key features where education systems show similarities and differences, and relate them to student performance on a variety of outcome measures.

As described in *Powerful learning* (Hopkins, Munro et al. 2011), we have learnt a great deal about high-performing educational systems over the past ten years. This is not only from PISA, but also from secondary analyses such as Fenton Whelan's (2009) *Lessons learned: how good policies produce better schools* and the McKinsey studies (Barber & Mourshed 2007; Mourshed, Chijioke & Barber 2010) *How the world's best performing school systems come out on top* and *How the world's most improved school systems keep getting better*. Despite learning more about the features of high-performing educational systems, up until recently,

successful efforts at systemic improvement have remained elusive. As we shall see in a little more detail later, there have been ambitious attempts to reform whole systems, but these have tended to be: i) oppressive and resulted in considerable alienation, such as some of the state-wide reforms in the USA; ii) well designed and centrally driven, but with impact stalling after early success, as with the literacy reforms in England; or iii) sustained, but usually due to factors outside the immediate control of educators and policy makers, such as in Finland. (Hopkins, Harris et al. 2011, p. 1)

In his paper, 'Large scale reform comes of age' (2009b), Michael Fullan reviewed the evidence on the success of large-scale improvement efforts over the past dozen years or so. He identifies three phases that such reform efforts have passed through with increasing effectiveness. The first is the pre-1997 period where the pressure for reform was mounting. Throughout the 1960s and 1970s there were examples of exemplary curriculum innovation, but none produced success at scale. Similarly in the 1980s and 1990s, although the impact of the international research on school improvement sponsored by the OECD and national strategies for reform such as the introduction of national curricula and inspection regimes spoke of ambition at scale, impact still remained serendipitous.

In the second period—1997 to 2002—there was evidence in some cases of whole-system reform in which progress in student achievement was clear. Let us look briefly at the three examples referred to earlier and their limitations.

▶ In the first example taken from the USA, Leithwood, Jantzi and Mascall (1999) reviewed the impact of a number of performance-based approaches to large-scale reform. Although there was some initial impact on test scores, this was not sustained over time. The fact that these reform strategies neglected to focus on instruction and capacity building must have contributed to their inability to impact positively on student achievement.

▶ In the second example from England, it is recognised that in 1997 the government was the first in the world to use an explicit theory of large-scale change as a basis for bringing about system reform (Barber 2008). The National Literacy and Numeracy Strategies were designed to improve the achievement of 11-year-olds in all 24 000 English primary schools. The percentage of 11-year-olds achieving nationally expected standards increased from 63% in 1997 to 75% in 2002 in literacy, and in numeracy the increase was from 62% to 73%. However, these achievements were not sustained post-2002 and subsequent success was the consequence of a different strategic approach.

▶ Finland, now recognised as one of the top-performing school systems in the world, is the third example. Hargreaves, Halász and Pont (2007) argue in their OECD review that between 1997 and 2002, Finland demonstrated that a medium-sized country (of five million people) could turn itself around through a combination of vision and society-wide commitment. It could also be argued, however, that in Finland much of their success was due to factors outside the control of the education sector, such as the degree of homogeneity in social structures and the considerable intellectual capital already existing in the country.

Fullan's third phase is characterised by the notion that 'Large-scale reform comes of age: 2003—to present'. In reflecting on this era of more successful reform efforts, he comments (2009b, p. 107):

Coming of age does not mean that one has matured, but that people are definitely and seriously in the game. As this happens the work becomes more analytical as well as action-oriented.

There is more convergence, but not consensus; debates are more about how to realize system reform, not so much what it is.

Before proposing, in the following section, a framework for thinking about how to 'realise system reform', it is important to emphasise the point made earlier about the contribution made by PISA to our understanding of the dynamics of educational improvement at scale. We will return to this point in more detail in Chapter Nine, but for the moment, it is important to remind ourselves of two issues.

The first is that as PISA has now been administered on four occasions (the fifth PISA round will be published in 2013) we have significant real-time information as to how national performance changes (or not) over time. As shown in Figure 1.2, the performance of some countries has remained stable—Finland, for example, has consistently scored very well—while the trajectories of others have moved both up and down. What explains the dramatic movement of

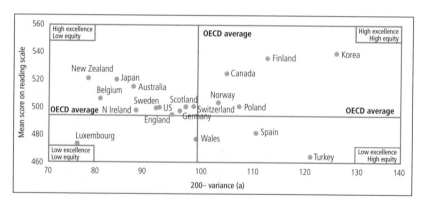

Figure 1.2 High excellence, high equity: raising the bar and narrowing the gap (Based on data from OECD 2011b)

(a) Total variance (between and within schools) is expressed as a percentage of the average variance in student performance across OECD countries. The OECD average is 101. For this chart, the variance is displayed as 200– variance, i.e. a country with a high relative variance of 120 will appear on this chart as 80 to the left of the chart.

Poland say, from the bottom right-hand segment to the top-left in a little over six years, or the equally dramatic fall of my own country of Wales from the top-left segment to the ignominy of the bottom-right? There are good explanatory reasons for both of these movements related to the policy choices made by respective national governments. The details need not concern us here, as they will be picked up in Chapter Nine—the point is that we are getting to a stage where we can predict cause and effect in system change related to the policy levers that governments, for whatever reasons, choose to select.

The second issue is also illustrated in Figure 1.2. Here the OECD compares national performance against two criteria. The first is 'excellence' represented on the vertical axis by mean performance on PISA scores, in this instance for reading; the second is 'equity' represented by the range of the distribution of scores in the national sample. If there is a wide distribution, that is, a long tail of underachievement, then the country is deemed low equity. Where the range is narrow, that is, all students perform at roughly the same standard, the country is regarded as high equity. When the OECD average for both dimensions is inserted (as illustrated in the diagram above), it enables a two-by-two matrix to be constructed. So in the high excellence/high equity segment is Finland and now Canada, with both Australia and England remaining in the high excellence/low equity segment. The advantage of this analysis is that it gives an indication not just of academic performance, but also of how far aims of social justice and moral purpose have been achieved.

When I became responsible for school standards during the Blair government in late 2001, Estelle Morris, the Secretary of State and David Miliband, the Minister of State for Schools, expressed their moral purpose for the English secondary school system in terms of moving from 'high excellence/low equity' to 'high excellence/high equity'. Sadly this was never quite achieved—the reasons for which will be discussed later in this book. It is however, salutary to note that

Ontario, Canada had similar aspirations underpinned by the same moral purpose, brilliantly and consistently articulated by the Premier Dalton Mcguinty, which *were* realised in the last PISA round. Again, the reasons for this will be discussed later; the point here though, is that both excellence and equity are achievable and within realistic time frames.

Linking school and system improvement

In reflecting on how to realise system reform, I suggested in my book *Every school a great school* (Hopkins 2007) that the key to managing system reform is by strategically re-balancing 'top-down' and 'bottom-up' change over time (DEECD 2011, p. 3). This view is gaining some support. For example, in the current reform context, Barber (2009) stresses the need for system leadership along with capacity building. Hargreaves and Shirley (2009) argue for a 'fourth way of change' that consists of combining top-down 'national vision, government steering and support' with bottom-up 'professional involvement' and 'public engagement', all for the purpose of promoting 'learning and results'.

I began to develop these ideas after assuming responsibility from Michael Barber for the National Literacy and Numeracy Strategies in England. The positive influence of these strategies on student performance described earlier attracted worldwide attention. What is significant about this experiment in large-scale reform is that following an initially impressive increase in student performance over the first three years, it remained relatively static for the next three years, and only thereafter was further progress made. This is a trend that has been noted in virtually every large-scale reform initiative. What usually happens is that early success is followed by a levelling off in progress and a subsequent lack of commitment to the program of reform (Hopkins 2009b, p. 204). I would argue that the uplift in standards in 2004 and 2005 following a four-year plateau was because in 2003 the National Literacy and Numeracy Strategies merged into a National Primary Strategy as a consequence of the White Paper, *Excellence and enjoyment* (Department for Education and Skills [DfES] 2003), the design of which was underpinned by many of the principles advocated in this book.

In hindsight, more thought should have been given at the start of the reform process as to how to build capacity for sustained improvement and how to manage the transition between national prescription and schools leading reform. In other words, in the terms described in the following chapter, how over time to effectively adjust the balance between 'outside–in' and 'inside–out' change. If this had been built into the overall strategy at the outset, as in the case of Ontario, Canada, then I believe that the plateau effect, the perverse effects of top-down change and loss of momentum would all have been minimised.

The argument goes something like this:

> *Most agree that when standards are too low and too varied, some form of direct state intervention is necessary and the impact of this top-down approach is usually to raise standards, but only in the short term. But when progress inevitably plateaus—while a bit more might be squeezed out in some schools, and perhaps a lot in underperforming schools—one must question whether this is still the recipe for sustained reform. There is a growing recognition that to ensure that every student reaches their potential, schools need to lead the next phase of reform. The implication is that a transition is needed from an era of prescription to an era of professionalism, in which the balance between national prescription and schools leading reform will change significantly.*
>
> *(DEECD 2011, p. 3)*

Achieving this shift is not straightforward. It takes capacity to build capacity, and if there is insufficient capacity to begin with, it is folly to announce that a move to professionalism provides the basis of a new approach (Fullan 2004a). 'The key question is "How do we get there?" We cannot simply move from one [phase] to the other without self-consciously building professional capacity throughout the system' (Hopkins 2005, p. 5). It is this progression that is illustrated in Figure 1.3.

It is worth taking a little more time unpacking the thinking underlying the diagram. Five further points in particular need to be made.

The first is to emphasise that this is not an argument against top-down change. Neither top-down nor bottom-up change work when conducted in isolation; they have to be in balance, in a creative tension. At any one time, the balance between the two will of course depend on context. The state reforms in the USA referred to previously employed a virtually exclusive top-down approach and failed to sustain improvement, simply because they did not adapt the strategy over time.

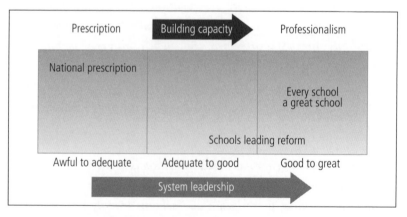

Figure 1.3 Towards large-scale sustainable reform
(Adapted from Hopkins 2007, p. 45)

Secondly, it must be realised that in England in 1997, for example, it was clear that more central direction was needed initially. This reflects the initial emphasis on national prescription as seen in the left-hand segment of the diagram above. Over time, the policy agenda and school practice moved towards the right-hand side of the diagram, which accounts for the subsequent rise in standards, following the period of levelling off.

Third, there is no suggestion that one always has to start from the left-hand side of the diagram and move in some sort of uniform way to the right. Some systems, Finland for example, may well start from the middle and then move into the right-hand segment.

Fourth, as discussed in detail in Chapter Nine, we are now gaining far more specific knowledge about what combination of strategies are needed to move a school and a system from 'awful to adequate', 'adequate to go od' and 'good to great'. Those countries and schools that utilise this knowledge strategically are able to make significant progress quite rapidly and seem to have solved the 'change–no change' conundrum described in Chapter Two as so prevalent in education.

Finally, as discussed in *Approaches to system leadership* (Pont & Hopkins 2008, p. 258), it should be no surprise to realise that the right-hand segment is relatively unknown territory. It implies horizontal and lateral ways of working with assumptions and governance arrangements very different from what we know now. The main difficulty in imagining this landscape is that the thinking of most people is constrained by their experiences within the power structure and norms of the left-hand segment of the diagram. We find some glimpses of this new landscape in Chapter Ten.

It needs to be reiterated that the transition from prescription to professionalism is not easy to achieve. In order to move from one to the other, strategies are required that not only continue to raise standards, but also develop social, intellectual and organisational capital (Hopkins, Harris et al. 2011, p. 14). Building capacity demands that we replace numerous central initiatives with a national consensus on a limited number of educational trends. There are four drivers— *personalised learning, professionalised teaching, networks and collaboration* and *intelligent accountability*—that provide the core strategy for systemic improvement. As we shall see in Chapters Three through Seven, these drivers also provide us with the background canvas onto which school and system reform can be sketched. For the moment, it is sufficient to acknowledge that although system reform is complex, it *is* doable.

Coda

The purpose of this chapter has been to explode the myth that high levels of student achievement cannot be achieved at scale and to paint the broad picture of school and system reform. Although it will take the whole book to satisfactorily explode this myth, a good start has been made here. In particular, evidence has been presented of schools and systems that have made the critical difference and frameworks have been proposed for strategic action. It has been argued that achievement at scale is only possible when the system works as such, when all the various moving parts are linked and pull together. The list below is an inventory of these moving parts.

Based on the best of global experience, these are the key ingredients of school and system reform. Beyond this, what recipes can be used to mix the ingredients for specific contexts is the concern of the discussion in the chapters that follow. The misinterpretation of these ideas has resulted in the proliferation of the myths about school and system reform that it is the duty of this book to explode. Building on previous work (DEECD 2011; Hopkins, Munro et al. 2011), these are the principles that characterise reform efforts in both high-performing educational schools and systems. Each principle has a high degree of operational practicality.

1. Ensuring that the achievement and learning of students expressed as **moral purpose** is at the centre of all that teachers do. This requires a focus on those strategies that have a track record of accelerating student achievement such as building student learning capability, personalising learning and the curriculum, assessment for learning and giving students a voice in their own learning.

2. As a consequence, it is the enhancement of the **quality of teaching**, rather than structural change that needs to be the central theme of any improvement strategy. The quality of teaching is necessarily related to system goals and targeted support that are likely to have a heavy emphasis in the first instance on the teaching of literacy and numeracy and the development of curiosity.

3. High levels of student learning and achievement will be partially achieved by **teacher selection policies** that ensure that only the very best people become educators and educational leaders. Almost by definition, this creates a positive school work culture and high levels of professional practice.

4. The development of this **professional practice** occurs within a system context where there is increasing clarity on the standards implied by the goals set, and the generation of the most appropriate curriculum and teaching strategies necessary to achieve those standards.

5. Putting in place ongoing and sustained **professional learning opportunities** that develop a common 'practice' of teaching and learning through blending theory, evidence and action through collaborative forms of enquiry.

6. To enable this, procedures are needed to provide **formative, ongoing and transparent data** (both assessment data and inspection evidence) on the performance of the student, school and system that facilitate improvements in learning and teaching.

7. Student and school performance is enhanced by teachers and leaders **'going deeper' and intervening early**, following diagnosis

that reflects a range of differential strategies based on performance, with targets being set that are related to implementation.

8. The development of professional practice, utilisation of data and early intervention using differential strategies takes place in schools where the **leadership** has:
   ▶ very high levels of expectation for both teachers and students
   ▶ an unrelenting focus on the quality of learning and teaching
   ▶ created structures that ensure an orderly learning environment and that empower and generate professional responsibility and accountability
   ▶ developed a work culture that takes pride in sharing excellence and has a high degree of trust and reciprocity
   ▶ when appropriate, supported leadership development across a locality.

9. **Inequities in student performance** are addressed through:
   ▶ good early education
   ▶ direct classroom support for those falling behind
   ▶ high levels of targeted resourcing
   ▶ utilising differential strategies at the school level.

10. Finally, **system level structures** are established that reflect the processes just described, linking together the various levels of the system through to the school and classroom, developing capacity by balancing professional autonomy and accountability and promoting disciplined innovation as a consequence of networking. These activities combine to produce a work culture that has at its core strong pressure to improve, takes seriously its responsibility to act on and change context and that embodies a commitment to focus, flexibility and collaboration.

Chapter 2

Strategies for improvement at the local level

The myth of school autonomy and the reality of change

Having set the scene in the previous chapter, we need now to sketch out in more detail the architecture of school and system reform. The myth that is particularly relevant to this chapter relates to autonomy. The myth of autonomy is currently centrestage given the increasing prevalence of 'right of centre' governments to embrace the trend towards the devolution of school management. The rhetoric is that if we let schools be free—release them from bureaucratic control and encourage independence, self-governance and making one's own decisions—then they will flourish. This is an attractive and populist image.

However we know from the evidence of PISA (OECD 2011b) that there is no correlation between decentralisation and achievement, and that the world's best performing educational systems sustain improvement by:

▶ establishing collaborative practices around teaching and learning
▶ developing a mediating layer between the schools and the centre
▶ nurturing tomorrow's leadership.

The McKinsey report on *Capturing the leadership premium* (Barber, Whelan & Clark 2010, p. 8) is unequivocal when it states:

> *Finally, differences in what leaders do are not directly related to the level of autonomy they are given. Internationally, there is no relationship between the degree of autonomy enjoyed by a school principal and their relative focus on administrative or instructional leadership.*

This evidence undermines the myth of a simplistic concept of school autonomy that assumes some inherent value added simply by giving schools freedoms to 'let a thousand flowers bloom', irrespective of their impact on student achievement. As Michael Fullan (2004b, p. 6) puts it:

> *... even highly supported decentralized strategies which seek 'a thousand flowers to bloom' do not take us very far (not enough flowers bloom; good flowers do not get around or amount to critical mass breakthroughs).*

Exploding this myth is not an exercise in negativity because the evidence that disproves it also helps us acquire a more sophisticated understanding of the contours of a new educational landscape. The framework for this was set out in the system reform diagram (Figure 1.3) at the end of the last chapter. By exploring the concept of school autonomy and its interpretation in the context of 21st century education, we should be able to see more clearly the connections between individual school improvement, local and system level reform. There is an important caution to be entered here however. As with all the other myths, just because it is wrong or misguided does not mean that the status quo should be endorsed. In most cases the myth is correct in identifying a problem, sadly; it is the solutions that are invariably wrong.

Despite policy trends that favour autonomy, the myth implies that schools working totally in isolation enhance system effectiveness. However, there is no contradiction in strong individual schools working in collaboration with other schools and agencies to support systemic improvement (Hopkins 2008). It is also important to acknowledge that there is an associated myth lurking here, to do with the appearance (or not) of change. For over four decades now, there have been incessant calls for change implying the need for improvement in education, yet as the old maxim goes—'the more things change the more they remain the same'. To quote one head teacher's comment in reflecting on the last 20 years of change in schooling in England: 'Everything has changed, but nothing has changed' (cited in Vacher 2007, p. 8). The paradox of 'change–no change' in education has proved to be a conundrum that continues to puzzle education practitioners, policy makers and researchers alike. This is a paradox that we address directly in this chapter and those that follow.

The responsibility of this chapter therefore is to explode the combined myth of school autonomy and the reality of change. The discussion will focus on how schools can effectively manage change by organising for improvement at the local level and build capacity to sustain both collective and individual improvement. These themes are addressed in the pages that follow by:

⬤ reviewing the evidence on successful district or regional level reform
⬤ distinguishing between development and maintenance in educational improvement
⬤ describing the key strategies for implementation and sustainability
⬤ proposing a transferable strategy for local reform—the powerful learning framework.

District or regional level reform

The research base on the impact of the district or regional role on student achievement has a relatively recent history. There are, however, a number of examples from the research on school districts in North America during the 1990s illustrating that under the right conditions, significant and rapid progress can be made in enhancing the learning of students (Fullan 2009b). As Fullan (2003, p. 50) describes it:

> ... people began to say, 'What does it take to achieve district-wide reform?' The majority of school districts do not have the conception, capacity, or continuity to be anything more than an episodic aggravation to school improvement ... but since 1990 we have seen an increasing number of districts that can claim success.

Subsequent to this, Elmore (2004) reported on the characteristics of successful school districts in California. These included:

> [showing] greater clarity of purpose, a willingness to exercise tighter controls over decisions about what [was] taught and what would be monitored as evidence of performance and ... [increased] delegation to the school level of specific decisions about how to carry out an instructional program. (DEECD 2011, p. 6)

Fullan (2007) also presented further analyses of effective district level reform in characterising the success of the New York school system. 'Here, strong vision coupled with intensive staff development on instructional practices and capacity building within a constructive accountability framework led to significant increases in levels of student achievement' (Hopkins, Harris et al. 2011, p. 9).

In the past five years, it has been possible to identify more recent examples of successful school reform at the district or regional level. Space precludes detailed discussion, but the following three examples in their different ways are illustrative of the way the most successful regions or districts have balanced top-down and bottom-up change, in order to make a real difference to student learning and achievement.

Example in action: England

Based on an authentic local authority partnership approach adopted by the London Borough of Bexley, this example illustrates the benefits of disciplined collaboration through an Accelerated Improvement Project (AIP). This approach was planned to incorporate the findings documented in *The logical chain: continuing professional development in effective schools* (Ofsted 2006c). It involved:

> school-based activity with a sustained focus on improving teaching and learning
> sustained work with AIP teachers in their classrooms
> activity that involved teachers working in a small team, allowing them to plan together, learn from each other and keep focused on the task
> a focus on making incremental changes that would be communicated to all staff and incorporated into further improvements as a way of sustaining changes
> including the AIP team in specific changes, thereby encouraging a responsibility for the leadership of that change
> establishing coaching and the 'buddy' system that ensured support for the transfer of knowledge and skills.

Example in action: Australia

The school improvement framework in Victoria—a state that has has traditionally performed well on PISA—has been regarded very highly by international agencies such as the OECD. It has also provided the shelter conditions within which the Northern Metropolitan Region's 'powerful learning' framework has been developed. Victoria's approach began with the Blueprint for government schools (Department of Education and Training 2003). It 'created a sense of urgency about the differential quality of the educational experience in government schools and was the catalyst for generating a [systematic] response to this challenge' (DEECD 2008, p. 3). This led to the development of a broadly based school improvement strategy that reflected the research and current knowledge about effective schools, leaders, professional learning and formative accountability. More specifically, the Blueprint identified three critical areas for reform:

▶ recognising and responding to diverse student needs
▶ building the skills of the education workforce to enhance the teaching–learning relationship
▶ continuously improving schools (Watterson & Caldwell 2011).

In commenting on the success of the Victoria strategy, Harvard Professor Richard Elmore (2007) said, 'There are few improvement strategies that are focused with such depth and complexity on the basic human capital problems associated with school improvement at scale'.

Example in action: United States

A third example of successful district reform is found in Montgomery County Public Schools (MCPS) in Maryland (Childress 2009). In the conventional educational jargon of the day, the district has engaged in a sustained, decade-long effort to 'raise the bar and close the gap' in terms of student performance. An illustration of their success is that the top quartile of performers in MCPS from 2003 to 2008 raised their scores significantly and the lower quartiles improved even faster. The following 'lessons' were noted as explaining their success.

▶ Implement common, rigorous standards with differentiated resources and instruction.
▶ Apply 'value chain' thinking to the K–12 continuum.
▶ Blur the lines between the traditional roles and responsibilities of the school board, leadership team, principals, teachers and parents.
▶ Create systems and structures that reinforce the behaviours necessary for success, and changes in beliefs will follow.
▶ Confront the effects that beliefs about race and achievement have on student performance and help teachers and students apply this knowledge to their day-to-day work in classrooms.
▶ Lead for equity.

The guiding image of successful school systems is their ability to balance top-down and bottom-up change over time, in the pursuit of sustained excellence in student achievement. As can be seen from the examples given above, those that are successful in doing this at the local, regional or district level seem to share the following characteristic commitments:

▶ They ensure that the *achievement and learning of students* is at the centre of all that teachers do.

▶ As a consequence, the *enhancement of the quality of teaching* is the central theme in any improvement strategy.

▶ To sustain this, they put in place ongoing *professional learning opportunities* that develop a common 'practice' out of the integration of curriculum, teaching and learning.

▶ This takes place in schools where *leadership* has high expectations and an unrelenting focus on the quality of learning and teaching.

▶ To enable this, procedures need to be in place to provide *ongoing and transparent data* to facilitate improvements in learning and teaching.

▶ Finally, *system level structures* are established that link together the various levels of the system and promote disciplined innovation as a consequence of networking.

It is no surprise that these characteristics reflect the more comprehensive list presented in the Coda to Chapter One. These three examples demonstrate the importance of a 'mediating layer' in systemic educational reform and provide more evidence to debunk the myth of autonomy. Shortly, the 'powerful learning' strategy developed in Melbourne's Northern Metropolitan Region will be described in detail. This will provide a more complete analysis of why the myth is wrong as well as pointing a way forward. Before this, however, it is important to highlight two features of organisational designs and change strategies that are necessary if a middle layer is to contribute effectively to systemic reform. These features also shed some light on the ancillary myth of the (non-) appearance of change.

Distinguishing between development and maintenance

In exploring the paradox of 'change–no change' in educational reform, it is now well established that it is the quality of the organisational conditions in the school that make it more or less likely that the paradox is resolved (Hopkins 2001). Given that, it is useful here to briefly review what these conditions are, and how they can be modified to support ongoing development in a school.

Matthew Miles was one of the first to understand the dynamic between the organisational condition of schools and the excellence of education they provide. This insight laid the foundation for much contemporary work in the area of educational change, school effectiveness and school improvement (Hopkins, Harris et al. 2011). In his seminal paper on organisational health, Miles (1975, p. 231) wrote:

> [There is] ... a set of fairly durable second-order system properties, which tend to transcend short-run effectiveness. A healthy organization in this sense not only survives in its environment, but also continues to cope adequately over the long haul, and continuously develops and extends its surviving and coping abilities.

Miles described a series of strategies designed to induce a greater degree of organisational health such as team training, survey feedback, role workshops, target setting, diagnosis and problem-solving and organisational experiment. Some of these strategies may have an anachronistic ring, but there are a number of common themes flowing through all of them that have a more contemporary flavour. Examples include self-study or review, the promotion of networking, increased communication, culture as a focus for change, the use of temporary systems such as school improvement groups and the importance of external support (Hopkins, Harris et al. 2011).

When we were developing the *Improving the quality of education for all* approach to school improvement (Hopkins, West & Ainscow 1996) we took seriously Miles' notion of organisational health and related it more directly to the organisational capacity of the school. Without an emphasis on capacity, a school will be unable to 'transform' itself or sustain continuous improvement efforts that result in student attainment. It is therefore important to be able to define capacity in operational terms. The Improving the Quality of Education for All (IQEA) school improvement project demonstrated that without an equal focus on the internal conditions of the school, innovative work quickly becomes marginalised. The 'conditions' have to be worked on at the same time as the curriculum and/or other priorities the school has set itself. Conditions are the internal features of the school, the 'arrangements' that enable it to get work done (Hopkins & Reynolds 2001, p. 469).

In terms of the IQEA project at least, it is these conditions that provide a working definition of the development capacity of the school. The conditions within the school that are associated with a capacity for sustained improvement are:

▶ a commitment to staff development and the establishing of a professional learning community
▶ practical efforts to involve staff, students and the community in school policies and decisions
▶ 'transformational' leadership approaches that are both instructionally focused and dispersed amongst staff within the school

- ❯ effective coordination strategies that ensure whole-school consistency of practice and high expectations
- ❯ serious attention to the potential benefits of enquiry and reflection that gathers data on both achievement and learning
- ❯ a commitment to collaborative planning activity that adapts external change for internal purposes (Porritt, Hopkins, Burney et al. 2009, p. 21).

As part of this work, we designed a methodology for enhancing the development capacity of the school (Hopkins, Ainscow & West 1994; Hopkins & Harris 2000). In taking this further, however, we began to realise that it was important to articulate the critical distinction between 'development' and 'maintenance'. This requires a school to be able to maintain its existing organisational functions to a high degree, but also to have the capacity to develop and change. The maintenance structure is concerned with relatively permanent systems and processes that are necessary for the school to get its work done as efficiently as possible. The development structure is there to develop new ways of working that, over time, add value to the school (Hopkins 2001). What usually happens, though, is that schools tend to overburden their maintenance system by asking it to take on development roles for which it was never designed. The separation of maintenance activities from development work is essential for the continuous improvement of a school and both need their separate infrastructures as shown in Figure 2.1.

As indicated in Figure 2.1, central to a school's development structure is a school improvement team. An effective school improvement team creates the capacity for development, while retaining the existing structures required both for organisational stability and efficiency. The role of the school improvement team is discussed in more detail in Chapter Eight; for now it is sufficient to acknowledge the crucial role of such teams and the individuals within them as the change agents of school reform at the local level.

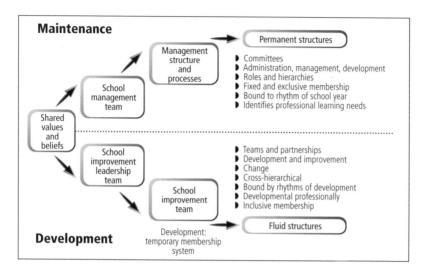

Figure 2.1 A model for maintenance and development

In tackling the complexities of school reform at the local level, the ability to distinguish accurately between the development and maintenance functions of schools is crucial. It is also important to recognise that a necessary requirement of all educational change agents operating both in and beyond the school is to ensure that these functions are fit-for-purpose and are actively working in harmony to support school improvement. In this regard, achieving the right balance between development and maintenance is of critical importance. In *The empowered school* (1991) David Hargreaves and I described three dimensions of the school's management arrangements as a mechanism for achieving this:

1. Frameworks that guide the actions of all who are involved in the school.
2. The clarification of roles and responsibilities so all know what they and others do.
3. The promotion of ways in which people can work together.

As can be seen from the discussion presented here, it is not just a question of being able to distinguish between the development and maintenance functions of schools. In the context of contemporary school reform, it is also about bringing these functions into alignment in order to achieve the greatest impact on school improvement and student achievement at the local level. In this regard, school leaders and other education practitioners need to ensure that their school management arrangements support maintenance, that is, preserving what has worked well and given the school its stability and reputation, as well as providing a means of dealing with new developments and of creating a new future. Achieving all this requires a relatively sophisticated understanding of the dynamics and phases of the change process, which is the focus of the following section.

Strategies for implementation and sustainability

The 'change–no change' conundrum in education described earlier has particular relevance in considering the implementation and sustainability of school reform strategies. Some 20 years ago, two of the wisest commentators on education reform—Michael Fullan and Matthew Miles—framed the issue in a number of ways that are outlined below. First, Fullan (1992, p. 2) whose analysis, sadly, still holds true in the present day:

> ... *educational reform not only does not work as the theories say it should, but more fundamentally ... it can never work that way. Educational reform is complex, non-linear, frequently arbitrary, and always highly political. It is rife with unpredictable shifts and fragmented initiatives. I am afraid that this is the nature of the beast in complex socio-political societies.*

At around the same time, Fullan claimed with Miles that the basic problem is that our 'maps of change' are faulty (Fullan & Miles 1992, p. 745). It is difficult to get to one's destination if the directions you are following are incorrect. It is these faulty assumptions that leave one helpless, de-skilled and frustrated at the inability to come to terms with a changing world. Although helpful critiques, neither of these comments help us understand why this is the case, or what to do about it.

A clue as to how to resolve this conundrum was given at the end of the last chapter in the diagram and discussion on systemic reform. We saw there that change strategies are always a combination of top-down and bottom-up approaches and that the general rule is that the worse the situation, the more directive and top-down one must be. This accounts for the prevalence of instrumental change strategies in the history of education reform. The critical point, though, is that as the school and system begins to improve and as confidence and competence increases, the balance needs to be adjusted to give more authority and control to those leading the changes—it needs to become more bottom-up, more empowering and strategies need to be employed that build professional capacity and confidence.

The following analysis explains the critiques of Fullan and Miles. The reason why reform efforts have been variously non-linear, arbitrary, political and fragmented is because policymakers and reformers have not understood the importance of rebalancing top-down/bottom-up change over time, in context-specific ways. Also, our maps of change are wrong, because most reformers default to top-down strategies irrespective of the particular context the school or system is in. Top-down, bureaucratic and authoritarian strategies actually reduce performance and create toxic cultures in schools and systems that are on the 'adequate to good' and 'good to great' journeys. This shift, later described by contrasting inside–out working with outside–in approaches, is crucial to resolving the change–no change paradox. It also helps explain why the crude application of the myth of autonomy is no panacea.

Besides this macro-level analysis, two other perspectives are essential to build into our change strategies if we are to ensure that they have the impact that our students deserve. The first is an understanding of the 'cycles of change' that relate to the implementation of specific strategies and the second is the 'challenge of individual change'.

In exploring the first of these, some of the pioneering work on understanding the implementation process undertaken in the 1980s and 1990s is still relevant for us today—see, for example, *Innovation up close* (Huberman & Miles 1984), *The new meaning of educational change* (Fullan 1991) and *Improving the quality of schooling* (Hopkins 1987a). In considering the current applicability of these perspectives in the context of 21st century school reform, what still remains of critical importance is an understanding of the change process as a series of three overlapping phases—initiation, implementation and institutionalisation. Although these phases often coexist in practice, there are some advantages in describing them separately. It is particularly important to understand what happens during each phase and what behaviours within each phase make for success.

Initiation is the phase concerned with deciding to embark on innovation, and of developing commitment towards the process. The key activities in the initiation phase are the decision to start and a review of the school's current state as regards the particular change. Miles' (1986) analysis of the stages of school improvement identified the following factors that make for successful initiation:

▶ the innovation should be tied to a local agenda and high profile local need
▶ a clear, well-structured approach to change

▶ an active advocate or champion who understands the change and supports it
▶ active initiation to start the innovation (top-down is okay in certain conditions)
▶ good quality innovation.

Implementation is the phase of the process that has received the most attention. It is the phase of attempted use of the innovation. The key activities occurring during implementation are the carrying out of action plans, the developing and sustaining of commitment, the checking of progress and overcoming problems. The key factors making for success at this stage, according to Miles (1986), are:

▶ clear responsibility for coordination (Head, Coordinator, external Consultant)
▶ shared control over implementation (top-down *not* okay); good cross-hierarchical work and relations; empowerment of both individuals and the school
▶ mix of pressure, insistence on 'doing it right' and support
▶ adequate and sustained staff development and in-service training
▶ rewards for teachers early in the process (e.g. empowerment, collegiality, meeting needs, classroom help, load reduction, supply cover, expenses, resources).

Institutionalisation is the phase when innovation and change stop being regarded as something new and become part of the school's usual way of doing things. The move from implementation to institutionalisation often involves the transformation of a pilot project to a school-wide initiative and often without the advantage of the previously available funding. Key activities at this stage according to Miles (1986) are:

▶ an emphasis on 'embedding' the change within the school's structures, its organisation and resources
▶ the elimination of competing or contradictory practices
▶ strong and purposeful links to other change efforts, the curriculum and classroom teaching
▶ widespread use in the school and local area
▶ an adequate bank of local facilitators (e.g. advisory teachers) for skills training.

Many change efforts fail to progress beyond early implementation because those involved do not realise that each of these phases have different characteristics and require different strategies for success to be achieved. Differentiating between the three phases is therefore helpful, as is the articulation of the appropriate activities at each stage.

Besides the specific activities required during each of the phases of initiation, implementation and institutionalisation, there are also generic skills and abilities identified from research and practice (Schmuck & Runkel 1985; Miles, Saxl & Lieberman 1988; Hopkins et al. 1996) that characterise the behaviours of effective change agents in this context. These are:

▶ to generate trust
▶ to understand and diagnose the state of the school's organisation
▶ to plan into the medium term and to see the bigger picture
▶ to work productively in groups
▶ to access the required technical resources and advice, be it research, good practice or specifications of teaching and learning
▶ to give people the confidence to continue.

There is, however, another key skill needed for managing the contemporary process of change. It is the ability to deal with complexity. As we have seen, traditional mindsets based on rational approaches to school improvement will not work in the current climate and, if employed, will probably make matters worse. Nowadays, however, one is rarely involved with just one innovation. A school can be going through a number of change cycles at any one time. This places great stress on the organisational capacity of the school and the confidence of those leading the change process. Once a school has developed the capacity to change, however, then successive cycles of innovation become much easier, and managing multiple cycles of innovation simultaneously becomes possible.

The second perspective referred to above—to understand the state of the school's organisation—relates to the challenge of individual change. One of the features of the change–no change paradox is that in terms of our moral purpose, change efforts and policy initiatives often focus on the wrong things. Most policy initiatives tend to focus on structural or curriculum issues that have little direct impact on the learning and achievement of students. In John Hattie's recent book *Visible learning* (2009), it is made clear that all of the empirical evidence suggests that it is teaching behaviours that most directly affect student progress. This presents a serious challenge to many teachers because it requires them to expand what is referred to as their 'circles of competence' and their repertoire of teaching strategies. It is exactly because change is a process whereby individuals need to alter their ways of thinking and doing that most changes fail to progress beyond early implementation. It is important to mention this theme initially here, but it is explored in far more detail in subsequent chapters.

In summary, the implications for successful school reform are that conditions need to be created both within and beyond the school at regional or district levels to ensure that individuals are supported through the inevitable, but difficult and challenging, process of change. This is particularly the case when there is, as there should be, an unrelenting moral purpose focused on improving student learning and achievement. With this in mind, there are two further points to be made. As will be noted in Chapter Five, the first is that tasks for students need to be set in their 'zones of proximal development' if significant progress is to be sustained; this applies to the professional learning of teachers too. If a new teaching approach is too exotic, too far from their existing practice, the change will be rejected because the jump is just too technically and psychologically difficult. An intermediate step must be identified that leads to a progressive expansion of teachers' repertoires of professional practices. Secondly, and in the same way, the school's 'development infrastructure' should be organised around the realisation that change is a process whereby individuals alter their ways of thinking and doing. The key features of such an infrastructure are explored in Chapter Seven.

The powerful learning framework

In deepening the analysis of strategies for improvement at the local level presented thus far, we now focus on the 'powerful learning' framework developed in the Northern Metropolitan Region (NMR) of Victoria, Australia. The approach adopted in NMR in utilising the powerful learning framework as a strategy for successful school reform at the local level is described in some detail here, in the belief that it can provide a transferable model for other settings (Hopkins, Munro et al. 2011). The educational goals and purpose of the region, as well as a model of improvement applicable to all schools across the region, is summarised in the publication *Powerful learning* (NMR 2009, p. 9) and expressed as follows:

> *These improvements represent a step change in the quality of our students' education. Our success will be marked by: students who are proud of their schools and what they have achieved; and*

parents who are confident that sending their child to a public school is a sound educational decision.

Successful school systems around the world—those that have high levels of equity in student achievement and success—are characterised by moral purpose and clarity of goals that have direct implications; not just for schooling, but also for the way society develops. This is also the case in the NMR that continues to strive to become a world-class educational system. The moral purpose for school reform in the NMR is to:

> *provide a high-quality education for all students regardless of background. This is to ensure that the conditions are in place to enable every student in the region to reach their potential. This moral purpose is reflected in a small number of tangible but ambitious objectives for student learning and achievement that are being vigorously pursued. These goals are also in line with the ... reform areas ... in the National Partnership agreements with the federal government.*
>
> *The goal is for all students in [the region] to be literate, numerate and curious, with schools continuing to provide a broad-based 21st century curriculum. (DEECD 2011, p. 8)*

Through setting such a goal and establishing the process of school reform to achieve it, the ambition is that in a relatively short space of time students, their parents, carers, teachers and other stakeholders will notice a real difference. For example, NMR defines the following goals for 2013 (NMR 2009, p 9).

- A student finishing primary school will demonstrate:
  - individual performance at or above national standards in literacy and numeracy
  - a sharp curiosity for learning.

▶ A student finishing secondary school will have:
  ▶ a clear well-defined pathway to further training and education.
▶ Parents and carers will have:
  ▶ a substantive and meaningful engagement with their child's school and teachers
  ▶ a clear understanding of their child's progress against national standards.
▶ Teachers will have:
  ▶ world-class professional skills
  ▶ high regard in their school communities
  ▶ continuing access to quality professional learning opportunities.
▶ The community will have confidence that:
  ▶ individual student performance meets national standards
  ▶ graduates of NMR schools are capable of making valuable contributions as citizens and employees.

If these are the goals, then the approach to school improvement adopted by the Northern Metropolitan Region is the means of achieving them. Based on the preceding principles, the model shown in Figure 2.2, identifies the crucial elements of an effective school, demonstrates their interdependence and provides a guide to strategic action. It has evolved from the 'integrated school improvement model' presented in Figure 1.1 in the previous chapter. This is an action framework designed to help both those working directly in schools and those working at district or regional level to more effectively manage the realignment of top-down and bottom-up change over time.

The overarching theory of action for the NMR school improvement strategy is if all the distinct but interrelated parts of the model detailed above (i.e. in the rings and each component of each ring) are aligned and working together, then all schools across the region as well as the

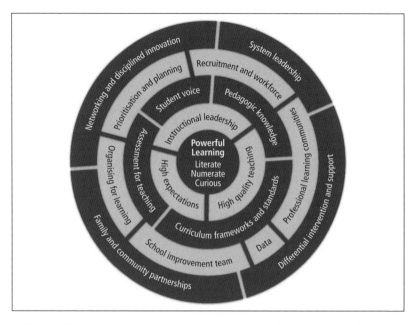

Figure 2.2 The powerful learning regional school improvement strategy framework (Reproduced from NMR 2009, p. 13)

system as a whole will improve. This approach not only illustrates how a region such as NMR is balancing top-down and bottom-up change in practical ways, it also introduces a new concept of successful change by moving from the inside out rather than the outside in. The main features of the approach are as follows.

▶ In the centre is powerful learning, which represents the school's goal that every student will reach their potential, together with a definition of achievement that embraces standards of literacy, numeracy and learning capability (curiosity). Such a learning focus will not only raise standards, but also reduce the range of performance in a school, thus simultaneously 'raising the bar and narrowing the gap'.

▶ Effective schools are not simply an amalgam of disparate elements. There are some essential features that need to be in place that lay the basis for greatness—these are the pre-conditions for effectiveness, upon which all else is built. Without these, a school will be unable to achieve or sustain excellence. These three features, represented in the second ring of the diagram, are:
  ▶ the importance of instructional leadership
  ▶ the quality of teaching
  ▶ high expectations.
▶ The next ring is comprised of those essential ingredients of effective classroom practice necessary for powerful learning:
  ▶ the teacher's repertoire of teaching and learning strategies, commonly known as pedagogical knowledge
  ▶ the organisation of curriculum in terms of frameworks and standards
  ▶ the way that learning is assessed in order to inform teaching
  ▶ the ways in which students are involved in their learning and the organisation of the school.
▶ The organisational conditions supportive of high levels of teaching and learning are detailed as the key elements found in the next ring; these are:
  ▶ collaborative planning that focuses on student outcomes
  ▶ professional learning that is committed to improvement of classroom practice
  ▶ regular use of data, enquiry and self-evaluation to improve teaching
  ▶ the recruitment of teaching staff and the deployment of the whole school workforce
  ▶ the identification of a school improvement team to provide the research and development capacity for the school
  ▶ the way in which the school is organised to most effectively promote learning.

▶ The broader systemic context of the school is represented in the outer ring of the diagram by reference to four obligations and opportunities enjoyed by all schools in the Northern Metropolitan Region:

  ▶ the opportunity to network with other schools in order to share good practice and engage in disciplined innovation

  ▶ the way in which schools embrace and respond to the needs and opportunities provided in their locality from parents, carers and communities

  ▶ the new opportunities for principals to engage in broader forms of 'system leadership' where they take on a range of roles in supporting other principals and schools

  ▶ the opportunity to engage in more purposeful reflection on the effectiveness of the school's provision provided by the region's regular reviews of schools and the subsequent planning and differential intervention and support determined by the school's current performance.

A further perspective needs to be added that is critical to an understanding of the NMR approach and its general applicability. Most school reform assumes that change comes from the outside–in. The logic goes something like this:

a high quality policy or program is developed and then implemented, with the assumption that it will impact upon the school and be internalised through the school's planning processes. In turn, it is assumed this will impact on classroom practices and will therefore positively affect the learning and achievement of students. (DEECD 2011, p. 11)

It is as if the drive comes from the outer circle of the diagram and permeates the various layers, hopefully reaching the powerful learning of students in the centre.

However, as has been pointed out in the previous chapter, in those schools that have made the jump from 'good to great', the linear logic of policy implementation has been inverted. Instead of doing outside–in better, or more efficiently, they start from the centre of the circle and move outwards; these schools begin at the other end of the sequence, with student learning. It is as if they ask, 'What changes in student learning and performance do we wish to see this year?' Having decided these, they then discuss what teaching strategies will be most effective at bringing them about, and reflect on what modifications are required to the organisation of the school to support these developments. Finally, they embed within their school improvement plans those policy initiatives that provide the best fit with the school's vision, values and goals for enhancing student achievement. It is these schools that appear to be the most effective at interpreting the national, state and regional reform agenda. The underlying purpose of the powerful learning framework described above is to generate this degree of confidence and agency in schools. In so doing, it exposes the paucity of simple autonomy as a recipe for systemic educational reform.

Coda

Debunking the autonomy myth is both tricky and vital. Tricky because it is ubiquitous as well as populist; vital, because if we allow the simple-minded form of autonomy to flourish, a few schools may well improve, but the variation in school performance will inevitably increase and social equity will remain a far off goal. This is why in order to sustain system-wide improvement, societies are increasingly demanding strategies characterised by diversity, flexibility and choice—hence the focus on powerful learning in the Northern Metropolitan Region. It is, however, moral purpose that drives contemporary approaches to learning and teaching. This is most vividly seen in the concern of the committed, conscientious principal who works with teachers in their school to match what is taught and how it is taught to the needs of the individual student, and involve them in that process. This by itself is just not enough. It is how schools collaborate and grow through diversity that is at the heart of system reform, and this is why autonomy as a panacea is so misguided.

Unfortunately the debate is often clouded by a dispute over structures, and this is where I have some sympathy with the autonomy lobby. They often point out that middle-tier organisations have become bloated, self-serving bureaucracies, more concerned with administration and their own careers than supporting the improvement of schools. Although an exaggeration, one can see their point! The debate should move away from structures, which in any case should be flexible and responsive to context, to the functions that the middle-tier performs to support systemic improvement.

The recent McKinsey (Barber et al. 2010) report *Capturing the leadership premium* recognises not only the need for quality school leadership, but also the importance of the middle tier to system reform. It is here where the debate should be located; the discussion of structure is second order as long as it is flexible enough to reflect and support local needs. Barber and colleagues (2010, pp. 23–4) argued that there is a growing body of evidence on the potential for the middle tier to support and drive improvement in schools and learning. Their review identified five practices that explain the contributions the middle tier can make.

1. Middle-tier leaders can help support weaker school leaders, both improving and supplementing their leadership to raise the overall effectiveness of leadership and management in a school. In the words of one Canadian system leader, 'Many principals cannot be successful without the best possible district leadership'.
2. The middle tier often plays a crucial role in identifying principals' development needs and providing appropriate development support.

3. Managing clusters and lateral learning. For example, in Victoria, regional network leaders are responsible for promoting and managing learning within their network and helping principals in their network put together a plan with specific goals.

4. In systems that go beyond self-identification, the middle tier usually plays a crucial role in helping identify and develop leadership capacity. Frequently this means ensuring that leaders are developing succession plans and identifying talent in their school. In other systems the middle tier also works directly with aspiring leaders.

5. Strengthening and moderating accountability. Despite different performance-evaluation systems and consequences, [effective] middle-tier leaders are all heavily involved in principal reviews and supporting them over the course of the year to achieve their school improvement goals.

It is axiomatic that middle-tier leaders also acquire and model change agent skills such as those described in this chapter, so helping to debunk the myth of change–no change as well as the myth of autonomy.

Finally, a comment on the use of the phrase 'powerful learning' to describe NMR's systemic improvement strategy; it is purposeful. It is not just an accurate description of a strategy that focuses directly on enhancing the learning of all students in the region, thus adding value to individual school improvement; it is also, in our experience, an idea that is capturing the imagination of teachers, parents and young people around the world (Hopkins 2008). Bearing all this in mind, in the next chapter we look at how powerful learning can be best expressed and delivered at the school level.

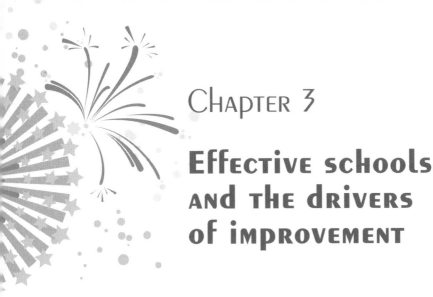

Chapter 3

Effective schools and the drivers of improvement

The myth that poverty is a determinant of student and school performance

Before moving into the substance of this chapter, it may be worth briefly rehearsing the argument so far. We began by emphasising the importance of moral purpose in educational change, then reviewed the history of school improvement efforts and linked that to a conception of, and a framework for, system reform. Keeping this big picture in mind, in the previous chapter we discussed the myth of autonomy, the role that the middle tier can play in system reform, the importance of the distinction between maintenance and development in organisational design and began to confront the paradox of change and no change. The way forward was illustrated by a case study of the importance of the local level in school reform. The NMR 'Powerful Learning' framework provides a strategy for local support where autonomous schools can more effectively work together. With this in mind, for the next six chapters starting here, we focus again at the school level, before returning to a consideration of a strategic perspective on system-wide reform in the final two chapters of the book.

In this chapter, a deeper discussion of the effective school is provided in an effort to explode the myth that poverty is a determinant of student and school performance. This is an important myth to explode for both social justice and strategic reasons. Not only is it morally wrong that poverty is a determinant of educational achievement, but it is also important to remind ourselves that those 'effective schools' that do break the association between poverty and achievement share similar characteristics. So by exploding this myth we also understand better the qualities of effective schools.

Significant quantitative data will be presented in this chapter to persuade even the most sceptical of the vulnerability of this myth. If we accept this as given for the moment, it may be helpful to discuss the implications of such evidence. Some time ago now, Joe Murphy reformulated the debate on school effectiveness by articulating the 'real legacy of the effective school movement'. He identified four aspects to the legacy (Murphy 1992, pp. 94–6):

1. **The educability of learners.** At the heart of the effective schools movement is an attack on the prevailing notion of the distribution of achievement according to a normal curve. There is a clear demonstration that all students can learn.
2. **A focus on outcomes.** Effective school advocates argue persuasively that one can judge the quality of education only by examining student outcomes, especially indices of learning. Equally important, they define success not in absolute terms, but as the value added to what students brought to the educational process.
3. **Taking responsibility for students.** The third major contribution of the effective schools movement is its attack on the practice of blaming the victim for the shortcomings of the school itself. The movement has been insistent that the school community takes a fair share of the responsibility for what happens to the youth in its care.

4. **Attention to consistency throughout the school community.** One of the most powerful and enduring lessons from all the research on effective schools is that the better schools are more tightly linked—structurally, symbolically and culturally—than the less effective ones. They operate more as an organic whole and less as a loose collection of disparate subsystems. An overarching sense of consistency and coordination is a key element that cuts across the effectiveness correlates and permeates our better schools.

This analysis represents a major contribution both to the effective schools literature as well as a challenge to school improvement. The legacy of the effective schools movement as outlined by Murphy leads away from the effective schools research per se into the territory of authentic school improvement (Hopkins 2001, p. 49). This leads to a basic assumption of this book, that there is useful and increasingly precise knowledge that can be transferred from school to school. This represents progress, because for some time there was another myth that all schools were unique and required distinct and idiosyncratic improvement strategies. We have moved well beyond that now and have a much clearer idea on how to successfully pursue change at the school and local level.

It is this evidence that will disprove the myth of poverty as a determinant of educational success; we now turn to a further discussion of these issues in addressing the following themes by:

▶ introducing the concept of a 'whole-school design' as a means of providing a more dynamic perspective on effective schools

▶ describing some of those schools that have 'made a difference' and identifying the reasons for their success

▶ overviewing the four drivers of reform that provide the focus for the next four chapters

▶ exploring the importance of development planning in achieving successful school reform.

The effective school and whole-school designs

The legacy from school effectiveness and the recent research into school improvement and system leadership focuses on the dynamics of improvement in schools that employ a more strategic and capacity building approach to change. In our book *System leadership in practice* two colleagues and I identified nine components that need to be worked on at the same time in order to build professional capacity for sustained improvement (Higham, Hopkins & Matthews 2009). They are presented below in a way that reflects the discussion in preceding chapters.

1. **Teaching and learning** is consistently good. There is a classroom ethos of high expectations and a shared 'good lesson' structure, a high proportion of time on task and good use of assessment for learning (AfL) to plan lessons and tailor to need.
2. The **curriculum** is balanced and interesting. Strategic planning integrates basics, breadth and cognitive learning with specific interventions in skills, grade enhancement classes and mentoring.
3. **Behaviour** promotes order and enjoyment. There are consistent rules for conduct and dress, with consistent implications for infringement consistently applied.
4. **Student attitudes to learning** are positive. Attendance is high, pastoral care is accessible, achievement is acknowledged and students have a voice in school decision-making.
5. **Leadership** provides a clear vision that is translated into manageable, time-bound and agreed objectives; commitment is established; data are used to tackle weaknesses and internal variation.
6. Dedicated time is allocated for a range of **continuing professional development** (CPD) opportunities. There is a focus on sharing experience of improving practice and individual needs are

identified as part of the development process, especially in addressing weak or poor teaching.

7. **Internal accountability** actively empowers practitioners through a culture of discipline. There are agreed expectations for teaching quality, and quality assurance processes are in place including peer observation.

8. **Resource and environmental management** are student focused. Use of funding streams, a whole-school team approach and the environment all support learning.

9. **Partnerships beyond the school** create learning opportunities. Parental engagement is encouraged and support agencies are used effectively.

These nine elements all link together to create a distinctive school culture as seen in Figure 3.1.

There are two relatively new features to schools that adopt this approach. The first feature is the emphasis on narrative and its impact

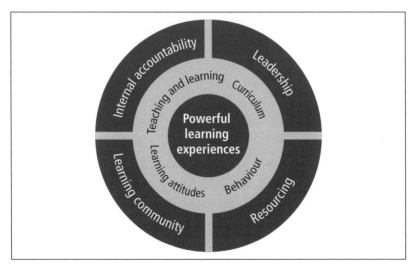

Figure 3.1 The nine components for strategic school improvement

on both strategy and culture. Narrative is integrative and cumulative, presenting a series of complex and interacting initiatives within a unifying story around the image of a journey. This is strategic insofar as it projects forwards integrating a wide variety of initiatives, and cultural insofar as it speaks both to the individual and the collective contribution.

The second feature is the emphasis on 'systems' and the transferability and sustainability of best practice. The characteristics of effective schools have been known for some time, but at a rather high level of generalisation. Recently, we have acquired a more textured understanding of what these effective practices look like and how they combine together in a more comprehensive framework. We are now at a point when these practices can be presented in an implementable form. Again the key point is twofold—although this knowledge is replicable from setting to setting, it must be integrated in order to have transformational impact.

Unfortunately this approach is often not adopted in practice, although as we see in the following section, when it is applied, it is unusually effective. At present, most schools adopt an idiosyncratic pick-and-mix approach, choosing to adopt some of their 'favourite' things without a clear implementation strategy. What is clear, however, is that there is a 'developmental sequence in school improvement narratives that needs certain building blocks to be in place before further progress can be made' (Hopkins, Harris et al. 2011, p. 15). This suggestion finds support in recent research (Higham et al. 2009) that identifies not only a clear strategic and capacity building process in most successful school improvement efforts, but also the specific adoption of practices proven to be effective elsewhere. These tend to be the planned use of another school's curriculum, teaching strategies, approaches to monitoring or behaviour policies.

This deliberate approach has also been taken even further, where proven effective practices are linked together to create a comprehensive whole-school design. The whole-school design approach holds such promise for school transformation, especially in an increasingly devolved and market-driven system, that it is surprising that it has not proven more popular. In the USA in the 1990s, there was a national competition to evaluate the effectiveness of some dozen whole-school designs that resulted in the *New designs for American schools* program (cited in Stringfield 2009). There is now good evidence to support the contention that 'Externally developed reforms have proven more likely to produce desired outcomes than locally developed reforms' (Stringfield & Nunnery 2010, p. 305).

In the recent past, the Outward Bound movement in the USA has taken the application of Outward Bound principles to schooling very seriously. In the 1990s they formed an 'Expeditionary Learning' program to provide a comprehensive school reform and school development model for elementary, middle and high schools. Inspired by their example, we have recently established a charity in the UK— Adventure Learning Schools (ALS)—which provides a strong illustration of this approach as it is quintessentially based on a whole-school design. The core elements are detailed in Figure 3.2.

The whole-school design illustrated in Figure 3.2 is based on experiential learning principles. It builds on the adventure learning concept of personal development through direct experience, but within a whole-school setting. The 'framework is designed to be specific and replicable, insofar as it contains the best of current knowledge of what makes for an effective school, but then infuses it with [an experiential] approach to learning' (Hopkins 2012, p. 3). The metaphor of the 'wilderness' embraces both urban and rural settings and is fully compatible with contemporary policy initiatives. The five elements of the design that form the outside of the star relate to most highly effective and high-performing schools. The middle element relates specifically to ALS and is what gives these schools their distinctive ethos. There are four key aspects to each core element and

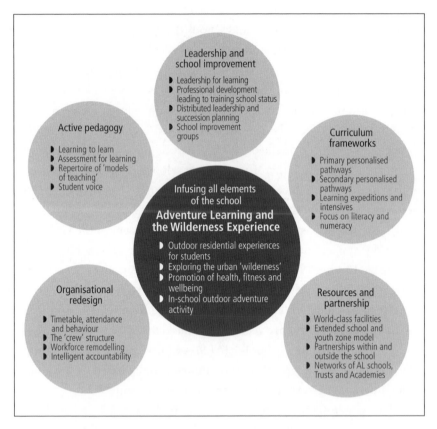

Figure 3.2 Core elements of the design of an Adventure Learning School (Adapted from Hopkins 2012)

each of these have a number of operational implications. We have published a handbook (Hopkins 2012) to describe the framework and a website which Adventure Learning Schools use to share their practices.

At the heart of ALS is 'a curriculum design that actively deepens subject expertise for all young people through engagement in learning both inside and outside the classroom'. There are five critical curriculum dimensions:

1. The first is the wilderness as an environment in which learning takes place, and which, through adventure and expeditionary challenges, enables young people to develop key skills and qualities. The outdoors also offers a vehicle for subject learning in the classroom, to enrich more traditional academic subjects with examples from the wider world.

2. The second is a curriculum that is delivered through active learning and has a predominantly enquiry-based approach. As a result, students acquire a range of learning skills through direct curriculum experience, assessment for learning and the expanded repertoire of teaching strategies utilised by staff.

3. Third is the flexible use of curriculum time. Utilising 'learning expeditions' which are extended lesson blocks to facilitate cross-curricular project-based work and 'intensives' that are opportunities for deep inquiry, catch-up or extended study by blocking out days and sometimes weeks every half term.

4. Fourth is a coherent curriculum experience that utilises the elements above, together with a range of additional learning entitlements related to the arts and the community. This ensures that the student completes each phase of the curriculum with a broad range of skills, knowledge and experiences that equip them for the next transition and eventually into adulthood.

5. The fifth is an unrelenting commitment to all young people achieving functional skills in literacy and numeracy. So at the secondary school level, for example, those students without the requisite skills participate in intensive literacy and numeracy programs so that they are capable of progressing in other curriculum subjects.

The purpose of this discussion of the framework for ALS is to illustrate the concept of a whole-school design and its possibilities in taking educational transformation to scale. As we shall see in the following section in considering the characteristics of those schools that have made a real difference, the development and implementation of a whole-school design illustrated in the work of Adventure Learning Schools potentially has wide applicability. The key point being made here is to emphasise the importance of the transference of proven practices from one setting to another in the pursuit of sustained systemic reform.

Schools that have made a difference

One of the encouraging features of the recent history of educational reform in both England and Australia is the progress that has been made in raising school standards. In England, for example, there has been almost a 20 per cent gain in literacy and numeracy at the primary school level and year-on-year gains in GCSE results in secondary schools. Although there is not comparable data in Australia at a federal level, Australia continues to perform well in PISA. There is also evidence of significant pockets of improvement in student outcomes in both states and regions, for example, as a result of specific school improvement efforts in areas such as NMR, or as a result of structural changes that have extended length of time in school such as in Western Australia and Queensland.

Despite these patterns of progress in recent years, still more needs to be done, and rapidly. The urgency of this quest is underlined by the statistics shown in Figure 3.3, which sadly reinforce the point that poverty remains the most significant contributor to poor school performance. There are, however, numerous examples of schools in both Australia and the UK that have managed to buck this trend, by breaking the link. In so doing, they have been successful in exploding the myth that a child's background is necessarily a determinant of their performance and that of their school.

In his study for the Office for Standards in Education in the UK, Peter Matthews studied twelve outstanding secondary schools (Ofsted

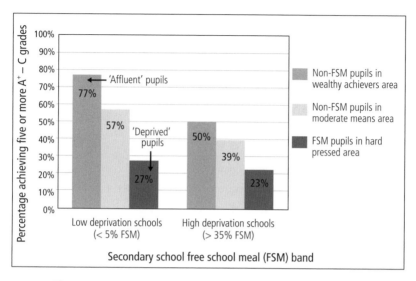

Figure 3.3 Deprivation as a key determinant of performance at school and pupil level

2009a) described as 'excelling against the odds' in terms of breaking the deprivation–attainment dependency illustrated in the statistics above. As Matthews (Ofsted 2009a, p. 5) says: 'The 12 outstanding schools studied in this report defy the association of poverty with outcomes; they enable such young people to succeed and reduce their disadvantage'. Although all the schools in Matthews' study were identified as being in the highest category of deprivation, that is, 35 per cent or more pupils were eligible for free school meals (FSM), they all:

▸ achieved over 80% good GCSE passes by students at the age of 16, with a sustained trajectory of improved attainment going forward
▸ had at least two recent inspection reports in which the school was judged as 'outstanding'
▸ received outstanding grades in their most recent inspection for teaching and learning, leadership and the school overall

- demonstrated a pattern of high contextual value-added (CVA) scores from Key Stage 2 (age 11) to Key Stage 4 (age 16).

What is so significant about these achievements is that the scale of the challenges faced by these schools is considerable. These include the following.

- A higher than average proportion of students come from poor or disturbed family backgrounds where support for learning and expectation of achievement are low.
- Many students are subject to emotional and psychological tension and regular attendance is a problem.
- A number of students are open to a range of 'urban ills' that often characterise poorer communities—drugs and alcohol, peer pressure of gangs and overt racism—which tend to attract behaviour which ranges from anti-social to violent.
- Getting such students ready and willing to learn, which schools strive to achieve by providing a better daytime alternative to being at home or on the streets.

In unpacking the reasons for the success of those outstanding schools described above, Matthews (Ofsted 2009a, p. 6) provides the following synthesis of what these schools do in practice to achieve such success and excel against the odds.

- They excel at what they do, not just occasionally but for a high proportion of the time.
- They prove constantly that disadvantage need not be a barrier to achievement, that speaking English as an additional language can support academic success and that schools really can be learning communities.

▶ They put students first, invest in their staff and nurture their communities.

▶ They have strong values and high expectations that are applied consistently and never relaxed.

▶ They fulfil individual potential through providing outstanding teaching, rich opportunities for learning and encouragement and support for each student.

▶ They are highly inclusive, having complete regard for the educational progress, personal development and wellbeing of every student.

▶ Their achievements do not happen by chance, but by highly reflective, carefully planned and implemented strategies that serve these schools well in meeting the many challenges that obstruct the path to success.

▶ They operate with a very high degree of internal consistency.

▶ They are constantly looking for ways to improve further.

▶ They have outstanding and well-distributed leadership.

In similar vein, the work of Vic Zbar and colleagues, commissioned by the Victorian Department of Education and Early Childhood Development, provides insights drawn from an examination of high-performing disadvantaged schools in Australia documented in the report *How our best performing schools come out on top* (Zbar, Kimber & Marshall 2008). Drawing on the evidence-base provided by both Matthews and Zbar from those secondary schools that demonstrate high levels of performance despite a baseline of deprivation and disadvantage, the following examples in action illustrate the features of those schools that have been successful in exploding the myth that poverty is necessarily a determinant of student and school performance. These examples are underpinned at their very core by a belief that, as Matthews (Ofsted 2009a, p. 6) emphasises, 'It is no longer acceptable to use a child's background as an excuse for underachievement'.

Example in action: England

Table 3.1 Features of schools that achieve, sustain and share excellence (Reproduced from Ofsted 2009a, p. 9)

Achieving excellence	Sustaining excellence	Sharing excellence
▶ Having vision, values and high expectations ▶ Attracting, recruiting, retaining and developing staff ▶ Establishing disciplined learning and consistent staff behaviour ▶ Assuring the quality of teaching and learning ▶ Leading and building leadership capacity ▶ Providing a relevant and attractive curriculum ▶ Assessment, progress-tracking and target-setting ▶ Inclusion: students as individuals	▶ Continuity of leadership ▶ Maintaining a strong team culture ▶ Continually developing teaching and learning ▶ Developing leaders ▶ Enriching the curriculum ▶ Improving literacy ▶ Building relationships with students, parents and the community ▶ No student left behind	▶ System leadership ▶ Partnering another school facing difficulties and improving it ▶ Acting as a community leader to broker relationships across other schools ▶ Developing and leading a successful school improvement partnership ▶ Working as a change agent or expert leader: National Leaders of Education

Example in action: Australia

St Albans Secondary College: Building a culture of achievement (Zbar et al. 2008).

▶ **Strong leadership.** The school's leadership sets high expectations for students and staff and has a set of key messages such as 'All kids can learn', 'You can all achieve', 'We expect you to participate in a learning community' and 'You have rights, but with that also comes responsibilities' (p. 64), which are continually reinforced and built into key policy areas.

▶ **Orderly structures.** Ensuring a safe, orderly learning environment as central to 'ensuring teachers can teach and kids can learn'. Students are 'expected to be in uniform, in class on time, attending school and ready to work' (p. 64). Expectations of academic success, social and community behaviour and student rights and responsibilities are regularly reinforced.

▶ **Curriculum documentation.** The curriculum is planned, based on clear expectations and documented electronically. The documentation includes the pedagogy and assessment and an acknowledged emphasis 'on how and what students learn'. A major in-school professional development program underpins this focus.

▶ **Positive work ethic.** Students' work ethic is made explicit and 'exhorts them to higher achievement' (p. 66). This comes with hard-edged expectations when needed and associated structures of challenge and support. The prime focus is to enable students to succeed, especially by having programs in place for students who lack the basics they require, or are at risk of falling behind.

▶ **Using data and celebrating success.** The school has developed a comprehensive data and assessment protocol to guide teachers' work. One benefit of knowing more from the data the school collects is the capacity it affords to recognise and reward student achievement.

At the same time as undertaking the study of successful secondary schools that have excelled against the odds, Matthews (Ofsted 2009a, p. 6) also recognised the pre-eminent position of primary schools, together with preschool providers of education and care 'when it comes to having a lasting impact on children's futures'. In his complementary study of primary education entitled *Twenty outstanding primary schools* (2009b), he identified twenty schools that do make a difference and have been successful in tackling the misconception that a child's background is in any way acceptable as an excuse for underachievement.

On the basis of similar criteria adopted in the selection of the secondary school sample, all the primary schools in this study:

▶ sustained excellence, indicated by being judged to be 'outstanding' in two or more inspections
▶ had a disadvantaged intake, indicated by over a quarter of pupils, that is, 50% above the average, being eligible for free school meals
▶ were judged as outstanding in terms of leadership and management, teaching and learning, as well as overall effectiveness
▶ achieved standards that compared favourably to national averages and were well above 'floor targets' at Key Stage 2 (age 11), that is, 65% of pupils attaining Level 4 in both English and mathematics
▶ had a contextual value-added (CVA) score exceeding 100, in the schools that had Key Stage 2 pupils.

In examining the ways in which these 20 schools make a difference, Matthews (Ofsted 2009b, p. 6), describes the following eight characteristics revealed during the course of school visits.

1. They provide affection, stability and a purposeful and structured experience.
2. They build—and often rebuild—children's self-belief.
3. They teach children the things they really need to know and show them how to learn for themselves and with others.
4. They give children opportunities, responsibility and trust in an environment that is both stimulating and humanising.

5. They listen to their pupils, value their views and reflect and act on what they say.

6. They build bridges with parents, families and communities, working in partnership with other professionals.

7. They ensure their pupils progress as far as possible and achieve as much as possible (outperforming both similar schools and many with fewer challenges).

8. In short, they put the child at the centre of everything they do, and high aspirations, expectations and achievement underpin the schools' work.

In focusing upon the primary phase of education and drawing further from the evidence-base on those high-performing schools that have demonstrated the creativity, competence and capacity to overcome the influences of deprivation, the examples in action that follow seek to provide: firstly, an exemplification of the common features of outstanding teaching and learning based on an analysis of the Ofsted inspection reports of the 20 outstanding primary schools in Matthews' study in the UK (Ofsted 2009b); and secondly, an illustrative case example from Dandenong North Primary School, based on an analysis of the characteristics of high-performing disadvantaged schools in Australia reported by Zbar et al. (2008).

Example in action: England

Features of outstanding teaching and learning:

▪ stimulating and enthusiastic teaching, which interests, excites and motivates pupils and accelerates their learning

▪ high expectations of what pupils can do

▪ consistency in the quality of teaching across the school

▪ development of good learning habits, with many opportunities for pupils to find things out for themselves

▶ highly structured approaches to reading, writing and mathematics, with some ability grouping
▶ well-planned lessons which provide for the differing needs of pupils
▶ stimulating classroom environments
▶ frequent praise and a valued reward system
▶ well-trained and deployed teaching assistants
▶ a close check on learning during lessons, with effective marking and assessment.

Example in action: Australia

Dandenong North Primary School: Ready and able to learn (Zbar et al. 2008)

▶ **Ready to learn in class.** The school does all in its power to ensure that students enter their classes able to learn and believing that this is their task. Substantial effort is put into ensuring that any student 'falling behind' is supported to come up to par and whatever the resources available, they are always directed towards getting more people working with students in and outside of the class.

▶ **The right people in place.** The central strategy used by the school to gain and maintain high results is ensuring it gets the 'right' people on staff, and that they are doing the right jobs in the school. Most important in this context is getting the mix of experience right.

▶ **Data as a circuit breaker.** In transcending beliefs regarding low expectations of students, the school has become attentive to its own data, examining in depth and determining how its students perform, resulting in raising the degree of expectation and challenge in the school. School review processes undertaken by staff 'promote ownership of data and understanding of what it means' (p. 45).

▶ **A focused approach.** Increased understanding of students and their needs is reflected in the very high property accorded to literacy and numeracy. There is a shared recognition that literacy in particular is fundamental to future learning success. Direct teaching plays a central role in the school, premised on the notion that 'we need to find out what [learners] do not know and teach it' (p. 45).

▶ **Layers of support.** There is a very strong sense of collegiality that promotes a culture of sharing and seeking support to 'do the best for all of the kids' (p. 46). All members of staff actively talk about teaching and learning with a focus on the classroom and the difference to student learning they make.

In their analyses both Matthews (Ofsted 2009a; 2009b) and Zbar et al. (2008) argue that that these schools do not succeed by accident, but for very clear reasons. Irrespective of phase and context, a number of common themes emerged from this work that are applicable to most or all of the schools involved. These include, for example, attention to the quality of teaching and learning; the assessment and tracking of students' progress; target-setting, support and intervention; attracting teachers; and growing leaders. It is important to stress, however, that the success of these schools is not due simply to what they do, but to the fact that it is rigorously distilled and applied good practice, cleverly selected and modified to fit the needs of the school. These schools do not value innovation for its own sake, but rather when it adds something extra. The practices described here are not 'off the peg' tricks; they mesh together and work synchronously as part of a clear framework for improvement.

The four drivers of school reform

What is apparent from the analysis of the schools that make a difference is that they have a very clear strategy for improvement that is integrated and focused on both raising achievement and building professional capacity in the school. Similarly, the transition from 'prescription' to 'professionalism' noted previously is not straightforward. In order to move from one to the other, strategies are required that not only continue to raise standards, but also build capacity within the system and school. This point is of key importance, as one cannot just drive to continue to raise standards in an instrumental way; there is also a need to develop social, intellectual and organisational capital. Building capacity demands that we replace numerous central initiatives with a national consensus on a limited number of educational trends (Hopkins 2009b).

As proposed in *Every school a great school* (Hopkins 2007), it seems to me that there are four key drivers that, if pursued relentlessly and deeply, will deliver both higher standards and enhanced professional capacity. Indeed, if a school or system were not emphasising these four themes, then I would question their ability to provide effective and personalised learning environments for their students. As introduced previously, the four drivers—personalised learning, professionalised teaching, intelligent accountability and networks and collaboration—are represented in Figure 3.4 as a 'diamond of reform'. The four trends coalesce and mould to context through the exercise of responsible system leadership. System leadership is the subject of subsequent discussion in Chapter Ten—it is the four drivers of school reform that are the focus here.

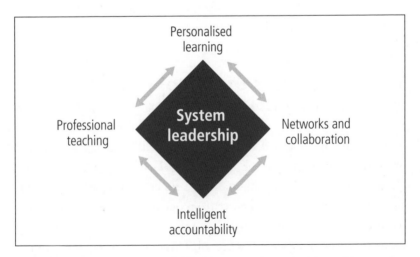

Figure 3.4 Four key drivers for building capacity and raising achievement (Reproduced from Hopkins 2007, p. 47)

1. Personalised learning

This is not a new idea.

> *Many schools and teachers have tailored curriculum and teaching methods to meet the needs of children and young people with great success for many years. What is new is the drive to make the best practices universal. It is [re-imagining] the education system around the learning needs and talents of young people that is the basis for every school becoming great. (Hopkins 2010c, p. 227)*

It is moral purpose that drives personalisation (DfES 2004c; Gilbert 2006; West-Burnham 2010). We see it most vividly in the concern of the committed, conscientious teacher to match what is taught and how it is taught to the individual learner as a person. This is not just a question of providing sufficient challenge or of aligning pedagogy to the point of progression that each learner has reached, even though that is vitally important. It is part of the teacher's concern to touch hearts as well as minds, to nourish a hunger for learning and help equip learners with both the proficiency and the confidence to pursue understanding for themselves (Hopkins 2010c). A successful system of personalised learning has clear implications: to raise standards by focusing teaching and learning on the aptitudes and interests of pupils and by removing any barriers to learning. The key question explored in Chapter Four is how collectively we build this offer for every pupil and every parent.

2. Professionalised teaching

Significant empirical evidence suggests that the quality of teaching is the most significant factor influencing student learning that is under the control of the school. A widely circulated international study (Barber & Mourshed 2007) concluded that:

▶ the quality of an education system cannot exceed the quality of its teachers
▶ the only way to improve outcomes is to improve instruction
▶ this means taking professional development into the classroom and making it routine (e.g. through peer observation, lesson study, demonstration lessons).

The phrase 'professionalised teaching' implies that teachers are on a par with other professions in terms of diagnosis, the application of evidence-based practices and professional pride. The image here is of teachers who use data to evaluate the learning needs of their students, and are consistently expanding their repertoire of pedagogic strategies to personalise learning for all students. It also implies schools adopting innovative approaches to timetabling and the deployment of increasingly differentiated staffing models. Crucially, the focus of professional development needs to be unrelentingly on the 'instructional core'. This concept is discussed in detail in Chapter Five and further in Chapter Seven, but in its simplest terms, the instructional core can be regarded as the transactions that occur between 'the teacher and the student in the presence of content' (City et al. 2009, p. 22). Later discussion also addresses the two broad categories of strategies—deductive and inductive—that have a proven track record of building such professional work cultures within schools.

3. Intelligent accountability

This refers to the balance between nationally determined approaches to external accountability on the one hand, and on the other the capacity for professional accountability within the school that emphasises the importance of formative assessment and the pivotal role of self-evaluation (Hopkins 2009b). In any debate on accountability it is important to distinguish between means and ends, methods and purpose. There are two key purposes for accountability. The first is as a tool to support higher levels of student learning and achievement; the second is to maintain public confidence. The means of achieving these will inevitably vary from country to country and from situation to situation. In general, where there are high levels of student achievement and small variations of performance between schools, then pressures from external accountability will be modest. However, in those situations where there is a need for more robust forms of external accountability it should always be designed to support teacher professionalism and the school's capacity to utilise data to enhance student performance (DEECD 2011). Most systems of national accountability are established on the four pillars of tests, targets, tables and inspection or review. In many systems, they are dominated by their external forms. As systems move to the more inside–out ways of working described earlier, they seek to redress the balance in favour of internal assessment. The intricacies of this direction of travel are discussed in detail in Chapter Six.

4. Networks and collaboration

The prevalence of networking practice in recent years supports the contention that there is no contradiction between strong, independent schools and strong networks—rather the reverse. Effective networks require strong leadership by participating head teachers, principals and other school leaders, as well as clear objectives that add significant value to individual schools' own efforts (DEECD 2011). Without this, networks wither and die, since the transaction costs outweigh the benefits they deliver. Nor is there a contradiction between collaboration and competition—many sectors of the economy are demonstrating that the combination of competition and collaboration delivers the most rapid improvements. Although evidence of effectiveness is still accumulating, it is becoming clear that networks support improvement and innovation by enabling schools to collaborate on building curriculum diversity, extended services and professional support. In turn, this aids development of a vision of education that is shared and owned well beyond individual school gates. Networks can therefore be the foundations for an innovative system of education (DfES 2005b; NCSL 2006b; Horne 2008). Indeed, it has been argued that it is *only* networks that can deliver a mix of 'vertical–central' and 'lateral–local' reform strategies necessary for transformation (Hopkins 2007; Higham et al. 2009). In short, the system itself has to become a more self-conscious and effective learning system in parallel with the learning organisation advocated for schools. This issue, together with those outlined above, is addressed in the discussion of innovation, networking and professional learning presented in Chapter Seven.

System leadership

As has already been argued, these key drivers provide a core strategy for systemic improvement through building capacity while also raising standards of learning and achievement. It is system leadership, though, again as we will see in later chapters, that adapts them to particular and individual school contexts. This is leadership that enables systemic reform to be both generic in terms of overall strategy and specific in adapting to individual and particular situations. It is system leaders who reach beyond their own school to create networks and collaborative arrangements that not only add richness and excellence to the learning of students, but also act as agents of educational transformation (Ballantyne, Jackson & Temperley 2006; Carter & Franey 2006; Hopkins 2009a). It is also important to realise, as they do themselves, that such leaders also operate in the context of the system of their own schools. Indeed, as we have already noted, 'their achievements do not happen by chance, but by highly reflective, carefully planned and implemented strategies' (Ofsted 2009a, p. 6). It is therefore instructive to discuss what these planning strategies look like before examining in more detail each of the four drivers for improvement in turn in the chapters that follow.

The importance of planning

It should be becoming clear that system leaders need to be able to think strategically in both the short and the medium term. Furthermore, this thinking needs to be underpinned by quality planning. Evidence of good practice and the lessons from research suggest that development planning needs to focus on both how to accelerate the progress and enhance the achievement of students *as well as* establishing effective management practices or organisational structures within the school. This approach to planning is neither top-down (i.e. focused in the main on management arrangements) nor bottom-up (i.e. committed to specific changes in individual classrooms); it is a combination of the two (Hopkins 2009b). It is this understanding that has led to a re-conceptualisation of how development planning can be used to enhance pupil progress and achievement. This also reflects the balancing act between what are often regarded as polar opposites in order to achieve a more dynamic approach to educational reform—in connection with systemic reform, school improvement, accountability and leadership for example.

This approach to development planning concerns the integration of three key foci:

1. pupil progress and achievement
2. the quality of teaching and learning
3. organisational redesign to support the first two (Hopkins & MacGilchrist 1998).

Schools adopting this approach identify clear learning targets for pupils and use development planning to achieve these by concentrating simultaneously on related improvements inside and outside the classroom. In particular, with regards to teaching, they place specific emphasis on the content of teachers' planning and on the type of teaching strategies that will enable the learning goals for students to be achieved (Hopkins 1998). Additionally, in considering the school's organisational re-design, they identify any modifications that are needed to the school's current arrangements (e.g. timetable, budget, staffing, staff development) and they plan for any changes that may be needed in the school's curriculum policies, schemes of work and assessment strategies.

The stronger the relationship between improvements inside the classroom (in terms of teaching) and outside the classroom (in terms of management arrangements), the more successful the school is in raising standards. In the past, for very understandable reasons, plans have tended to concentrate on organisational structures or maintenance activities, with the result that, for many schools, the plan had little significant impact on pupils' learning. This was often as a consequence of schools' planning being focused on staff activities rather than student outcomes. The key lesson here is that when schools plan for both of these aspects of development in a strategic way, it does make a difference where it matters most, namely in the classroom for pupils (Hopkins & MacGilchrist 1998).

Figure 3.5 illustrates the interface between whole-school development and classroom practice by integrating the three key foci detailed above. At the heart of the model is pupils' progress and achievement supported by the quality of teaching and learning in the classroom. Outside the classroom are the key management arrangements and practices that support and provide the context for quality learning experiences within the classroom.

In any action plan for student achievement, the classroom should be the main focus for improvement. The priorities for development must also be rooted in evidence about pupils' progress and achievement. Targeted action can then address:

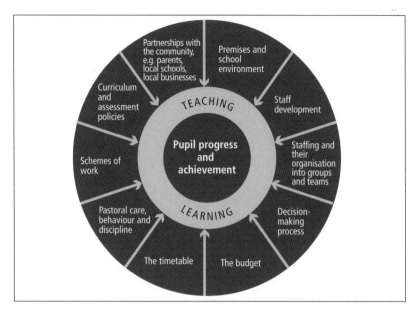

Figure 3.5 The interface between whole-school development and classroom practice (Adapted from Hopkins & MacGilchrist 1998)

▶ specific improvements in pupil outcomes
▶ changes in teaching practices
▶ any modifications needed to school-wide provision, management or organisational arrangements to support developments in the classroom.

An action plan for student achievement will therefore need to include the following:

▶ Specific targets related to pupils' learning, progress and achievement that are clear and unambiguous.
▶ Teaching and learning strategies designed to meet the targets.
▶ Evidence to be gathered to judge the success in achieving the targets set.

▶ Modifications to management arrangements to enable targets to be met.
▶ Tasks to be done to achieve the targets set and who is responsible for doing them.
▶ Time the plan will take.
▶ How much it will cost in terms of the budget, staff time, staff development and other resources.
▶ Responsibility for monitoring the implementation of the plan.
▶ Strategies for evaluating its impact over time (Hopkins 1998).

There is more to planning than this though, and although such a protocol is necessary, it is not sufficient for the purposes we have for school improvement. We also need to consider three other key processes: firstly, how priorities are set; secondly, how they are managed over time; and thirdly, how implementation is linked to evaluation.

1. Setting priorities

In setting priorities for development rather than maintenance schools need to choose priorities that:

▶ focus on pupil progress and achievement
▶ are manageable and few in number
▶ relate to the school's vision
▶ are sequenced over time (Hopkins & MacGilchrist 1998).

The following figures are adapted from *The empowered school* (Hargreaves & Hopkins 1991). Figures 3.6a and b use criteria related to urgency, need and desirability; size and scope; distinguishing root and branch innovations and forging the links between priorities.

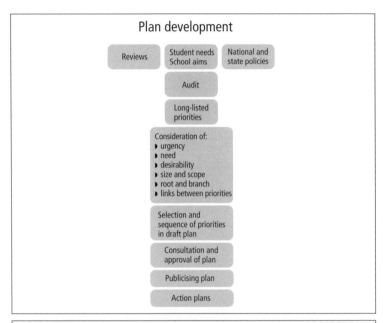

Figures 3.6a and b Selecting priorities
(Adapted from Hargreaves & Hopkins 1991)

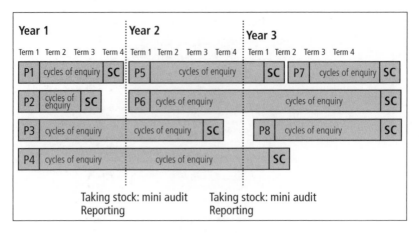

Figure 3.7 Sequencing priorities
(Adapted from Hargreaves & Hopkins 1991, p. 47)

P = Priority for development
SC = Success checks which take place at the end of work on a priority

2. Managing priorities over time

Successful schools have established a rolling program of policy review and revision spanning a number of years related to the particular priority for student learning and achievement being worked on at that point in time. As shown in Figure 3.7, this has given these schools the space to use the development plan to achieve an explicit classroom focus.

3. Linking implementation to evaluation

As distinct from previous approaches that focused on the management of external change and the implementation of school-wide policies, this approach to development planning begins with the learning needs of students and moves out from there. After setting targets for student learning, progress and achievement, the plan focuses on developing a strategy for enhancing teaching and creating powerful learning experiences, and then on the organisational redesign required to support such changes in classroom practice. This will inevitably have a 'knock on' effect for the timetable, the budget, staffing arrangements, professional development provision and possibly the premises. The schedules for these basic aspects of the work of the school will, therefore, need to take account of current and future priorities in the development plan (Hopkins 1998).

It is also important to stress that planning is an active process; if it is to affect the learning of students, it will need to pay attention to both implementation and evaluation. What is critical is that evaluation is not regarded as a 'big bang' at the end of the process but is from the outset integrated with classroom implementation, as seen in Figure 6.1. The key to the integration of implementation and evaluation of school improvement activities is the action plan used by groups of teachers. An action plan is a working document that describes and summarises what needs to be done to implement and evaluate a priority. It serves as a guide to implementation and helps to monitor progress and success. There are three key elements to the enquiry aspect of the action plan.

1. The *success criteria* against which progress and success in reaching targets can be judged.
2. The allocation of responsibility to *assess progress*.
3. How *success* is subsequently judged.

To summarise, the integration of implementation and evaluation within development planning is supported through the identification of success criteria and the use of regular progress and success checks. Although these frameworks are important in supporting the link between implementation and evaluation, it is the enhancing of the professional judgements of teachers that ensures the consistency of practice so necessary in breaking the association between poverty and achievement.

Coda

This myth is a tough nut to crack and sadly we cannot claim to have fully exploded it. What we have demonstrated, however, is that poverty *is not necessarily* a determinant of student and school performance. The examples from England, UK and Victoria, Australia demonstrate unequivocally that this is the case. From the school effectiveness legacy and more recent research, we have also learnt that there are clear specifications of both the organisational culture and the specifics of teaching, learning and curriculum that can be transferred effectively and efficiently from one school setting to another. The transfer of specifications of good practice is still an underutilised strategy in the war—and the word is used rightly here— to ensure that poverty cannot for much longer be regarded as a determinant of, or as an excuse for, not achieving educational success. The critical point is that the elimination of poverty as a determinant is not the result of aspiration, as important as that is—rather it is the consequence of deliberate actions by teachers fuelled by moral purpose and facilitated by strategic whole-school planning.

I have been discussing these issues recently with my friend, the leading American school improver, Sam Stringfield. I invited him to share his thoughts on implementing school reform in the current context with me. This is his eight-point email response.

1. Be very clear with yourself on desired outcomes of the reform, and quantitative measures of success. Have four or fewer goals. I'd recommend national or state measures and student attendance as two of them, but that's just me.
2. Get buy-in from the school heads and the local authority or region on those goals and measures, or don't start. No point in wasting your and their time.

3. If at all possible, have all of the primaries or secondaries in a region or a geographically identifiable subgroup all working together. If they aren't willing to share, the reform is doomed.

4. Tell the heads and teachers at first meeting, 'I know a lot about school improvement and teacher effectiveness. You are the world's leading experts on your school(s). Either we co-construct change or we won't get change. You in? Right. Let's get going'.

5. Engage the teachers and heads with more data analyses than they have ever seen before. Have them engage the students, too.

6. Plan on cross-site professional development and inter-visitation.

7. Assume that it will take more professional development time and local investment than you wish were true—assume a minimum of three years.

8. The more concrete stuff to look at and use in classrooms, the better.

There is much wisdom in the contemporary theory and practice of school reform that underpins Stringfield's proposals. Many of the points he makes also have resonance with the best of what we know about effective schools (and indeed regions or districts) that have been successful in severing the dependency relationship between poverty and performance in education. Stringfield's analysis is also helpful in illustrating how the four drivers for improvement—personalised learning, professionalised teaching, intelligent accountability and networks and collaboration—introduced in Chapter One provide the core strategy for systemic improvement. It is these topics that provide the focus for the next four chapters.

Chapter 4

Personalising Learning

The myth that it is the curriculum rather than the learning that counts

Despite its relatively recent history, the idea of 'personalisation' has nevertheless become widely popular in many countries besides Australia and the UK, as an approach to reforming public sector services towards more effective provision in meeting the individual needs of service users (Bentley & Miller 2006). Personalisation is a very simple concept. It is about putting citizens at the heart of public services and enabling them to have a say in the design and improvement of the organisations that serve them (DfES 2004c). As Charles Leadbeater (2005, p. 14) describes it, in essence, personalisation is concerned with learning about 'what it is that the people we serve in public services really want'. In attempting to capture what this means in practice for the education sector in particular, he provides the following definition:

> *At its root personalisation is about education, about morality, human social goals, connecting with the internal motivations that*

we need to unlock for people to really learn; it's about moving from seeing education as meeting and imposing external standards to meet external yardsticks, to working on internal motivation and aspiration.

In education this can be understood as 'personalising learning'—the drive to tailor education to individual needs, interests and aptitudes, in order to fulfil every young person's potential and enhance their ability to learn. The moral dimension of personalisation to which Leadbeater refers was directly reflected in the introduction of the concept of 'personalised learning' into the English education system in 2004 (Miliband 2004; DfES 2004a, 2004c), which had very clear moral and strategic purposes in mind. These purposes were informed by an increasing understanding of the nature of systemic reform. Thus moral purpose was defined by the commitment to ensure that *every* student was enabled to reach their potential, whatever that was, through making satisfactory progress year-on-year. At the same time, the strategic purpose was informed by the realisation that the top-down reforms of the first Blair term had served their purpose, and in the quest to continue to raise standards, a new approach to improvement had to be found.

The introduction of an emphasis on personalised learning was part of a deliberate effort to shift the education system from an outside–in to an inside–out way of working. This approach was not focused on the slavish adoption of externally developed or imposed curricula, but the use of proven practices as tools to raise standards of achievement, as well as building student and teacher capacity for learning. In this way, personalising learning can be viewed as 'a unique opportunity to combine policy and professional imperatives' (West-Burnham 2010, p. 5). John West-Burnham (2010, pp. 7–8) further describes the moral imperative for adopting such an approach to personalising learning in the present day like this:

It is not just another initiative with a range of techniques. It is perhaps best seen as a powerful opportunity to focus on the core purpose of schools—the quality of the learning of every individual—by developing a direct link between policy and practice. [It] is perhaps the most effective way of translating the rhetoric of the learning-centred school into the actual reality of every learner's experience. It also offers models to transform the quality of the working lives of adults in schools.

The four drivers described in this and subsequent chapters have the unique capability of improving both performance and the ability to learn at the same time. This applies at the student, teacher, school and system levels. It also explains why the concept of personalisation is so congruent with the approach to inside–out working described in this book. In order to build a successful system of personalised learning:

We must begin by acknowledging that giving every single child the chance to be the best they can be, whatever their talent or background, is not the betrayal of excellence, it is the fulfilment of it. (DfES 2004d, p. 8)

A system that responds to individual pupils, by creating an education path that takes account of their needs, interests and aspirations, will not only generate excellence, it will also make a strong contribution to equity and social justice (Leadbeater 2005; Department for Children, Schools and Families 2007).

This discussion also serves to challenge the perception that it is the curriculum rather than the learning that counts, the myth that provides the focus for this chapter. Recent analyses from research, policy and practice suggest that although the curriculum and in particular, curriculum choice, curriculum materials and curriculum breadth are important (DfES 2006; Gilbert 2006; West-Burnham 2010), it is an emphasis on learning rather than the curriculum that provides the key to personalisation within the school system. David Hargreaves (2006) underlines this point in describing the 'gateways' to personalising learning. Here, 'deep learning' is seen to comprise three components: 'learning to learn', 'assessment for learning' and 'student voice' (Simms 2006). At the same time, 'design and organisation' are recognised as a key element of 'deep leadership', and 'mentoring and coaching' as a core component of 'deep support' (Vacher 2007). These key components of personalising learning, that also serve to explode the myth of curriculum dominance, are explored in this chapter by focusing on:

> learning to learn
> assessment for learning
> curriculum design and entitlement
> giving students a voice.

Learning to learn

At the heart of personalized learning is its impact, not just on test scores and examination results, but also on students' learning capability. If the teacher can teach the student how to learn at the same time as assisting them to acquire curriculum content, then the twin goals of learning and achievement can be met simultaneously. (Hopkins 2010c, p. 230)

In describing teacher strategies for the 'personalised classroom', the DfES report *Making good progress* (2006, p. 16) sets out the challenge for achieving this in the following terms:

The personalised classroom gives the pupils more opportunities to get involved, be curious, develop interests and call for the help they need. The challenge for pupils is to take responsibility for their own learning; and the challenge for the education system is to engage their instinct to learn.

There is now an increasingly sophisticated literature on how children learn (Wood 1998), the different types of multiple intelligences (Gardner 1999) and the descriptions of a range of learning styles (Kolb 1984). As increasing numbers of educators have taken on board learning to learn programs, these reference points have been extended to embrace understandings about the application of emotional intelligence theory in classrooms and schools (Goleman 1996; Elias, Kress & Hunter 2006). This trend has also encouraged the development of skills for building learning power such as those captured in Guy Claxton's popular '4 R's' model (2002; 2007)—resilience, resourcefulness, reflectiveness and reciprocity—which has been widely adopted in the UK (Barnes & Smith 2007; Sims 2006). Although a discussion of these literatures is beyond the scope of this chapter, it is instructive to show how they have influenced the way in which personalised learning is currently defined.

A fundamental aspect of personalized learning is ... the ability of learners to respond successfully to the tasks that they are set, as well as the tasks they set themselves—in particular to:

▶ *integrate prior and new knowledge*
▶ *acquire and use a range of learning skills*
▶ *solve problems individually and in groups*
▶ *think carefully about their successes and failures*
▶ *evaluate conflicting evidence and to think critically*
▶ *accept that learning involves uncertainty and difficulty.*

The deployment of such a range of learning strategies is commonly termed meta-cognition, which can be regarded as the learner's ability to take control over their own learning processes. (Hopkins 2010c, p. 230)

As Emma Sims (2006, p. 6) illustrates in unpacking the meaning of achieving deep learning through a personalised approach, the development of metacognitive skills is central to the success of any learning to learn program:

Key to the effectiveness of learning to learn programmes is the development of meta-cognitive skills, in other words, thinking about and reflecting on one's own learning. Through the development of meta-cognition students are encouraged to monitor, evaluate, control and reflect on their own learning, thus making a powerful contribution towards their development as confident and independent learners.

As discussed in an earlier article (Hopkins 2010c, p. 230),

The key point is that within whatever context learning takes place, it involves an active construction of meaning. This carries implications for the management of learning opportunities, in particular that an active construction of meaning requires [the application of] practical, cognitive and other learning strategies. As learning is [interactive] it can occur only as the learner makes sense of particular experiences in particular contexts. This making sense involves connecting with an individual's prior knowledge and experience. Thus, new learning has to relate to, and ultimately fit with, what individuals already understand.

This is where Vygotsky's (1962) insights extend, in my opinion, Bruner's tripartite integration of cognitive development, knowledge and teaching. His articulation of the 'zone of proximal development' has two key components. The first relates to the necessity to focus instruction at that margin between what the learner already knows and what they can learn in the company of a more experienced or knowledgeable other, such as a teacher or a peer. Ensuring that teaching occurs within the learner's zone of proximal development is a 'meta principle' for personalising learning. The second aspect of Vygotsky's theory is not just identifying the learning zone, but how to operate within the zone. It is here where the concept of scaffolding is so powerful. Scaffolding refers to the interactional support through dialogue, designed and led by the more competent other, in order to maximise the child's learning. This leads to the gradual withdrawal of support as the child gains knowledge and competence. This interactive view of learning is mirrored in Chapter Five by a discussion of how a teaching strategy can also be a model of learning.

While this exploration of the learning process is central to developing our understandings of the importance of learning to learn as a core component of personalisation, it is of equal importance to address the skills of learning that need to be taught and acquired. These skills can be broadly interpreted as including 'personal skills and strategies to enable self-management and direction ... and skills for further study and employability' (West-Burnham 2010, p. 12). This leads to a consideration of what skills are needed for 21st century learners and what frameworks are used to develop them. The general conclusion to be drawn is that there are significant skills gaps among learners emerging from the analysis of employer needs in the UK. For example, in Wales, the *Generic skills survey* (Future Skills Wales [FSW] 2003) revealed a lack of IT skills as the most common problem, followed by communication skills, showing initiative and problem solving (cited in Welsh Assembly Government 2008, p. 2).

It is realisations such as this that have led to the pursuance of a personalised skills agenda in the education sector in the UK, with varying emphases upon 'key skills' in England (DfEE 1999a; 1999b), 'core skills' in Scotland (Her Majesty's Inspectorate for Education 2001) and 'future skills' in Wales (FSW 2003). In recent years this has resulted in the implementation of a *Skills framework for 3- to 19-year-olds in Wales* (Welsh Assembly Government 2008), which incorporates a clear focus on functional skills in the areas of ICT and numeracy, thinking skills and personal skills in communication. This framework was introduced in the clear recognition that, as Estyn (2002) describes in setting out a vision for schools in Wales in the 21st century:

> *Schools will need to devote attention to developing attitudes to learning—affecting the disposition of learners and developing their learning skills—as well as to delivering formal instruction.*

Similarly, in Scotland, the introduction of the *Curriculum for excellence 3* (The Scottish Government 2008) has been underpinned by a skills framework incorporating 'skills for learning, skills for life and skills for work' (The Scottish Government 2009). This framework also pays attention to, among other things, functional skills in literacy and numeracy, 'thinking skills across learning' and personal skills including 'working with others' and 'personal learning planning'. This move towards embedding skills within the curriculum has been observed as a broad pattern across numerous countries internationally by Whitby and Walker (2006, p. 7) in their international review detailing a 'thematic probe' of the teaching and learning of skills in primary and secondary education. Among the countries studied, Tasmania (Australia) identified 'thinking skills' incorporating 'two key elements of enquiry and reflective thinking' as a priority across the whole curriculum. Here, both 'thinking skills and the skills of learning to learn' were defined as integral to the purpose of education (Whitby & Walker 2006, p. 10).

While there is clearly some variation of emphasis in considering these examples of embedding a skills agenda in the education systems of each country, there appears to be a general consensus that the skills for personalising learning, including those related to learning to learn, fall into three broad categories: functional skills; thinking and learning skills; and personal skills. In line with the argument presented in the following chapter, the most appropriate way of embedding these skills is through improved guidance, and training in teaching and learning across the curriculum. This has the great advantage of teachers becoming more proficient themselves in integrating the teaching and learning of skills into subject content. There are a variety of teaching and learning strategies that can be employed, and these could be championed by a variety of national or locally based agencies. These include:

▶ **subject specific programs** that contribute to pupils' understanding, thinking and learning of key skills in a subject context
▶ **discrete skills programs** (learning to learn lessons) that enable an explicit focus on skills with reference to a broad range of subject content and contexts
▶ **cross-curricular programs** that connect specific learning skills with a focus on subject content to help students transfer their learning between lessons.

So in summary, as we have seen in the examples above, the clarity provided by a single skills framework, especially when it is allied with better guidance and training on pedagogy, will itself create greater coherence across any national curriculum. This is the necessary foundation for ensuring that the essence of personalisation is available for every student and, in turn, it is a critical building block in ensuring that every school is able to simultaneously meet the twin goals of learning and achievement for all young people (Hopkins 2010c). It also provides a sustained argument—particularly in light of the demand for skills analysis—that it is learning rather than curriculum that counts.

Assessment for learning

It is no surprise that the advent of personalised learning has taken almost two decades to emerge as a potential strategy for improving learning and raising achievement. In England, successive governments since the early 1990s have favoured assessment-led reform not only to improve the quality of teaching and learning and to raise standards but also, importantly, to provide more credible forms of public accountability (Broadfoot & Murphy 1995; Gipps 1994; Black 1998). The establishment of a national assessment and testing infrastructure in England was, therefore, the main government priority at that time and inevitably these large-scale, legislated assessments received the most attention at system level.

The attempt to make these national statutory summative assessments fulfil a range of other purposes—formative, diagnostic and evaluative—led to what can be described as a 'formative assessment movement'. Consequently, the research base for formative assessment has seen a dramatic increase and has been influential in shaping what has become known as 'Assessment for Learning' (AfL). As a result of the publication of the seminal research *Inside the black box* (Black & Wiliam 1998) which identified the links between assessment and learning, the authors were confident enough in their findings to present a strong case for the consideration of the development of formative assessment in the drive to raise standards. In countries that have sought to emulate the assessment systems in England, for example in Australia, researchers have similarly reinforced the need to embrace alternative approaches to assessment beyond a singular emphasis on test results.

There are alternative approaches for schools and teachers to demonstrate accountability that places less emphasis on test results. Important questions need to be considered and mistakes that other national systems have encountered need to be avoided in Australia. (Klenowski 2011, p. 17)

The emergence of AfL as an outcome of the formative assessment movement has subsequently been closely coupled with the evolution of the concept of personalised learning within the English education system. The identification of 'assessment for learning and the use of evidence and dialogue to identify every pupil's learning needs' as one of the five key components of personalised learning (DfES 2004c, p. 8) established the foundation for this. Subsequent endorsement in the publication of the Gilbert report *2020 Vision* (2006, p. 16) gave further weight and impetus to the development of AfL as a key component of personalised learning, stressing the importance of ensuring that 'assessment for learning is embedded in all schools and classrooms so that its benefits are fully realised'. The authoritative definition of AfL by the Assessment Reform Group (ARG 2002) subsequently used by the DfES in introducing their *Assessment for Learning Strategy* (2008) states that:

Assessment for learning is the process of seeking and interpreting evidence for use by learners and their teachers to decide where the learners are in their learning, where they need to go and how best to get there.

Understandings of this definition and its application in practice were further expanded by the ARG (2002) in detailing what have now become widely known as the ten principles of AfL. The principles state that assessment for learning should:

1. be part of effective planning of teaching and learning
2. focus on how students learn
3. be recognised as central to classroom practice
4. be regarded as a key professional skill for teachers
5. be sensitive and constructive because any assessment has an emotional impact
6. take account of the importance of learner motivation
7. promote commitment to learning goals and a shared understanding of the criteria by which they are assessed
8. ensure learners receive constructive guidance about how to improve
9. develop learners' capacity for self-assessment so that they can become reflective and self-managing
10. recognise the full range of achievements of all learners.

In examining differing conceptions of assessment for learning amongst education practitioners, research conducted by Eleanore Hargreaves (2003) indicated that the summary definitions of AfL fell into six broad categories:

▸ monitoring pupils' performance against targets or objectives
▸ informing next steps in teaching and learning
▸ teachers giving feedback for improvement
▸ teachers learning about children's learning
▸ children taking some control of their learning and assessment
▸ turning assessment into a learning event.

These definitions highlighted the dichotomy between a focus on learning processes and a focus on performance. Those teachers who understood AfL to be about monitoring pupil performance against targets or objectives described the process as setting targets based on assessments and adjusting the learning experiences in order for children to meet those targets. The emphasis here was on the teacher setting the targets. Other teachers in the study described AfL as a process of deciding the 'next steps' in learning and that assessment should feed back into teaching once again emphasising the teacher's role and taking the next steps towards a given standard. This latter perspective is the one being argued for here. It is the emphasis on pupils' learning rather than performance, relating to the process of how children learn and what they need to do to improve, rather than a concentration on proving what they know, understand and can do. This position is reflected by Watkins (2001, p. 7) who argues, in what to some seem paradoxical terms, that 'a focus on learning processes can enhance performance, whereas a focus on performance can depress performance'.

The reasons why certain voices have become dominant in promoting understandings of and approaches to AfL can be seen in the perceptions of what appears to be most valued—learning processes, or performance against given standards. Hargreaves' suggestion that the duality of assessment of/for learning may not sit at opposite poles of the assessment spectrum is based on the premise that the 'black box' research represents a particular version of assessment characterised primarily by a measurement and objectives conception of assessment and learning. Similarly, the assessment strategy promoted by the DfES, National Strategies and the Qualifications and Curriculum Authority in England, is based on their interpretation of the definition of AfL provided by the Assessment Reform Group (2002).

It is revealing therefore that Dylan Wiliam, co-author of the founding publication *Inside the black box* (1998), views this situation 'as a "tragedy"—one he blames on the interference of government and on himself' (Stewart 2012). Although it is acknowledged that most teachers and schools are familiar with the term 'assessment for learning', the problem, according to Wiliam (cited in Stewart 2012), is that they have not understood it properly:

There are very few schools where all the principles of AfL, as I understand them, are being implemented effectively ... The problem is that government told schools that it was all about monitoring pupils' progress; it wasn't about pupils becoming owners of their own learning.

The vision for AfL that Wiliam had intended to portray is most clearly captured by Dann (2002, p. 153) who defines it as 'assessment [which] is not merely an adjunct to teaching and learning, but offers a process through which pupil involvement in assessment can feature as part of learning—that is assessment as learning'. The notion of assessment *as* learning is complex and translating that into day-to-day classroom practice requires that practitioners have a thorough understanding of assessment processes and the theories that underpin them. Such changes in classroom assessment represent major paradigm shifts in thinking about learning, schools and teaching (Hargreaves, Earl & Schmidt 2002). Classroom assessment requires that teachers use their judgements about children's knowledge, understand how to include feedback in the teaching process and decide how to meet students' varying learning needs (Tunstall & Gipps 1995). The significant change required in disseminating the idea of formative assessment as 'assessment as learning' has been controversial and like all challenging educational developments has taken time to show impact across the system. What has emerged over the past ten years, however, has been the need to consider formative assessment as a coherent whole and not a series of techniques practised in isolation. An important feature of the shift in mindset has been in relation to the necessity of students being active participants in the learning process, which of course is the essence of personalisation.

In conclusion, then, some ten years on from the ARG's establishment of the principles of AfL, it is important to reflect on the lessons learnt from the implementation of assessment for learning at both school and system levels. As we have identified in discussion in earlier chapters, system-wide reform often falters at the implementation stage, where national strategies such as those for assessment for learning fail to take hold with any consistency, because the initiative is not properly or fully implemented. Despite the worldwide popularity of AfL among education practitioners, there is certainly a perception, in England at least, that it 'has not had the impact it should have done because of the lack of a proper strategy for teacher professional development' (cited in Stewart 2012).

As described in the introduction to this book, in successfully moving potentially powerful initiatives such as AfL to scale at school and system levels, we need to implement with precision and energy, then study the effort, reflect on it, re-energise and refine. It is encouraging to note that these lessons have been learnt and applied, for example through the involvement of 'Learning Teams' of teachers in local authorities operating across the UK (Clarke 2008), where strategies for formative assessment have been subject to action research by teachers in classrooms. This has served not only to increase practitioner understanding of the strategies and underlying principles, but has also refined teachers' thinking and helped to create a frame of reference for effective practice. As Clarke (2008, p. 11) has commented:

The acid test of effective formative assessment ... is not how well written the strategies are, or how many good techniques are in use, but the extent to which pupils are, as a result of our work, actively engaged in thinking, learning and assessing that learning.

Curriculum design and entitlement

It is somewhat ironic to have a section in a chapter intended to disprove the myth of curriculum dominance, which focuses on the curriculum! Of course, the myth has some validity and of course the curriculum is important. The broader implications of the myth are discussed elsewhere in the chapter; the key question here is how curriculum design and entitlement can help—in a very practical way—to both support learning and at the same time deliver a national curriculum in an effective manner. While it is acknowledged that there is a need to design and create curriculum and timetabling models that enable opportunities for learning within and outside the classroom, this raises even deeper questions about curriculum planning particularly in the English and Australian school contexts.

It is the curriculum that provides the means for every school to become a great school and for every student to realise their potential. Yet in many educational systems the curriculum is often a barrier to achieving the forms of personalised learning so necessary for such a transformation. One way of both pinpointing the curriculum issue and of drawing the argument together is to pose the question 'What does it mean to be educated?' at any particular phase of education.

Being educated at any particular age has four central elements:

▶ a breadth of knowledge gained from a curricular entitlement
▶ a range of skills on a developmental continuum that reflects increasing depth at ages 7, 11, 14, 16 and, in many cases, 18
▶ a range of learning experiences
▶ a set of key products, projects or artefacts.

It also means that students are sufficiently articulate to:

▶ sustain employability through basic skills
▶ apply their knowledge and skills in different contexts

▶ choose from and learn in a range of post-14 study (assuming an entitlement curriculum up until then)

▶ draw on wider experiences to inform further learning and choice.

Most National Curricula do not meet these desiderata. Although the following proposals were originally based on our understanding of the Key Stage 3 (11–14) curriculum in England, they represent a broader attempt to imagine a structure that enables schools and teachers to personalise the curriculum across all stages of education.

The first is to **focus on core study.** Functional literacy, numeracy and communication could be clarified as expected attainment at the end of the KS3 curriculum. ICT would also need to be explicitly added to a suggested core of mother tongue, maths and science. Functional skills would similarly need to be embedded across the curriculum.

The second would be a **condensed statutory curriculum in non-core subjects combined with an optional entitlement.** In many countries this is referred to as the 'essential curriculum'. This means that the statutory curriculum content and processes in non-core subjects would be reduced. As a rule of thumb in most national systems this would mean that the content removed would be approximately 20–25% of current specifications. The reduction could be re-designated as an optional entitlement. The entitlement would make up a number of components in the breadth of study currently set out for each subject. Schools would be required to teach a minimum number of components.

Third, the flexibility of an **optional entitlement** would allow schools to guarantee time to:

▶ secure essential knowledge and teach common learning skills through the curriculum

▶ organise the curriculum to meet the needs of a range of abilities, tailoring support for underachieving and underperforming students, and to stretch gifted and talented students.

Fourth, there needs to be **clarity on common learning skills.** This requires that a common framework of skills be identified across the whole curriculum. As is seen elsewhere in the book, this would include: enquiry; problem-solving; creative thinking; information processing; reasoning; evaluation; communication. Students would develop each skill to a deeper level as they progressed through each stage of the curriculum. It is also necessary to look systematically across non-core subjects to consider how the spread and transmission of skills could best be improved to develop learning and raise attainment.

Finally, there is the need to **champion effective pedagogy.** There needs to be external support to help schools organise the curriculum to meet the needs of a range of abilities. It must also help teachers bring curriculum knowledge and common learning skills together in the classroom.

The clear prize from pursuing these actions would be a curriculum tailored to the needs, talents and aptitudes of all students. This would ensure that every student had the core and common skills required to learn at each stage of education, and that the best students were properly stretched.

An example of this approach is found in our work with Adventure Learning Schools that has already been referred to in Chapter Three. It is given as an exemplar of school-based curriculum development in schools, not as a model to be followed slavishly. At the heart of Adventure Learning Schools is a curriculum design that actively deepens subject expertise for all young people through engagement in learning both inside and outside the classroom. The expected results of these curricular experiences for secondary students are described in Table 4.1.

Table 4.1 Outcomes of curricular experience at Key Stage 3 and beyond
(Reproduced from Hopkins 2012)

By the end of KS3 students have:	By the age of 19 students have:
▶ at a minimum, achieved national standards in literacy and numeracy ▶ developed skills, knowledge and products in all key curriculum areas ▶ developed a range of personal, learning and thinking skills ▶ undertaken a wide range of additional experiences related to the arts, environment and community service ▶ reinforced the skills above and also developed confidence, resilience and greater social and global awareness through adventure learning.	▶ at a minimum, reached functional levels of literacy and numeracy and achieved qualifications related to further or higher education and the world of work at least at Level 2 and ideally at Level 3 ▶ developed a range of skills to enable them to become self-directed learners and produced a 'masterpiece' in their chosen specialism ▶ undertaken a wider portfolio of artistic and environmental experiences, together with a deeper engagement in community service ▶ developed their own leadership capacity, through facilitating adventure learning opportunities for other young people.

This example, admittedly based in the English secondary school context, illustrates how school-based curriculum development can be used in a powerful way to promote both personalised learning and the particular values and aspirations the school has for its students. The broader point is that in taking school reform to scale, it is the whole-school design that infuses all elements of the school, from the leadership to the pedagogy, to the organisational structures and the range of partnerships these schools will need.

To summarise, a move to a true enquiry-focused curriculum as in Adventure Learning Schools can bring the huge benefits of engagement, motivation and retention of skills, knowledge and attitudes; in other words—much more powerful learning experiences. This approach does, however, bring with it the associated difficulties for the teacher in monitoring to ensure that the curriculum is broad, balanced and relevant and fulfils the statutory requirements.

Giving students a voice

Despite the plethora of innovation and change in contemporary education it is ironic that the consumers of education—the students—are rarely consulted or involved. Consultation with students about things that matter in school can provide a rich and powerful source of data that can be used by teachers to enhance student efforts and attainment. Student voice, however, is not just about them having the opportunity to have a say in decisions in school that affect them. It also entails students playing an active role in their education and schooling as a result of schools becoming more attentive and responsive, in sustained and routine ways, to their views and needs. This is an essential component of personalised learning.

Research by Jean Rudduck (Rudduck & Flutter 2004) has shown that there is potential in the consultation of students to strengthen their commitment to learning and this is due to a range of impacts that student voice has, such as:

▶   developing their capacity to reflect on learning, leading to a greater control over how they learn and how to improve it
▶   making students feel respected and listened to in the school and developing a positive sense of self
▶   developing new capacity to take up more roles and responsibilities
▶   giving students a sense of belonging and a positive membership of the school and the classroom
▶   seeing teachers more positively.

Such potential however, is very much dependent on successful implementation. Activities that involve students in decision-making have to be well thought through, rather than treated as just another task to be completed. They also have to move beyond the tokenism that sadly often accompanies efforts to secure student voice. The ladder of participation shown in Table 4.2, based originally on Arnstein's (1969) work, gives a helpful indication of the progression of activities in student voice from non-participation to learner empowerment for both implementation and self-evaluation (Hart 1992; Rudd, Colligan & Naik 2006).

Table 4.2 The ladder of participation

Type of participation	Type of involvement	Level of engagement
Manipulation	Students are **directed** by teachers and tend not to be **informed** of the issues. Students may be asked to 'rubberstamp' decisions already made by teachers.	Nonparticipation
Decoration	Students may be **indirectly** involved in the decisions but they are not fully aware of their **rights, involvement or how decisions might affect them**.	Nonparticipation
Informing	Students are merely **informed** of decisions, actions and changes but **their views are not actually sought**.	Nonparticipation
Consultation	Students are kept **fully informed** and encouraged to express their opinions but have **little or no impact on decisions and outcomes**.	Tokenism

Table 4.2 (continued)

Type of participation	Type of involvement	Level of engagement
Placation	Students are **consulted** and **informed**. Students views are **listened to** in order to inform the decision making process but this does not guarantee any changes they may want.	Tokenism
Partnership	Students are **consulted** and **informed** in decision-making processes. Decisions and outcomes are the result of **negotiations** between teachers and students.	Tokenism
Delegated power	Teachers still **inform** the agenda for action but students are given **responsibility** for managing aspects or all of any initiatives or programs that result. Decisions are **shared** with teachers.	Learner (student) empowerment
Learner (student) control	Students **initiate** agendas and are given **responsibility** and **power** for management of issues and **to bring about change**. Power is **delegated** to students and they are **active** in designing their education.	Learner (student) empowerment

The ladder of participation provides a framework for implementation, but within this there is a range of specific activities that need to interlink, to be monitored for the quality of implementation and, through the feedback collected, lead to change. Schools are now using a range of activities such as:

- peer support
  - buddying systems
  - peer tutoring
  - peer teaching
  - circle time
- organisational change structure
  - school councils
  - school governors
  - students on appointment panels
  - School Improvement Plans, e.g. draw-and-write
  - Healthy Schools
  - Ofsted
  - Every Child Matters agenda
- engagement with teaching and learning
  - lead learners classroom observation
  - Assessment for Learning
  - student-led learning walks
  - students as researchers
  - students as co-researchers
  - evaluating work units
  - departmental development plans
  - classroom consultation.

The above activities will clearly support schools in improving their practice. Further exploration of the idea of a 'student as a researcher' and the 'student as a co-researcher' is also worthy of note in that it can produce significant data for the school, but also support students' thinking and learning and leadership skills significantly. This emphasis has led to the development of models where students are seen as 'co-researchers' with teachers or as 'researchers' themselves. The work of Michael Fielding (2004) on student voice is relevant here. Although his work is not a step-by-step model of action research, he provides a clear conceptual framework for student participation in action research for transformation.

Fielding sees 'students as co-researchers' as partners in the inquiry to be conducted and in the development of instruments and analysis. However, teachers are the driving force and the research lies predominantly with them. The following example explains the process:

> *Thus, a primary school teacher keen to develop more independent learning with her Year 1 students asked them their view of independence in learning, what it meant, what it felt like, what it looked like. She and the class discussed these matters, developed an observation schedule, jointly videoed lessons, sat down and looked at the video data, discussed what it meant to them, and developed new learning and teaching practices together. Here the teacher learned things about independence in learning from her engagement and dialogue with her student co-researchers that she could not have done from traditional action research. Similarly, her students as co-researchers learned things about independence in learning, about their individual and collective agency that they could not have learned in other ways. (p. 307)*

As implied, 'students as researchers' places students in the role of the researcher. Students are trained in research and attend the same training sessions as their teachers and are responsible for identifying the topic of the investigation, selecting the methods of data gathering and analysis. Teachers assist students in the process but 'student leadership is constitutive and distinctive of this approach' (p. 307). Fielding argues that the premise of this model is that students have a different standpoint from that of teachers and thus, different understandings of similar issues and their importance. This can result in both innovation and renewal.

It is clear that the role of student voice in these increasingly deep ways is central to the learning culture established in outstanding schools. Genuine transformation in learning is more likely to be realised through the active participation of students in the research and educational process and the belief that students can be radical agents of change. The following examples from England and Australia provide examples of the richness of incorporating this aspect of personalised learning into the fabric of the school.

Example in action: England

In reporting on the findings of Leading curriculum innovation in practice (Carter & Sharpe 2007) it was noted that developing pupil voice emerged as a pronounced strand in a number of innovation projects. These schools recognised the potential power of pupils to shape the learning environment and learning methodologies. This work presented a number of key points for school leaders (p. 14).

▶ School leaders need to have an overwhelming belief in the rightness and relevance of this approach as they are likely to meet some staff resistance.

▶ It is important to have a persuasive rationale and to engage in rigorous discussions—but be prepared to be directive if this is the only way.

▶ The language of learning can intimidate pupils. A common terminology and frame of reference are essential—use of models like the 'Rs' can assist dialogue.

▶ Parents may not recognise work like this from their own educational experience. It will need explanation.

▶ There is no point in embarking on initiatives like this unless the school is serious about acting on the results they stimulate.

▶ Staff and pupils require training, for example, in feedback skills.

▶ Developments like this can only thrive in conditions of trust and where there is a collaborative spirit. The business of learning thus becomes a shared enterprise.

Example in action: Australia

As part of our school improvement work in the Northern Metropolitan Region in Melbourne we have been systematically interviewing students and feeding their opinions back into the school's improvement strategy. The synthesis of this material falls into seven themes (Franey 2012). These indicate the students' views and desires under each of the following headings.

▶ Key Focus Area 1—Learning progress
  ▶ Start each topic with what we know.
  ▶ Know how we are going to be assessed.
  ▶ Know how we can assess each other's work.
  ▶ Talk to an adult about our learning and how we can reach our goal.
  ▶ Know that we have learnt in each lesson.
  ▶ Be able to say what we have learnt each day.

▶ Key focus areas 2 and 3—Learning experiences and our environment
  ▶ Orderly learning environment with a behaviour plan which is fair.
  ▶ I feel safe.
  ▶ Teacher uses my name.
  ▶ We do active things to learn.
  ▶ I am trusted to work on my own outside the classroom.
  ▶ I like some silent time for writing.
  ▶ Work that is not too easy or too hard.
  ▶ I can ask questions.

▶ Key Focus Area 4—Learning partnerships
  ▶ Speaking with adults about their learning.
  ▶ Schools invite people from outside into the classrooms.
  ▶ Links with other schools.
  ▶ See teachers learning and that they talk about their learning.
  ▶ Learning in groups and that everyone knows what they are doing.
  ▶ Work with other pupils and also with different classes.

▶ Key Focus Area 5—Learner leadership
  ▶ I would like to know what leadership is.
  ▶ Our ideas are important to improve learning.
  ▶ We like it when we are involved in solving problems.
  ▶ I think we could help the school get better if we get better.

- If we have more responsibility we know we have to be sensible.
- It would be good to have the chance to be a leader, just for a while.
- Key Focus Area 6—Learning manifesto
  - It would be good to know about all the different ways we learn in the school.
  - We would like to say which ways of learning are most enjoyable.
  - We could tell other people about how we learn in our school.
  - Our parents would know more about all the different ways we learn.
  - We want to tell people how proud we are of our school.
- Key Focus Area 7—Learner goals
  - It would be good to think about learning goals.
  - Helpful to have goals or targets on display and in our books.
  - I want to tell people how much I love learning.
  - It would be great if adults spoke to me about my goals for learning.
  - I wonder if my teacher has a learning goal.

Coda

Much evidence has been presented in this chapter to support the claim that in terms of student achievement it is the learning that counts. The focus has been on a particular approach—personalised learning—and for the important reason that it is learning skill that will endure into the future, while as we progress into the 21st century curriculum content will have an increasingly short half-life. It is on this basis that it is claimed that the myth of curriculum dominance has been exploded. Of course, this is not to say that the curriculum is unimportant—that would be foolish—but within any given curriculum context, it is how a school addresses learning that is the critical issue in terms of student progress and achievement.

There are two other, somewhat contradictory but ultimately complementary, points to be made in connection to this myth. The first is that assuming a curriculum is in place in the school, focusing on the quality of teaching and learning will make the most rapid progress in terms of student achievement and learning. Secondly, in line with the curriculum argument outlined earlier, if the curriculum is developed on an enquiry basis, then this can only complement the emphasis on personalised learning.

In concluding, here are three further perspectives that support the argument for personalised learning. The first is a quote from Peter Matthews' (Ofsted 2009a, pp. 42–43) work on those schools that make the difference:

> *These schools use a range of strategies to provide students with the skills they need to talk about their own learning and experience of education. They listen very carefully to what the students have to say and use such feedback to improve teaching. In some cases, this is about students' general experience of learning, but the schools are not afraid to use student observers or other techniques to gather feedback about what individual teachers are doing well, what they could do to improve and how they could modify their teaching to match students' needs more closely. As well as, arguably, providing the most useful feedback that a teacher can receive, this is also highly motivating for students. Apart from the fact that it leads to better lessons, the students feel that they are in a genuine partnership with the school and that their views are valued. The message is very clear: 'We are here to enable you to learn and we are committed to doing it as well as we possibly can'.*

Secondly, if we are serious about personalised learning then we need to be clear as to the typology of the skills students should gain in order to develop their personal effectiveness and employability. We should also appreciate that the demand for skills is rapidly changing. Figure 4.1 illustrates this shift in the USA that should be fairly representative of other developed economies.

It is clear from these data that skills such as 'routine manual' (e.g. factory work), 'non-routine manual' (e.g. driving a bus) and 'routine

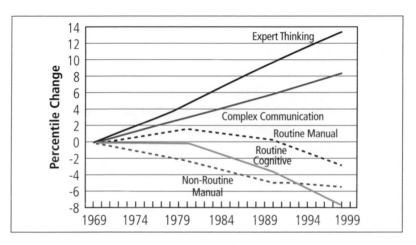

Figure 4.1 How the demand for skills has changed
(Reproduced from Levy & Murnane 2004, p. 50)

cognitive' (e.g. office work) have declined significantly since the 1980s. Yet the dilemma for educators is that these are the skills that are easiest to teach and assess, and as our economies know to their cost, they are also the easiest to digitise and outsource. The skills where the demand is increasing significantly are those termed 'non-routine analytic' which refers to the ability to problem solve and apply knowledge (these are the skills that PISA tests) and 'non-routine interactive' which is best described as emotional intelligence. This data provides confirmation, if any was needed, of the central importance of ensuring that the skills of problem solving and collaboration are centrally important in the educational provision of any 21st century school.

The final comment is inspired by the UN Convention on the Rights of the Child (1989). The four basic principles include the child's right to be heard (*Article 12 – The views of the child*). This confirms, I believe, the emphasis in this chapter on personalised learning and in particular the importance of student voice. Such an approach to the personalisation of learning demands a substantive and skilful response from the teacher. These are the themes that we address in the following chapter.

Chapter 5

Professionalising teaching

The myth that teaching is either an art or a science

Despite having written extensively about the quality of teaching over the years, I have recently had a breakthrough in my thinking about the impact of teaching on learning and the nature of the professional development of teachers. This has occurred as a consequence of two lessons that I have learnt. The first learning is related to my leading a significant number of 'instructional rounds' in Australia and the UK which have involved the extensive study of classroom practice and the subsequent generation of hypotheses about the relationship between learning and teaching and vice versa. The second is the increasing popularity of assessing the impact of teaching and learning through using the statistical technique of 'effect size'. This approach has been widely disseminated by John Hattie (2009) in his book *Visible learning*. The accessibility of John's work has encouraged me to use this approach more frequently in my own.

Both of these lessons speak directly to the myth that teaching is either an art or a science, when of course it is both. This polarisation has a long history and reflects a dualism—that teachers only learn from experience on the one hand, and that there are prescriptions related to research evidence that need to be in lock step on the other. Despite the self-evident foolishness contained in both these positions, reaching a concordat has taken much time and even now has not been fully achieved.

The argument I am making in this chapter, reflected in my previous work on teaching and learning, is that the various theories of action and models of teaching and learning are simply tools that teachers can use to create more powerful learning experiences. But such research and strategies should not be regarded as panaceas to be followed slavishly. Research knowledge and the various specifications of teaching can have limitations, especially if they are adopted uncritically. Such knowledge only becomes useful when it is subjected to the discipline of practice through the exercise of the teacher's professional judgement. For, as Lawrence Stenhouse (1975, p. 142) said many years ago, such proposals are not to be regarded 'as an unqualified recommendation, but rather as a provisional specification claiming no more than to be worth putting to the test of practice. Such proposals claim to be intelligent rather than correct'.

It is at this nexus that theory and practice productively coalesce. The framework for thinking about teaching that I first proposed in the late 1990s as seen in Figure 5.1 was intended to be comprehensive and resolve this dichotomy.

The three perspectives on high quality teaching in the outer circles reflect, as we shall see later in the chapter, propositions based on research and practice that relate the impact of different aspects of teacher behaviour to the learning of students. It is the routine of fine teachers to combine these elements through a process of reflection to create an individual style. Consequently, it may be that critical systematic reflection is a necessary condition for quality teaching. This is not reflection for reflection's sake, but in order to continue to develop a mastery of one's chosen craft.

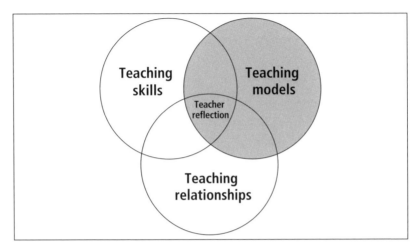

Figure 5.1 Four ways of thinking about teaching
(Reproduced from Hopkins 2007, p. 76)

When presenting the framework and leading workshops on teaching and learning, I placed great emphasis on the 'models of teaching' approach developed by Bruce Joyce (Joyce & Weil 1996; Joyce, Calhoun & Hopkins 2009). This was for two reasons. The first was that, at the time, I naively believed that teachers were reasonably well acquainted with the knowledge base on teaching skills, given that the area had been well researched, was supposed to be covered in the teacher training curriculum and had ostensibly influenced the Ofsted school inspection framework in the UK. The second was that I had been heavily influenced by the work of Bruce Joyce. The title of a book that we had written together, *Models of learning: tools for teaching* (Joyce et al. 2009), reflected an approach that provided the critical pedagogic tools for linking teaching to learning and for promoting learning skills, while at the same time raising achievement.

Until recently I could never quite work out why fewer teachers than I thought would go on to adopt this approach and incorporate it into their personal repertoires and styles. My experience with the instructional rounds process helped me understand why my initial assumptions were wrong. It became clear that a good majority of teachers did not have a specific or systematic grasp of the essential basics of pedagogy and without this they did not have the essential tactical skills to incorporate the models of teaching approach into their professional repertoire of practice. The approach was beyond their 'zone of proximal development' and although they were attracted to the idea, they lacked the basic skills to implement it. That is why my original approach to implementing the framework for thinking about teaching, although superficially attractive, failed to gain traction. It is also the critical reason for regarding teaching as both an art and a science.

I explore these issues more deeply in this chapter by:

▶ introducing the concept of the 'instructional core' and 'theories of action' and their whole-school application

▶ describing the theories of action for teachers emerging from instructional rounds

▶ reviewing the 'models of teaching' approach

▶ reflecting on the science of teaching through the use of effect size.

Instructional core and whole-school theories of action

The elephant in the room of professional teaching, and it has been resident for some time, is the lack of a professional practice that provides a language and a set of behaviours or processes to connect teaching to learning. There are two key problems here: the first is the individualised and atomised nature of teaching as a profession; the second is that teaching is a profession without a practice. These two tendencies interact in intricate and resilient ways.

I have been helped to understand the nature of this complexity through conversations with Richard Elmore, and more recently through reading the book he has co-authored with his colleagues entitled *Instructional rounds in education* (City et al. 2009). In that book they contrast the individualism that too often characterises teaching, where the person and the practice are intertwined, with professionals who are those that share a common practice and open it up to public scrutiny. Professionals believe that the only way to improve one's practice is to allow yourself to appreciate that your practice is *not* who you are. It is, instead, a way of expressing your current understanding of your work, your knowledge about your work and your beliefs about what is important about the work. All these things can change—*should* change if you are a professional—as your knowledge, skill, expertise and understanding of your work increases. The real insight here is that you can maintain all the values and commitments that make you a person and still give yourself permission to change your practice. Your practice is an instrument for expressing who you are as a professional; it is not who you are. How we define practice is, therefore, critical and Elmore and his colleagues (City et al. 2009, p. 3) mean something quite specific:

> *We mean a set of protocols and processes for observing, analyzing, discussing and understanding instruction that can be used to improve student learning at scale. The practice works because it creates a common discipline and focus among practitioners with a common purpose and set of problems.*

It is the lack of such a practice that has inhibited recent reform efforts from unleashing the potential of our students. We need to reach down into the classroom and deepen reform efforts by moving beyond superficial curriculum change to a more profound understanding of how teacher behaviour connects to learning. In particular, it requires a direct and unrelenting focus on what many are now calling the 'instructional core'. It is worthy of note that, here and in the remainder

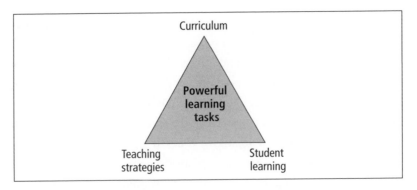

Figure 5.2 The instructional core

of this chapter, the words instruction, pedagogy and teaching are used synonymously, reflecting as they do American, European and Anglo-Saxon definitions of the same concept.

As seen in Figure 5.2, in its simplest terms 'the instructional core is composed of the teacher and the student in the presence of content' (City et al. 2009). Although there are a number of principles associated with the definition of the instructional core, two features in particular require emphasising from the outset.

The first feature is that one element of the instructional core cannot be changed without impacting directly on the other two. Yet most change efforts focus on only one—curriculum innovation, or professional development or student voice. The three need to be regarded as a whole if authentic change in student achievement is to occur. It is the relationship between the teacher, the student and the content—not the qualities of any one of them by themselves—that determines the nature of instructional practice. Each corner of the instructional triangle has its own particular role and resources to bring to the instructional process.

The second feature is more subtle but even more important. It is an understanding that the 'instructional task' is at the centre of the instructional core. The instructional task is the actual work that students are asked to do in the presence of instruction. It is not what teachers think they have asked students to do, nor what the prescribed curriculum says they should be doing, but what students are actually doing and the sense they make of it that is fundamental. This is why in *Models of learning: tools for teaching* (Joyce et al. 2009, p. 7) we claimed that:

> *Learning experiences are composed of content, process and social climate. As teachers we create for and with our children opportunities to explore and build important areas of knowledge, develop powerful tools for learning, and live in humanizing social conditions.*

Unless we make the instructional task the focus of our enquiry, then we can have no confidence that learning will be enhanced and that consequently, the outcomes of educational reform will remain capricious. We must continuously remind ourselves that it is the tasks that students undertake that predict their performance (Doyle 1983).

The model of the instructional core provides the basic framework for how to intervene in the instructional process so as to improve the quality and level of student learning. The following five principles guide the work (City et al. 2009).

1. Increases in student learning occur only as a consequence of improvements in the level of content, teachers' knowledge and skill and student engagement.
2. If you change any single element of the instructional core, you have to change the other two to affect student learning.
3. The tasks students do predict their performance; so the real accountability lies in the tasks the students perform.

4. We learn to do the work by doing the work: people have to engage in sustained description and analysis of instructional practice before they can acquire either the expertise or the authority to judge it.

5. In developing a practice around the instructional core, description comes before analysis, analysis before prediction and prediction before evaluation.

Taken together the potential contained in the implementation of these principles is to create a new instructional culture within the school. This requires adopting strategies that have the ability to build a common language of instructional practice as well as of building within and across schools—the connective tissue by which the culture is propagated—and of focusing greater attention on the knowledge and skill requirements of doing the work. The approach works iteratively from the existing knowledge base of individual teachers to develop theories of action that discipline and deepen the culture of teaching and learning of all teachers in the school. Critical to the success of the instructional rounds approach has been the development of 'theories of action'. A theory of action is a link between cause and effect: *if* we take a particular action, *then* we expect that action to have specific effects. A theory of action connects the actions of teachers with the consequences of their actions—the learning and achievement of their students.

As the experience with the instructional rounds has continued to deepen in Wales (Caerphilly County Borough Council 2012), in Australia (NMR 2011) and elsewhere, five important lessons have been learnt.

▶ The first was that despite the phase or context of schooling, the theories of action were in most cases very similar.

▶ Second, this is not a 'pick and mix' approach—all the theories of action have to be integrated into the teacher's professional repertoire if they are to impact in a sustained way on student learning.

▶ Third, and most importantly, all the theories of action were characterised by an approach to teaching that has enquiry at its centre.

▶ Fourth, some of the theories of action relate to the school and some to the practice of individual teachers.

▶ Fifth, all of the theories of action have a high level of empirical support in the educational research literature.

To summarise, through the instructional rounds process an approach to teaching has been developed from the practice of teachers—in Victoria, Australia; London, England; Caerphilly, Wales; and elsewhere—that if consistently applied will enhance not just the achievement, but also the spirit of enquiry of all students. The whole-school theories of action emerging from the instructional rounds process are as follows:

1. When schools and teachers set high expectations and develop authentic relationships, then students' confidence and commitment to education increases and the school's ethos and culture deepens.

2. When teacher directed instruction becomes more enquiry focused, then the level of student achievement and curiosity increases.

3. By consistently adopting protocols for teaching, student behaviour, engagement and learning is enhanced.

4. By consistently adopting protocols for learning, student capacity to learn, skill levels and confidence are enhanced.

The implications of these whole school theories of action are discussed in more detail in Chapter Eight. Meanwhile, it is to the 'theories of action for teachers' that we now turn in the commentary presented below.

Theories of action for teachers

Harnessing learning intentions, narrative and pace

When teachers set **learning intentions** and use appropriate **pace** and have a clear and strong **narrative** about their teaching and curriculum, then students are more secure about their learning, and achievement and understanding is increased.

It has become very clear from instructional rounds that when teachers are clear about their learning intentions then the students become more engaged and feel more secure in their learning. But it is about more than just setting a learning intention or goal; importantly it is also about linking the intention to the learning outcome and success criteria for the lesson, as well as ensuring curricular progression. This becomes the basis for the narrative of the lesson. Teachers with a strong sense of narrative are able to engage with diversion, knowing how to bring the discussion back on track. Pace is also necessary to keep the lesson lively and, through increasing tempo, deal with potential low-level disruption. A learning intention for a lesson or series of lessons is a statement that describes clearly what the teacher wants the student to know, understand and be able to do as a result of the learning and teaching activity. In formulating the learning intention it is essential to consider three components:

- an action word that identifies the performance to be demonstrated
- a learning statement that specifies what learning will be demonstrated
- a broad statement of the criterion or minimum standard for acceptable performance, e.g. 'By the end of the lesson you will be able to describe foundation concepts and questions in ...'

Setting challenging learning tasks

When **learning tasks** are purposeful, clearly defined, differentiated and challenging then the more powerful, progressive and precise the learning for all students.

In many of the instructional rounds conducted, we found that, by and large, most students did not find the tasks they were set very challenging. Yet it is the tasks that students do that predict their performance. This requires setting tasks that are within the student's 'zone of proximal development' and differentiated, if their learning is to progress. Usually, this involves having three or four 'graded tasks' available for each group with scaffolding around the task to ensure success. In *Looking in classrooms*, Good and Brophy (2008) identified the six components listed below as central to scaffolding support for pupils carrying out tasks.

1. Develop student interest in accomplishing the intended goal of the task.
2. Demonstrate an idealised version of the actions to be performed.
3. Simplify the task by reducing the steps.
4. Control frustration and risk.
5. Provide feedback that identifies the critical features of discrepancies between what has been produced and what is required.
6. Motivate and direct the student's activity to maintain continuous pursuit of the goal.

Closely associated with scaffolding is the gradual transfer of responsibility for managing learning. As students develop expertise they begin to assume responsibility for regulating their own learning, by asking questions and by working on increasingly complex tasks with increasing degrees of autonomy.

Framing higher order questions

When teachers systematically use **higher order questioning,** the level of student understanding is deepened and their achievement is increased.

Hattie's research on *Visible learning* (2009, p. 182) tells us that questioning is the second most prevalent teaching method, after teacher talk. Most teachers spend between 35% and 50% of their time in questioning. Questioning has a positive impact on student learning—but this effect is associated more with higher order questioning which promotes higher order thinking and curiosity. The evidence suggests that most teachers ask low-level questions, related more to knowledge acquisition and comprehension. Research studies suggest that 60% of teachers' questions recall facts and 20% are procedural in nature. Bloom's taxonomy (Anderson & Krathwohl 2001) of learning objectives is widely used as a basis for structuring questions, particularly higher order questions.

▶ **Knowledge**—recall previous material learnt
▶ **Comprehension**—demonstrate understanding of facts and ideas
▶ **Application**—solve problems by applying knowledge, facts and skills learnt in different ways and situations
▶ **Analysis**—examine information and break into parts, make connections and support ideas and arguments
▶ **Evaluation**—present judgements, recommendations and opinions
▶ **Synthesis**—compile information in different, more creative ways; choose other solutions.

The following sequence works well, as this approach makes everyone responsible for generating an answer, particularly when combined with some of the simple cooperative techniques described later in this chapter.

- ‣ Frame a question to the whole class.
- ‣ Allow students time to think—'wait time'.
- ‣ Only then, call on someone to respond.

Connecting feedback and data

When teachers consistently use **feedback and data** on student actions and performance, then behaviour becomes more positive and progress **accelerates**.

Feedback is one of the most powerful influences on student achievement. That is clear from both psychological theory and research. In *Visible learning*, John Hattie (2009, p. 173) provides a powerful insight, as he describes his attempts to understand feedback:

> *It was only when I discovered that feedback was most powerful when it is from the student to the teacher that I started to understand it better. When teachers seek, or are at least open to, feedback from students as to what students know, what they understand, where they make errors, when they have misconceptions, when they are not engaged—then teaching and learning can be synchronized and powerful. Feedback to teachers helps make learning visible.*

In considering data and feedback that moves beyond the purely academic, Hattie suggests that a behavioural focus on student performance helps students to recognise the linkage between effort and outcome. In addressing this behavioural dimension of student performance and achievement, it is recommended that the teacher should:

- ‣ model beliefs
- ‣ focus on mastery
- ‣ portray skill development as incremental and domain specific

▶ provide socialisation with feedback
▶ portray effort as investment rather than risk.

Committing to assessment for learning

When **peer assessment and assessment for learning** (AfL) are consistently utilised, student engagement, learning and achievement accelerates.

The generally accepted definition of Assessment for Learning (AfL) has been defined previously as: 'The process of seeking and interpreting evidence for use by learners and their teachers to decide where the learners are in their learning, where they need to go and how best to get there' (Assessment Reform Group 2002). This may be organised differently in different schools, but the rationale is always the same.

▶ Clear evidence about how to drive up individual attainment.
▶ Clear feedback for and from pupils, so there is clarity on what they need to improve and how best they can do so.
▶ Clarity for students on what levels they are working at, with transparent criteria to enable peer coaching.
▶ A clear link between student learning and lesson planning (Hopkins 2006).

The OECD project on formative assessment (2005) concluded that it is one of the most useful strategies in improving student performance. The following practices most consistently emerged during their research:

▶ establishment of classroom cultures that encourage interaction and the use of assessment tools
▶ establishment of learning goals and tracking individual student progress
▶ use of varied instruction methods to meet diverse student needs

▶ use of varied approaches to assess student understanding
▶ feedback on student performance and adapting instruction to meet learner needs
▶ active involvement of students in the learning process.

Teachers need to continue to develop their understanding of how students learn so they can help them to: reflect on how they learn; develop learning strategies and apply them in different circumstances; and engage in high quality dialogue with teachers, peers and others.

Implementing cooperative group structures

If teachers use **cooperative group structures/techniques** to mediate between whole class instruction and students carrying out tasks, then the academic performance of the whole class will increase as well as the spirit of collaboration and mutual responsibility.

Cooperative group work has a powerful effect in raising pupil achievement because it combines the dynamics of democratic processes with the discipline of academic enquiry. It encourages active participation in learning and collaborative behaviour by developing social as well as academic skills. The approach is highly flexible and draws on a wide range of methods—individual research, collaborative enquiry and plenary activities—and allows the integration of them all into a powerful teaching tool. It is most commonly used as part of the direct instruction model, both as part of teacher instruction and the structuring of group activities, although at times the teacher will use the approach to structure a whole lesson or series of lessons.

There is a wide range of strategies that comprise cooperative group work. They are all underpinned by the following five principles (Johnson & Johnson 1994):

1. **Positive interdependence:** When all members of a group feel connected to each other in the accomplishment of a common goal—all individuals must succeed for the group to succeed.
2. **Individual accountability:** Where every member of the group is held responsible for demonstrating the accomplishment of their learning.
3. **Face-to-face interaction:** When group members are close in proximity to each other and enter into a dialogue with each other in ways that promote continued progress.
4. **Social skills:** Human interaction skills that enable groups to function effectively (e.g. taking turns, encouraging, listening, clarifying, checking, understanding, probing). Such skills enhance communication, trust, leadership, decision-making and conflict management.
5. **Processing:** When group members assess their collaborative efforts and target improvements.

Cooperative group work requires pupils to practise and refine their negotiating, organising and communication skills, define issues and problems and develop ways of solving them. This includes collecting and interpreting evidence, hypothesising, testing and re-evaluating.

Models of teaching

Imagine a classroom where the learning environment contains a variety of models of teaching that are not only intended to accomplish a range of curriculum goals, but also designed to help students increase their competence as learners. This is captured by Joyce et al. (2009) in the following description.

▶ In such classrooms the students learn models for memorising information, how to attain concepts and how to invent them.

▶ They practise building hypotheses and theories and use the tools of science to test them.

▶ They learn how to extract information and ideas from lectures and presentations, how to study social issues and how to analyse their own social values.

▶ These students also know how to profit from training and how to train themselves in athletics, performing arts, mathematics and social skills.

▶ They know how to make their writing and problem solving more lucid and creative.

▶ Perhaps most importantly, they know how to take initiative in planning personal study, and they know how to work with others to initiate and carry out cooperative tasks.

▶ As students master information and skills, the result of each learning experience is not only the content they learn, but also the greater ability they acquire to approach future learning tasks with confidence and to create increasingly effective learning environments for themselves.

Bruce Joyce developed this approach in his pioneering work *Models of teaching* that was first published in 1972 and is now in its eighth edition. Joyce describes and analyses over 30 different models of teaching—each with their own 'syntax', phases and guidelines—that are designed to bring about particular kinds of learning and to help students become more effective learners. It is in this way that the use of 'teaching models' forms part of an overall strategy for enhancing teacher professionalism and the key tool for personalising learning (Hopkins 2010b). Models of teaching simultaneously define the nature

Table 5.1 Examples of the relationship between models of teaching and learning skills

Model of teaching	Learning skill
1. Whole-class teaching	Extracting information and ideas from lectures and presentations
2. Cooperative group work	Working effectively with others to initiate and carry out cooperative tasks
3. Inductive teaching	Building hypotheses and theories through classification
4. Mnemonics	Memorising information
5. Concept attainment	Attaining concepts and how to invent them
6. Synectics	Using metaphors to think creatively

of the content, the learning strategies and the arrangements for social interaction that create the learning environments of students. Models of teaching are also models of learning. How teaching is conducted has a large impact on students' abilities to educate themselves. Each model has its own core purpose that relates not only to how to organise teaching, but also to ways of learning—examples of this relationship are given in Table 5.1.

Of the six models of teaching outlined above, three of the models are considered in more detail below, namely: inductive teaching, cooperative group work and synectics. Before moving on to a more detailed consideration of each model and its implications for practice, however, it is important to be clear about what is meant by a 'model of teaching'. An initial distinction would be to regard the evidence on teaching skills as providing the teacher with *tactical* knowledge, whereas the research on models of teaching gives teachers *strategic* knowledge about how to create whole classroom settings to facilitate learning. There is a need to become increasingly specific about those teaching strategies that promote more effective learning. This is for two reasons. First, this is the best way to communicate professional knowledge to other teachers. Second, in the belief that a good teaching strategy is also a good learning strategy, it is by the same token the best way to communicate them to our students. In order to achieve this, establishing clarity of the concepts and precision on principles is required, especially if professional knowledge is to be put to the test of practice.

Inductive teaching

Inductive teaching is a model of teaching that encourages pupils to build, test and to use categories. It nurtures logical thinking and allows pupils of all abilities to process information effectively.

The inductive teaching model is a powerful way of helping pupils to learn how to construct knowledge. The model focuses directly upon intellectual capability and is intended to assist pupils in the process of mastering large amounts of information. Within teaching there are numerous occasions when pupils are required to sort and classify data. In many cases, however, the sorting process is viewed as an end in itself. Pupils are usually required to understand the 'one correct way of classifying'. Teachers know that there are usually many ways of classifying, but they choose one for simplicity. The inductive method allows pupils to understand a variety of classifications in a structured way that includes a variety of teaching techniques within one method. Without opportunity for re-classification or hypothesising, learning potential is limited and the development of higher order thinking is restricted.

Well planned inductive teaching should mean that the students:

▶ work collaboratively to solve problems
▶ discuss with each other, often using higher order thinking skills

▶ teach each other, thus memorising facts and concepts more easily
▶ demonstrate their skills by seeking and freely expressing reasons for their views
▶ discuss alternatives before deciding, challenging each other, being prepared to compromise and showing a willingness to change their mind
▶ learn from what other pupils are thinking and respect their ideas and opinions.

The inductive model of teaching consists of a number of discrete phases that cannot be rushed or omitted. Inductive inquiries are rarely brief because the very nature of the inquiry requires pupils to think deeply. The inductive model in synthesis is the collecting and sifting of information in order to construct categories or labels. This process requires pupils to engage with the data and seek to produce categories in which to allocate the data. It requires them to generate hypotheses based upon this allocation and to test out these hypotheses by using them to guide subsequent work. The syntax of the inductive teaching model is characterised by the following six phases:

1. Identify the domain
    ▶ Establish the focus and boundaries of the initial inquiry.
    ▶ Clarify the long-term objectives.
2. Collect, present and enumerate data
    ▶ Assemble and present the initial data set.
    ▶ Enumerate and label the items of data.
3. Examine the data
    ▶ Thoroughly study the items in the data set and identify their attributes.
4. Form concepts by classifying
    ▶ Classify the items in the data set and share the results.
    ▶ Add data to the set.

- Re-classification occurs, possibly many times.
5. Generate and test hypotheses
   - Examine the implications of differences between categories.
   - Classify categories, as appropriate.
   - Reclassify in two-way matrices, as well as by correlations, as appropriate.
6. Consolidate and transfer
   - Search for additional items of data in resource material.
   - Synthesise by writing about the domain, using the categories.
   - Convert categories into skills.
   - Test and consolidate skills through practice and application (Hopkins & Harris 2000).

Cooperative group work

Cooperative group work is a model of teaching where pupils, working together in small groups on a range of academic problems, can develop both their social and their intellectual skills.

As a model of teaching, cooperative group work has a powerful effect in raising pupil achievement because it harnesses the synergy of collective action. It combines the dynamics of democratic processes with the processes of academic enquiry. It encourages active participation in learning and collaborative behaviour by developing social as well as academic skills. Thus the model requires pupils to practise and refine their negotiating, organising and communication skills; define issues and problems and develop ways of solving them, including collecting and interpreting evidence, hypothesising, testing and re-evaluating.

Well planned cooperative group work should mean that the students:

➤ depend on each other to get a task completed
➤ have individual responsibility to the rest of the group
➤ discuss with each other, often using higher order thinking skills
➤ teach each other, thus memorising facts and concepts more easily
➤ develop better social skills, which encourages positive feelings among group members.

The model is highly flexible and draws on a wide range of methods—individual research, collaborative enquiry and plenary activities—and allows the integration of them all into a powerful teaching tool. The teacher is able to conduct a more subtle and complex learning strategy that achieves a number of learning goals simultaneously. Thus, styles can vary from didactic to 'light touch' teaching where teacher is more an adviser and guide than a director (Hopkins & Harris 2000). Some examples of cooperative group activities are seen below.

Using cooperative group strategies: two detailed examples (NMR 2011, p. 25)

Numbered heads

In an English lesson the learning intention is to extend competence in punctuating direct and indirect speech. The teacher explains the cooperative group strategy before implementing it. There are five key steps:
➤ The class divides into named groups of four.
➤ Each student is allocated a number.
➤ From a displayed passage of unpunctuated dialogue and description each group is asked to identify the direct speech.
➤ A bell rings after two minutes of discussion—this is a call for silence.
➤ A number is called and the student with that number responds by identifying the direct speech.

Jigsaw

In 'Jigsaw', the teacher is more an adviser and guide than a director.

In Food Technology a teacher sets up a question or problem for enquiry. Topics might include food hygiene in the home, safe practice in the kitchen, processed versus organic foods or dangerous additives. There are five key steps:

▶ Students divide into equal-sized groups, called Home Groups.
▶ Each group is given an identical task and list of roles or jobs.
▶ For five minutes, groups discuss the 'problem' and allocate roles/jobs.
▶ Home Groups then divide: those with identical jobs form new Expert Groups tasked with collecting relevant information.
▶ After a period of research, students return to their Home Groups and expert knowledge is pooled.

Using cooperative group strategies: five brief examples (NMR 2011, p. 25)

Twos to fours, or Snowballing

Students work in pairs on a task. They then join with another pair to explain and compare what they have achieved.

Rainbow groups

A way of ensuring students experience working alongside a range of others is to give each child in a group a number, or a colour. After groups have worked together, students with the same number or colour form new groups to compare what they have done.

Envoys

This strategy helps students find support without necessarily having recourse to the teacher.

If a group needs to check something, or to obtain information, one group member is sent as an 'envoy' to the library, or book corner or another group. The envoy then reports back.

Listening triads

In groups of three, students take the roles of Talker, Questioner or Recorder:

▶ The Talker explains or comments on an issue or activity.

▶ The Questioner prompts and seeks clarification.

▶ The Recorder makes notes.

▶ When the learning activity concludes, the Recorder reports on the conversation.

In summary, cooperative forms of teaching quicken and deepen learning and enhance a wide range of cognitive abilities. In particular:

▶ The model enhances certain higher cognitive abilities, including the capacity to form and reform concepts and transfer knowledge across domains.

▶ The model helps pupils develop the basic skills of memorisation— with 'deep' learning the capacity to memorise, hold and recall information is much enhanced.

▶ The model creates a cohesive context for learning that supports both able and less able pupils alike.

▶ The model encourages positive feelings among members, reduces loneliness and alienation, builds relationships and provides affirmative views of other people (Hopkins & Harris 2000).

Synectics

Synectics is a model of teaching that encourages pupils to make connections between concepts and to produce new ways of thinking about a topic or idea.

Synectics as a model of teaching aims to increase the creativity of both individuals and groups. The model is premised upon using creative thought to generate new and different ways of thinking about an issue or a problem. A main tool within this model is the use of analogies to increase pupils' creative expression, empathy and insight (Hopkins & Harris 2000). The model stresses the relationship between creative activity and a deeper understanding of ideas. It emphasises the use of metaphoric associations to create new perspectives on a topic or issue. The model is not confined to only those subjects that most readily encompass the use of metaphoric thinking such as English or drama, but can be used within all subject areas to promote higher-level thinking. Within all fields (i.e. the arts, the sciences, engineering) creative processes are used to foster the same intellectual processes, although in science this may be called innovation and in engineering it may be termed invention. Synectics offers a different way of problem solving that is the antithesis of logical thought. The model requires pupils to think in a range of ways that may be considered illogical or ridiculous. In order to move pupils away from learnt solutions and the usual ways of thinking about a problem, synectics uses three types of analogy to encourage creative thought (Hopkins & Harris 2000).

1. **Direct analogy** requires a simple comparison of two objects or concepts. For example, pupils may be asked in a biology lesson, 'How is blood like a waterfall?' or 'Why is skin like glass?' The main purpose of this comparison is to elicit features that present both concepts in an extended and new way. Thinking about the way in which the two elements or ideas are similar and different allows pupils to be creative and imaginative. It also allows new connections to be made between quite different concepts.

2. **Personal analogy** requires pupils to empathise with the ideas or problems to be compared. Pupils are encouraged to express how they feel as if they were immersed in the problem. The purpose of personal analogy is to encourage empathy and involvement. It requires pupils to imagine the situation or problem from a perspective other than their own.

3. **Compressed conflict** requires pupils to provide a two-word description of an object, person or situation. The words selected have to be opposites, or seem to contradict each other. The aim of the two-word description is to compress meaning by using only two frames of reference with respect to a single concept. This task requires creative thinking and is another way of helping pupils to make new connections between ideas and to engage in higher order thinking (Hopkins & Harris 2000).

The most effective use of synectics develops over time. In the short-term it can extend pupils' thinking about different concepts and problems, but used repeatedly it will engender creative thinking skills that will improve pupils' learning generally. Synectics helps pupils to develop their creative capacity and to refine their creative thinking skills for use in all subject areas. It helps pupils stretch their ideas and to reformulate them in ways that contribute to creative thinking and higher order thinking skill development. The synectic model of teaching has six discrete phases, although certain components such as personal analogy may be used in isolation within a lesson to generate creative thinking (Hopkins & Harris 2000).

▶ **Phase one:** description of the present condition
▶ **Phase two:** direct analogy
▶ **Phase three:** personal analogy
▶ **Phase four:** compressed conflict
▶ **Phase five:** direct analogy
▶ **Phase six:** re-examination of the original task.

The tangible outcomes of using a synectics approach are captured by Fisher and Moss (2012). In detailing their experience of the use of synectics in practice at Dallam School in the UK, they claim that the approach:

▶ generates a positive, shared classroom experience
▶ enhances participation levels and depth—risk of being wrong is lost
▶ enhances problem-solving skills
▶ is very enjoyable
▶ demonstrates that the creative invention process is the same in all subject areas—the same underlying intellectual processes
▶ brings creative process to consciousness (i.e. metacognitive)
▶ shows that the analogistic state is the best one for exploring and expanding ideas
▶ brings fresh perspectives to issues and ideas
▶ promotes recall and retention
▶ enhances personal flexibility and behaviour.

Towards a science of teaching and learning

The exciting point to be made in this section of the chapter is that when the individual theories of action and models of teaching are tested against the research evidence, their effectiveness is found to have a strong empirical base. As noted in the introduction, the concept of 'effect size' is currently used to describe the magnitude of the gains in student learning to be expected from a change in teacher behaviour—in this instance, the adoption of the theories of action or models of teaching.

Effect size refers to the impact that the practice has on the curve of normal distribution, moving it, as seen below, more to the right. Effect size provides a means of gauging the effect of a particular school, change in teaching method or classroom organisation on learning and achievement. By the same token, it can also be used to predict what can hope to be accomplished by using that practice. The computation of effect size involves the meta-analysis of a large number of empirical studies that measure the impact of a specific teacher behaviour on student learning. First developed as a statistical technique by Gene Glass and colleagues, it was subsequently adopted by Bruce Joyce to measure the impact of models of teaching on learning and by ourselves in relation to the theories of action (Glass, McGaw & Smith 1981; NMR 2011; Joyce et al. 2009).

Figure 5.3 illustrates the effect size of using higher order questions. In this case it is 0.73 of a standard deviation that is the metric utilised by effect size analyses. This means that the average student in the 'experimental group'—where the teacher used higher order questions—would be performing at the about the 65th percentile level, compared with the 50th percentile level in the 'control group' where the teacher was using closed questions.

John Hattie (2009) in his book *Visible learning* has computed the effect size for over 800 influences on student learning. Hattie has developed his own 'barometer of influence' that provides a heuristic way of expressing the concept. Although both developmental and

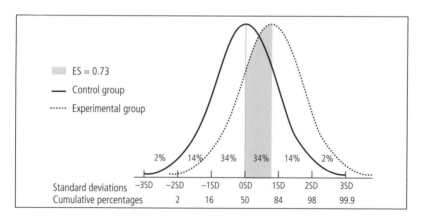

Figure 5.3 Effect size for higher order questions
(Reproduced from NMR 2011, p. 4)

teacher effects are important, we should always aim to be adopting practices that are in the zone of desired effects. As Hattie (2009, p. 19) comments:

> *The development of this barometer began not by asking whether this or that innovation was working, but whether this teaching worked better than possible alternatives; not by asking whether this innovation was having positive effects compared to not having the innovation, but whether the effects from this innovation were better for students than what they would achieve if they had received alternative innovations.*
>
> *For each of the many attributes investigated in* Visible Learning, *the average of each influence is indexed by an arrow through one of the zones on the barometer. All influences above the 0.40 point are labelled in the 'zone of desired effects' as these are the influences that have the greatest impact on student achievement outcomes.*

As seen in Figure 5.4, five of the teacher theories of action described in the previous section are in the zone of desired effects, according to Hattie's barometer of influence.

Bruce Joyce, as intimated above, was an early adopter of effect size and a means of measuring the impact of *Models of teaching* on student learning (Joyce et al. 2009). This is a summary of the effect sizes of the four families of the models of teaching:

- **information processing**—a mean effect size over 1.0 for higher order outcomes
- **cooperative learning**—a mean effect between 0.3 and 0.7
- **personal models**—a mean effect of 0.3 or more for cognitive, affective and behavioural outcomes

▶ **behavioural models**—a mean effect between 0.5 and 1.0—best representatives are for short-term treatments looking at behavioural or knowledge of content outcomes.

The increasingly widespread use of effect size provides an understandable, accessible and reliable methodology for linking together the art and science of teaching in the pursuit of ever higher

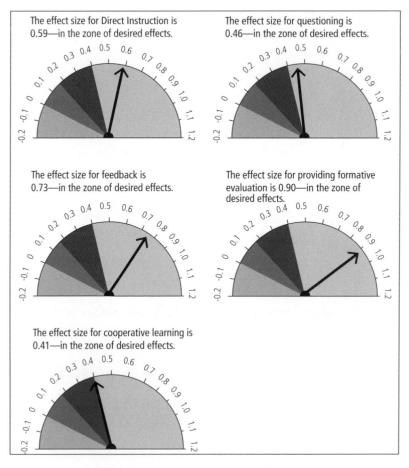

Figure 5.4 Hattie's barometer of influence

levels of student learning. The challenge for all school improvers is to develop increasingly powerful specifications and strategies for teaching that will push the normal curve of distribution further to the right.

Coda

This is good science! In exploding the myth that teaching is either an art or a science, and establishing that it is both, the argument of this chapter has followed the traditions of good science, in working from observations, to developing propositions and then testing their value in practice. The theories of action for teaching and learning have emerged inductively from the work of hundreds of teachers. They have not been imposed by academics or policy makers, but are the outcome of deliberate and rigorous observation and reflection on the part of committed practitioners. Having synthesised many instructional rounds and established a composite set of theories of action, we tested them against the research evidence. Their validity and reliability having been established, they were then subjected to a further cycle of implementation and reflection, and even more precise specifications are sought to the benefit of student learning. This is the quintessential linkage of the art and science of teaching.

There are no ceilings to the performance of quality teachers and they are teachers who deliberately integrate art and science.

Outstanding teachers take individual and collective responsibility to base their teaching on the best knowledge and practice available. But they then take those ideas and strategies and critically reflect on them through practice in their own and each other's classrooms. It is through reflection that the teacher harmonises, integrates and transcends the necessary classroom management skills, the acquisition of a repertoire of models of teaching, and the personal

aspects of her teaching into a strategy that has meaning for her
students. (Hopkins 2000, p. 144)

It should now be obvious that the evidence from research on teaching can help teachers become more creative in devising effective learning environments for the students. There is a danger that centrally designed curricula can become blueprints that inhibit autonomy in teaching and learning. In that respect the models of teaching presented here are *specific* rather than *prescriptive*. Although they define the nature of the educational encounter, they do so in order to encourage teachers to experiment with the specificity, rather than being bound by the prescription. Within the spirit of the process model of curriculum, as described by Stenhouse (1975), this approach is liberating or emancipatory because it encourages independence of thought and argument on the part of the pupil, and experimentation and the use of judgement on the part of the teacher. When teachers adopt this experimental approach to their teaching they are taking on an educational idea, cast in the form of a curriculum proposal and testing it out within their classrooms.

Thus, as Bruce Joyce elegantly phrased it, the operational repertoire of the teacher is the critical element in the calculus of effects. Some years ago, we conducted a comparative study of policies aimed at improving teacher quality for the OECD. Six characteristics of high quality teachers (Hopkins & Stern 1996) were identified:

- commitment
- love of children
- mastery of subject didactics
- a repertoire of multiple models of teaching
- the ability to collaborate with other teachers
- a capacity for reflection.

Although it is convenient to group teachers' desired capacities and behaviours into categories, these attributes all interact in practice. For example, one French teacher elegantly defined teacher quality as '*savoirs, savoir-faire, et savoir-être*'. This is translatable perhaps as 'knowledge, knowing how to do, and knowing how to be' (Hopkins & Stern 1996, p. 503). This phrase reflects the essential fusion of the meshing of art and science in teaching.

Chapter 6

Intelligent accountability

The myth that external accountability results in sustained school reform

The global interest in school reform has accelerated in recent years partially as a consequence of a system-level desire in many countries to move up the PISA league tables. In many cases this has resulted in a common curriculum of policy options. Some commentators have reacted positively to such a policy consensus and have posited an international process of 'mutual learning' resulting in the adoption of a similar range of policy options. I am not so sanguine and believe it is more a case of what Halpin and Troyna (1995) have called 'policy borrowing' largely for symbolic purposes. 'Faddism'—the adoption of any current vogue, irrespective of its fit to a particular problem or challenge, just to be seen to be doing something—is a well-documented response to the pressure for external change at the school level (Slavin & Madden 1999). It seems to me that 'policy borrowing' is the same phenomenon raised to a system level on an international scale.

One of the central features of policy frameworks within education systems worldwide is the introduction of structures and processes for external accountability. Think, for example, of *No child left behind* in the USA, the 'My School' website in Australia and league tables, national testing and school inspection in England. It is important to recognise, however, that the use of large-scale educational assessment for external accountability purposes is not a new concept, as Peter Hill (2010, p. 416) describes: 'The practice of basing selection for the bureaucracy on results achieved in national examinations or tests can be traced back to the Han dynasty (206BC–220AD).' Although large-scale testing may well be efficient in stratifying a society, one could ask whether it has a role to play in decreasing inequity and enabling all to reach their potential. Furthermore, it's only recently, as a result of the effective schools movement, that schools have begun to be held to account for student performance. There is also a further sleight of hand at work here, illustrated in the quote from Hill (2010, p. 417) below:

The shift in logic from the notion that it is possible to create schools that systematically adopt mechanisms for bringing about ongoing improvements in student learning to the notion of holding schools and school systems directly accountable for the progress of their students as measured by scores on tests was a small one, and one that resonated well with increasingly frustrated and anxious voters who were losing confidence in the capacity of public school systems to deliver a quality education.

The myth to be exploded here is that the introduction of an external accountability policy will necessarily have a positive and sustained impact on student achievement scores. As with all the other myths there is a grain of truth in the proposition, but it is not a panacea. It is certainly true that such an approach is efficient in selecting students for elite positions on the basis of competitive examinations. It is also true that the use of external accountability measures in seriously underperforming and dysfunctional schools or education systems will administer a short, sharp, shock—either shaking them out of complacency, or directing their attention to a limited number of measurable goals. The problem is that such top-down strategies have a very limited half-life. Once the school or system has begun to improve and to take ownership of its own development, then the continuing pressure for external accountability becomes oppressive, alienating and counter-productive. The 'levelling off' of literacy achievement in English primary schools in the early 2000s is an example of this phenomenon. Although external accountability may be a useful strategy at the early stages of an improvement process, its continued use will reduce both performance and motivation. Not only this, but such an approach gives little guidance as to how to create more productive, instructional and curriculum pathways for students. This in essence is the myth.

This is not to argue that the concept of accountability in education is redundant; far from it. The point is that as a school or system continues to improve, there must be a concomitant shift away from external to internal forms of accountability, which help build more effective instructional opportunities for students and serve to decrease the variation between them, by both raising the bar and closing the gap. The relationship between external and internal forms of accountability needs to reflect that implied by the system reform diagram presented in Figure 1.3 at the end of Chapter One. In the move from prescription to professionalism, any accountability framework needs to be able not only to fulfil its original purpose, but also to build capacity and confidence, particularly in designing productive learning environments for students. There will always be a place for some form of external accountability in any system, but it will move over time from being the key driver of improvement to a function that maintains high aspirations, ensures quality and triggers intervention when necessary. The concept of 'intelligent accountability' in education was developed as a way of illustrating this progression. The term was first coined by John Dunford of the Secondary Heads Association in the UK (SHA 2003, paragraph 45, p. 9):

Intelligent accountability is a framework to ensure that schools work effectively and efficiently towards both the common good and the fullest development of their pupils. It uses a rich set of data that gives full expression to the strengths and weaknesses of the school in fulfilling the potential of pupils. It combines internal school processes with levels of external monitoring appropriate to the state of development of each individual school.

How the concept of accountability in education evolves through the phases of system development and in the process becomes increasingly intelligent is the key issue addressed in this chapter. In exploding the myth that external accountability results in sustained school reform and presenting the idea of intelligent accountability as an impactful alternative, the discussion that follows focuses on four key themes:

▶ a framework for intelligent accountability
▶ tracking student progress
▶ school self-evaluation and review
▶ school performance and formative assessment.

A framework for intelligent accountability

The debate surrounding external accountability is often a fraught one with staunch advocates on both sides. For example, Sir Michael Barber (2004, p. 10), part-architect of the English system of external accountability, claims that:

For pupils and the performance of the system the benefits have been huge. Standards of achievement have been put in the spotlight, expectations have been raised, teachers' efforts have been directed to making a difference and performance has undoubtedly improved.

Many others, however, have been highly critical of the accountability framework. Oft quoted examples are of teachers 'teaching to the test', schools increasing their 'competitiveness' in league tables through adjusting their admissions policy and adopting examinations that for whatever reason offer more passes or are deemed easier. Many would also agree that an over-emphasis on external accountability increases the degree of dependence and lack of innovation within the system (Hopkins 2007).

As argued in the introduction, the solution is not to abandon the accountability framework, but to make it more intelligent by achieving a more even balance between external and internal accountability. Most forms of accountability are externally dominated—the clarification of expected standards at various ages, the setting of targets to be met, the publication of results at school and local level and the use of inspection schemes to ensure quality. Once in place, these pillars of the external accountability framework are often difficult to dismantle. Because of the resilience of external forms of accountability, it is necessary to compensate by increasing the emphasis on internal forms of accountability as confidence and competence in the school or system increases. The most common approaches are: the use of teacher assessment; bottom-up target setting; progress measures of student performance; value-added measures of school performance; and schools publishing their own profiles of strengths, weaknesses and benchmark comparisons. It is these forms of accountability that both allow a sharper fix on the focus of personalisation and develop the professional skill of the teaching staff involved. As a consequence, when the balance between external and internal accountability becomes more even, it also becomes more intelligent (Hopkins 2007).

In drawing a picture of an intelligent accountability framework in *Every school a great school* (Hopkins 2007) I set out a comprehensive schema for balancing internal and external accountability. In doing this I drew on my experience in England where I was partially responsible for helping that system move from one dominated by external forms of accountability, to one where there was a better balance with internal forms. I must stress that I am not advocating the English framework as an ideal, although it does serve to raise issues that are generalisable to other contexts, particularly in mapping the shift from externally dominated forms of accountability to more intelligent accountability informed by a better balance with bottom-up school reform efforts. As indicated previously, in the mid-1990s the education policy framework in England was dominated by external forms of accountability based on the 'four pillars' of tests, targets, tables and inspection. A summary of this position is seen in the 'Pre-1997' column of Table 6.1.

Table 6.1 Summary of the accountability framework in England pre-1997, in 2004 and in the future (Reproduced from Hopkins 2007, p. 103)

	Pre-1997	2004	Future
Tests	External/ summative tests at KS1–3, GCSE and A-level	External (with pilots in teacher assessment)/ summative (with drive on AfL)	Synergy between formative and summative; external and internal
Targets	Top down/school-level, but no targets required at KS1 and 2	Top down at KS3 and GSCE. Bottom-up at KS1–2/improved pupil-level data	Bottom-up, school-owned/ student-level to drive individual performance
Tables	Raw data at KS2, GCSE and A level	Raw and value-added from KS2 to GCSE	Raw results and contextual value-added
Inspection	External/detailed, long notice, massive preparation	External/focused: shorter notice, significant preparation	External/focused, combined with self-evaluation

Although by 2004 a better balance had been achieved between internal and external accountability measures as indicated in the '2004' column of Table 6.1, the preferred direction of travel was towards the position indicated in the 'Future' column as described in more detail below:

‣ **Tests**—a mixed economy with a presumption of external testing in core subjects at key stages, but with a gradual move to teacher assessment in other cases.

‣ **Target setting**—with a move to bottom-up school-owned targets, informed by individual student-level data, to drive up performance.

‣ **Tables**—with a move to contextual value-added tables, combined with the school profile to give a clear picture of progress.

‣ **Inspection**—with a move to short duration inspections with minimal observation, informed by self-evaluation; small teams; and a short, sharp report with clearer recommendations for improvement (Hopkins 2007, p. 103).

One of the most contentious issues in most systems is that of testing. Interestingly, there is a marked difference in approaches between high-performing school systems. Finland, for example, eschews any form of testing, whereas it is dominant in South Korea and Singapore. Context and cultural specificity obviously apply here and in the latter two cases testing has been an important strategy in securing rapid improvement from a relatively low baseline. My own preference would be for a mixed economy with the balance of testing shifting from internal to external as students move through school stages. Looked at from the perspective of the previous two chapters, there are strong arguments for moderated teacher assessment being the default approach to assessment. If it is done properly, it can be very reliable and links well to personalised learning, supports teacher professionalism and through external moderation encourages the transfer of curriculum innovation between schools. As the effectiveness and reliability of teacher assessment and school self-evaluation increases, capacity is built into the system, and the need for 'high stakes' testing can be confined to key points of transition in a narrower range of subjects. This leaves the opportunity open for schools to become increasingly responsible for their own assessment through a 'chartered examiner' approach, with a national or local perspective being given through randomised sampling (Hopkins 2007).

The way in which the accountability system has evolved to achieve a better balance between internal and external accountability is seen in the diagram below which includes reference to standards as well as performance management. It represents a reasonable, if not ideal, balance between internal and external assessment and provides a platform for building capacity and professional accountability towards the next phase of reform (Hopkins 2007).

Table 6.2 A framework for building intelligent accountability

	Internal	External
Test	▶ Assessment for learning using a range of tools at all stages ▶ Teacher assessment	▶ External tests at regular (two yearly) intervals together with randomised national testing ▶ Test results published
Targets	▶ Targets for every child—part of the learning culture ▶ Self-evaluation identifies priority areas for targets and action ▶ Use pupil performance data to inform target levels	▶ Schools must set targets at all stages ▶ High quality data means LA or region can check targets are stretching ▶ Floor targets bite on low performers

▶

Table 6.2 (continued)

	Internal	External
Tables	▶ VA and CVA help establish strengths/ weaknesses relative to peers	▶ Raw at key stages ▶ VA at key transition points
Inspection	▶ Rigorous self-evaluation throughout school required to demonstrate sound management	▶ Every 3 years at no notice ▶ More frequent in weak schools
Standards	▶ Benchmarks used as a framework in which to consider students' individual learning paths	▶ National standards set at range of ages and all students assessed against them
Performance management	▶ To be based on portfolios emerging from teachers' involvement in triads related to specifications of teaching and learning	▶ 360 degree assessment ▶ Diagnostics all linked to professional development

Any system of accountability at the system level will not be easy to achieve and will inevitably be politically contentious. This will always be the case. The problem is that changes to the accountability framework are usually achieved piecemeal, rather than as part of a strategic and purposeful rebalancing. Because of this, opponents of accountability will perceive the framework as continuously open to change through attrition. This is inevitably destabilising and no way to build a platform for schools utilising an inside–out way of working to achieve successful school reform. It is therefore important to make clear that the move towards intelligent accountability is part of an explicit strategy in pursuit of building capacity within the system to ensure that the personalisation of learning and the professionalisation of teaching lead to success for every school in terms of student achievement. The following two sections of this chapter look in more

detail at tracking student progress and school self-evaluation as two of
the most prominent strategies for achieving this.

Tracking student progress

Central to the concept of intelligent accountability is the shift from the
use of data for the purposes of holding schools to account to using
school data directly to monitor the progress and drive the performance
of students. According to PISA (OECD 2010, p. 46):

> *Although the use of standardised tests tends to be unrelated to
> school performance, it does relate to levels of equity within school
> systems. School systems that have high proportions of students in
> schools that use standardised tests tend to show a lower impact of
> socio-economic background on learning outcomes within schools.*

It is clearly implied by this analysis that those schools that use data to
monitor the progress of their students significantly reduce the variation
in student achievement and performance within the school. This is
further reinforced by research findings (NCSL 2006a) from the study
of reducing within-school variation in pupil outcomes in England,
where *Tracking for success* (DfES 2005a) and the *Making good
progress* initiative (DfES 2006) have further illustrated the importance
of tracking student performance, both for the individual student and
for the cohort as a whole. As Peter Matthews (Ofsted 2009b, pp.
18–19) points out in evaluating the practice of 20 outstanding primary
schools that have excelled against the odds:

> *An undoubted feature of all the schools' success is the rigour of
> their assessment. This starts in the Early Years Foundation Stage
> classes where continual observation and assessment of individual
> children are key activities ... With older children, assessment is an*

integral part of teaching and learning ... In Key Stage 2, the schools make much use of tests to supplement and benchmark teacher assessments ... This allows progress to be tracked ... and challenging targets to be set.

Although some schools still analyse their student level data using their own, often idiosyncratic, methods, many schools are finding that national or regional schemes serve their purposes best. Among the best of current approaches to tracking student progress are those outlined in the following sections.

Student tracking in the Northern Metropolitan Region, Australia

The implementation of student tracking systems in the region was a two-stage process. The first stage, led by Professor Patrick Griffin from the University of Melbourne, focused not just on testing of students, but also on the nature and purpose of Professional Learning Teams (PLTs). The PLTs evaluated student performance and growth and used tests to provide feedback for teachers to adjust their teaching.

Professor Griffin emphasised that PLTs were about teachers challenging each other on the impact of their teaching on student performance and that judgements on performance can only be made on the basis of what students say, make, do and write. In terms of testing, Professor Griffin emphasised three key points:

1. The tests are fair.
2. In heterogeneous groups of students there will be three or four 'zones of proximal development' and teachers should ensure that their teaching meets the needs of those groups.
3. Teachers should review progress of students on a regular basis to ensure teaching is targeted appropriately and also to adjust student groupings.

While Professor Griffin's work had, and continues to have, a profound impact on teacher culture, it was, by the nature of its reliance on the University of Melbourne, not readily accessible by all teachers in the region. So, in 2008, all schools were provided with a licence for Philip Holmes-Smith's 'Student Performance Analyser' (SPA), which is now widely used in schools across Melbourne's north. SPA can be used by all teachers and allows teachers to manage and analyse data from a range of sources including NAPLAN (National Assessment Program—Literacy and Numeracy), ACER (Australian Council for Educational Research) tests, online adaptive tests and other data such as teacher judgements.

The data is analysed in four different ways:

1. SPA instantly identifies students who are performing one or more years below expected level, at expected level or one or more years above expected level.
2. SPA shows trends over time.
3. SPA shows the growth from one test period to the next.
4. SPA provides item analysis for individual test items (SREAMS 2011).

Teachers in professional learning teams now regularly review the progress of various student groups and adjust both their teaching and the composition of student groupings on the basis of data from SPA.

Using Fischer Family Trust data to track student performance in the UK

The Fischer Family Trust (FFT) data analysis project began in 2000. Following initial development work with schools in Islington, Local Authorities (LAs) in England were invited to join the project in 2001. Initially, 45 LAs joined and this grew to all LAs (150+) by 2004. In parallel, work with all LAs in Wales was undertaken from 2002 onwards.

The overall aims of the project are to support the processes of self-evaluation, target setting and, consequently, school improvement through the provision of data, analyses and support. Key principles which the project aims to embody are that:

▶ data should provide questions not answers
▶ data analysis should be used by schools to promote discussion, evaluation and planning
▶ analyses are available for different groups of pupils, and a range of indicators, to help identify strengths or areas for development/ intervention
▶ information about the past (previous attainment and value-added) should inform, but not determine the future (FFT 2007).

The project involves the matching and analysis of national datasets (around 650 000 students per year for each stage) covering attainment at different Key Stages (KS). Initially, this included National Curriculum assessments (both test and teacher assessment data) at KS1 (age 7), KS2 (age 11), KS3 (age 14), KS4 (age 16) and KS5 (ages 17–19). More recently, analyses using data from the Foundation Stage Profile (age 5) have been added. Analyses cover a range of levels from overall indicators to individual subjects (including the full range of subjects now taken at KS4 and KS5).

From 2003 onwards, data on attainment has been linked to details collected through the school census. This has enabled detailed analysis about the progress made by students with different characteristics (e.g. gender, ethnicity, language) and also led to the development of contextual value-added models. Rather than focusing on just one model, analyses have always provided a range of approaches— including attainment, value-added and contextual value-added. Also, a range of indicators is used. This is because no one model or output measure is appropriate to all situations and an overly simplistic approach does not provide the information needed to support detailed self-evaluation.

The introduction of the online system 'FFT Live' in 2005 provided schools and LAs with more immediate and more flexible analyses and is now the main delivery method. FFT Live is used widely by schools and LAs across England and Wales. As the project has developed it has become increasingly clear that key issues in the effective use of data are ethos and levels of data literacy. Schools where data is used in a top-down approach with little room for discussion tend to be less successful in using the data to enhance expectations than those where the data is used and presented in a manner which encourages discussion with individual students, active participation and agreed targets. Developments in recent years have introduced new areas on FFT Live, notably:

▶ Student Explorer, which provides a set of tools to enable users to select students with particular characteristics, look at their 'history' and inform planning for their specific needs. This can also help to identify students who, for example, have considerably more potential than might be thought if their previous attainment alone was used.

▶ Analyses to enable groups of schools to compare outcomes and progress. Where this is done within an ethos of collaboration it is usually more effective than when imposed from above.

▶ Looking to the future, the project aims to continue to provide a wide range of analyses to support the varied needs and contexts of users. Research into patterns and trends within the data will continue to inform such developments.

These approaches to tracking student progress have the advantage of both emphasising student progress as well as giving whole-school data to allow for comparisons. When choosing an approach, schools must not only be intelligent consumers, but be clear about how they contribute to a whole-school approach to intelligent accountability as seen in the following sections.

School self-evaluation and review

Before discussing contemporary approaches to school self-evaluation a short history lesson may be instructive. There was a marked change in the character of school improvement efforts in the late 1970s and early 1980s, which was largely the result of an increase in demands for school accountability. In the United Kingdom, for example, the reaction to the pressure for accountability took the form of a variety of local authority schemes for school self-evaluation. At this time, it was viewed as one of the few improvement strategies that could not only strengthen the capacity of the school to develop or renew itself, but also provide evidence for accountability purposes as well as a structure for managing the change process. The OECD *International School Improvement Project* (ISIP), in particular, took a leading role in conceptualising and disseminating examples of school evaluation (Bollen & Hopkins 1987; Hopkins 1987b, 1988).

Research (Hopkins 1987b) on school self-evaluation efforts suggested that schools found carrying out a full review very time consuming. It also found an apparent lack of rigour and objectivity in the evaluation processes used and, more importantly, difficulties in impacting directly on classroom practice. It was for these reasons that more comprehensive strategies for self-evaluation including development planning were advocated. In England in 1989 when the then Department of Education and Science issued its first advice, development planning was regarded as a means of helping schools manage the extensive national and centrally driven change agenda, and also enabling schools 'to organise what it is already doing and what it needs to do in a more purposeful and coherent way'

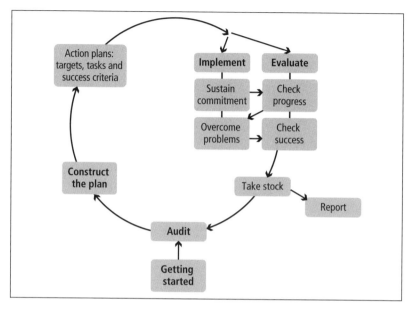

Figure 6.1 The planning process
(Reproduced from Hargreaves & Hopkins 1991, p. 66)

(Hargreaves et al. 1989, p. 4). Priorities for development are planned in detail for one year and are supported by action plans that are the working documents for teachers. The priorities for subsequent years are sketched in outline to provide the longer-term program (Hopkins 2007). An overview of the planning process is shown in Figure 6.1.

Research into school improvement during the 1990s (Hopkins et al. 1996; MacGilchrist et al. 1995; MacGilchrist, Myers & Reed 1997), as was seen in Chapter Three, showed that schools that exhibited best practice in development planning used it as a strategy to enhance directly the progress and achievement of students. The focus was on students' learning, their progress and achievement; what was needed to improve it and how this was best supported. Crucial to this shift was the closer integration of implementation and evaluation as illustrated in Figure 6.1 (Hopkins 2007).

So although school self-evaluation lost popularity during the late 1980s and early 1990s, it is now enjoying a renaissance. This seems to be due to its links to student learning where the work of John MacBeath (2006) is important, the enhancing of teachers' professional judgement, whole school improvement (Ofsted 2006b) and as we shall see, new forms of inspection (Hopkins 2007). As the Office for Standards in Education in England acknowledge in setting out inspection guidance for school self-evaluation (Ofsted 2011, p. 2):

> *Rigorous self-evaluation is at the heart of effective school improvement. The accuracy and clarity of the school's self-evaluation helps to inform the inspectors' initial view of the quality of leadership and management and the school's capacity to improve ... During the inspection inspectors will need to focus on the impact which the school's self-evaluation has in driving improvement and demonstrating the school's capacity to improve.*

In identifying the factors that contribute to effective self-evaluation, recommendations from Ofsted's report *Best practice in self-evaluation* (2006a) stress the importance of a strong impact and outcomes focus. In reporting on research findings from schools, colleges and local authorities, the survey showed 'that good self-evaluation led to improved outcomes for children and young people' (p. 2). The report also acknowledges that although participants' institutions were at very different stages of development, all 'were revising their self-evaluation systems to cope with change' (p. 2). In light of this, there was a recognised need to ensure that self-evaluation systems and processes are closely aligned with development planning priorities and rigorously focused on improving the quality of teaching and learning (2006a, p. 2):

> *... self-evaluation should focus specifically on the impact provision makes on outcomes for children and young people; the views of a*

wide range of stakeholders should be used to inform it. The findings from self-evaluation should inform priorities in development planning, and schools ... should identify the precise characteristics of strong and weak pedagogy to help them focus more rigorously on improving the quality of teaching and learning.

The contribution of this enhanced, more holistic and contemporary approach to school self-evaluation to intelligent accountability in England was most concretely expressed in *A new relationship with schools* (DfES 2004d). Central to this was the role of schools evaluating themselves through the 'Self-Evaluation Form' (SEF) (DfES 2004b). The SEF required schools to provide evidence on their performance, on their strengths and weakness, identify precise issues as their key priorities for improvement and plan on how they intend to improve them. These were then fed through into the 'School Improvement Plan' where schools set specific targets for each of these areas (Hopkins 2007).

A new relationship with schools (DfES 2004d, pp. 7–10) poses the following questions, shown by Ofsted (2006a) to be most frequently used by schools where evaluation was perceived to be effective:

▶ Does the self-evaluation identify how well our school serves its learners?

▶ How does our school compare with the best schools and the best comparable schools?

▶ Is the self-evaluation integral to our key management systems?

▶ Is our school's self-evaluation based on a good range of telling evidence?

▶ Does our self-evaluation and planning involve key people in the school and seek the views of parents, learners and external advisers and agencies?

▶ Does our self-evaluation lead to action to achieve the school's longer-term goals for development?

Of course, these questions are very important in self-evaluation, but in order to increase the quality of the process we have to be aware that it is a dynamic and continuous one (Ofsted 2006a; Blanchard 2002). It constantly needs revisiting, incorporating the processes of analysis, reflection, evaluation and target setting. This way it becomes more powerful and a part of the school's improvement culture.

In preparing this section, I inevitably reviewed the work that we did on school self-evaluation some 25 ago. Interestingly and happily, that advice and commentary still holds good today. In concluding this section then, I cite with minimal editing the characteristics of effective school self-evaluation taken from that work (Hopkins 1988, p. 117):

▶ *School self-evaluation is a systematic process, not simply reflection.*

▶ *Its short-term goal is to gain valid information on the progress of students and school functioning.*

▶ *The evaluation leads directly to action.*

▶ *It is a group activity that involves participants in a collegial process.*

▶ *Optimally the process is 'owned' by the school i.e. it exemplifies inside–out working.*

▶ *Its purpose is school improvement, the raising of achievement and the establishing of the 'problem-solving' school.*

School performance and formative assessment

The argument to this point goes something like this: there is dominance in current policy formulations on forms of external accountability. As previously argued, this approach has its place, particularly in giving a short, sharp jolt to a system or school that is under-performing. As a strategy for enhancing student learning and achievement and reducing inequity in the system, however, it has serious limitations.

An alternative approach has been proposed in this chapter— through altering the balance between external and internal forms of accountability with the aim of creating those conditions conducive to enhanced levels of student learning and achievement. Strategies for tracking student progress and for school self-evaluation are critical here, as are the approaches to assessment for learning discussed previously in Chapter Four. In this section the argument is sustained by discussing some of the lessons that schools need to heed in order to ensure that the pressures for external accountability are translated into the conditions for enhancing student learning. After reviewing these lessons, examples are given of schools that have made this journey and then some guidelines for formative assessment at the school level are proposed.

Peter Hill's work is particularly helpful here. In the chapter already cited, Hill (2010, p. 420) says this: 'While large-scale assessment for accountability purposes is now widespread, much remains to be done to ensure that it is effective'. He then proposes a series of lessons to assist school and systems in achieving this goal:

- **Lesson 1**—Ensure that what you seek to measure, the use you make of the results and what you intend to achieve by using results in this manner are in alignment.
- **Lesson 2**—Build into the accountability system tests that probe students' ability to apply the knowledge and understandings they have learnt in school to solving real and challenging problems.
- **Lesson 3**—Make certain that you have a way of confirming whether gains on accountability tests reflect real improvements in learning.

▶ **Lesson 4**—Avoid policies and perceptions of high-stakes negative consequences for those charged with bringing about improved performance.

▶ **Lesson 5**—Be cautious in assuming that providing schools with detailed information on the performance of their students on accountability tests is going to be useful to teachers in improving instruction.

▶ **Lesson 6**—Make use of multiple indicators in judging the performance of a school, including measures that give an indication of trends over time having adjusted for student intake characteristics.

▶ **Lesson 7**—Involve the profession (as well as stakeholders, especially parents) in the design and implementation of the accountability system. Accept the notion of reciprocal accountability and ensure that you can provide schools and teachers with the capacity to meet your expectations.

The application of these lessons can be seen in the following case study examples drawn from England and Australia, which present practical illustrations of how performance has been successfully managed in both primary and secondary school contexts.

Example in action: England

Keys to the sustained success of Berrymede Junior School (Ofsted 2009b, p. 30)

Teaching, leadership and teamwork

▶ an insistence on high-quality learning and teaching, and continuous self-evaluation

▶ excellent communication and team work, with teaching assistants playing a key role

▶ an induction and 'buddy' system for all new staff, including lunchtime supervisors
▶ support for succession planning through the development of middle and senior leadership skills.

Targets and tracking
▶ close, termly tracking of each child's progress
▶ individual targets—every child has a 'promises book' (the name used by a child) which has their targets for English and mathematics
▶ targets for the curriculum, each class and groups within a class, reviewed every six weeks
▶ extensive analysis and use of data, with standardisation of assessment across all year groups.

Developing positive attitudes to learning
▶ rewards for children that enhance positive attitudes, such as 'stars of the week' badges, certificates and team points, Year 6 leaders and elected Head Boy and Girl
▶ an exciting and relevant curriculum which makes full use of space in and outside the building
▶ displays of children's work that celebrate their achievements and stimulate further learning.

Involving parents
▶ Close links with parents through 'reading record books', two outreach workers who are accessible to parents and pupils at the beginning and end of a school day and an 'open door' policy.

Example in action: Australia

Hume Central Secondary College: an integrated strategic approach (Zbar 2011, p. 12)

The school's explicit instruction model, based on John Hattie's research (2009), supports teachers to adopt a common lesson planning approach based on what has been proven in practice to work. This in turn supports peer observations of classroom practice, through triads the school has established, and from 2011 it is expected that peer coaching, which is part of all job descriptions in the school, will include around seven observations a year.

Use of the model is underpinned by the systematic use of data to enable teachers both to know their students well and to know what and how to teach. Data is used to inform meetings of the leadership team, including data that illustrates how each student has performed in relation to NAPLAN and other tests and analyses of how different students performed against expected levels in the VCE. Data is also used to identify and target students who are especially at risk due to poor attendance.

To support a relentless focus on achieving 'two years learning in one', the school has also instituted regular reporting to parents about the progress of their children through the year. Parents now receive a progress report every three weeks, which enables the school to more proactively work with students to help them to succeed and ensure timely engagement with parents. Students at Hume Central receive around 12 reports a year which reinforce the expectation they will work hard and achieve as a result.

These case examples give some indication of how schools are creating an intelligent accountability culture in the pursuit of higher outcomes for their students. Crucial to this approach is how information and knowledge is best presented to most effectively generate action. Some years ago Matthew Miles set out some of those conditions under which knowledge is best acted on and added some comments on this process (cited in Hopkins 1988, pp. 170–1):

▶ **Clarity:** The knowledge must be understood clearly, not be fuzzy, vague or confusing.
▶ **Relevance:** The knowledge is seen as meaningful, as connected to one's normal life and concerns, not irrelevant, inapplicable or impractical.
▶ **Action images:** The knowledge is or can become exemplified in specific actions, clearly visualised. Without such images, knowledge-based action is unlikely.

▶ **Will:** There must be motivation, interest, action orientation, a will to do something with the knowledge.

▶ **Skill:** There must be actual behavioural ability to do the action envisioned. Without skill, the action will be either aborted or done incongruently with the knowledge undergirding it.

Matthew Miles continues this analysis by commenting that although there is a rough sequence from clarity to skill, the conditions are interactive. For example, seeing clear action images may result in an increased relevance, or added skill may increase will, since a good outcome is expected. In line with a theme emphasised throughout this book, Miles adds a further reflection. He remarks that it is sad, but true, that plenty of school improvers think that skill can be developed through reading, lectures or watching videotapes. It can't.

Improving skill requires doing, practice, getting feedback, reshaping the doing until the doing makes sense, is smooth and gets you where you want. We know this about skiing, tennis and golf, but not quite it seems about those behaviours in educational change. (Miles 1987, pp. 3–4)

This crucial point is addressed in more detail in Chapter 7.

Coda

Exploding the myth of external accountability is relatively easy to do. Although PISA suggests that improving countries do use standardised testing particularly in the early phases of a reform program, higher levels of student performance and increased equity—reducing the variation in student achievement—is enhanced when data are used to map the progress of students. The PISA report *What makes a school successful?* continues (OECD 2010, p. 47):

> *One explanation for the positive association between the prevalence of standardised tests and improved equity in school systems is that such tests provide schools with instruments to compare themselves with other schools. This, in turn, allows schools to observe the inequities among schools, which could be considered the first step towards redressing them. The results from PISA also show higher levels of socio-economic equity in school systems that use achievement data to make decisions about the curriculum and track achievement data over time.*

Another OECD project that has global reach but this time on teacher attitudes—the TALIS project—points to school leadership as playing a crucial role in shaping teachers' working lives and development:

> *Schools with strong instructional leadership are those where teachers engage in professional development to address the weaknesses identified in appraisals, where there are better student–teacher relations, where there is greater collaboration among teachers, and where greater recognition is given to innovative teachers. (OECD 2010, p. 31)*

The key issue in drawing this chapter together and in exploding the myth of external accountability is to point to the crucial idea of data being used formatively to create the most effective learning conditions in schools for students. This is a point that is also made in a book by Michael Fullan, Peter Hill and Carmel Crévola (2006) ambitiously entitled *Breakthrough*. In this book Fullan and his colleagues examine the pedagogic implications underpinning much of Fullan's recent work, some of which we have already reviewed (Hopkins 2007).

Simply put, they claim that there are numerous examples of good curricula that provide the necessary degree of specification and well-designed teaching approaches that work effectively in classroom settings when used at the right time with the right students (Hopkins 2007). What was missing, they argued in 2006, was a clear focus on formative assessment. They identified the following four key features of classroom practice that were virtually non-existent at the time (Fullan et al. 2006).

1. A set of formative assessment tools tied to the learning objectives of each lesson that give the teacher access to accurate information on the progress of each student on a daily basis, and that can be administered without undue disruption to normal classroom routines.
2. A method to allow the formative assessment data to be captured in a way that is not time-consuming, of analysing the data automatically and a means of converting it into information that is powerful enough to drive instructional decisions not some time in the future, but tomorrow.
3. A means of using the assessment information on each student to design and implement lessons that deliver differentiated instruction that optimise the effectiveness of classroom teaching.
4. A built-in means of monitoring and managing learning, of testing what works and of systematically improving the effectiveness of classroom instruction so that it more precisely responds to the learning needs of each student in the class.

They conclude:

> *One can think of instances where current practice comes close to achieving one or more of the above, but we are aware of none that integrates all four ... If classroom instruction could be organized*

... this would lead to quantum, ongoing improvements in the rate of student learning but, more important, to a transformational change in thinking about teaching. This is because, for the first time, classroom instruction would be organized so that teaching followed the student. (Fullan et al. p. 37)

The inspirational sentiment contained in the final sentence captures well the spirit of intelligent accountability proposed in this chapter. The OECD quotes at the start of this section have confirmed the fallibility of the myth of external accountability in school reform. Then the example from *Breakthrough* gives a powerful image of intelligent accountability in action. The important point is that the various strategies for intelligent accountability combine to form a coherent framework for formative evaluation that has a sharp and sustained focus on using the knowledge to enhance the learning and outcomes of students. We turn in the next chapter to consider how these evolving practices can contribute more directly to system reform.

Chapter 7

Innovation, networking and professional learning

The myth that innovation and networking always add value to school reform

This myth is a tricky one, for it flies in the face of conventional wisdom. Everywhere we go in this postmodern world of ours we are being encouraged to be innovative, to grasp the future and to embrace transformational change. That is all well and good, but if basic knowledge management practices are not in place, then innovation, which by definition builds on the best of existing knowledge, will be futile. I remember a challenging conversation with Charles Clarke who was at the time in 2004 the Secretary of State for Education in the UK when I was Chief Adviser on School Standards. He was asking me why teachers did not have the educational equivalent of the *Lancet* (a weekly review of research and current practice) as the medical profession did. I tried to explain, somewhat apologetically, that by and large teaching is not systematically influenced by existing research, let alone conditioned by cutting-edge discoveries. I also added that, sadly, current practice was rarely shared in an actionable form. This was a salutary moment that encouraged me to think and act more deeply in addressing the problem.

There seem to be four interrelated issues here:

▸ The first is that, at present, teaching cannot be called an evidence-based profession. Although research-based practice is ostensibly a prominent feature of many teacher education, leadership development and school improvement programs, it is not systematically embedded in the day-to-day professional practices of educators across the system.

▸ Secondly, there is no explicit professional agreement on what is good practice. This problem is compounded or compensated for by 'faddism'—a tendency to pick up new or popular ideas that are adopted in a superficial way. When subsequently and predictably they have little impact on student performance they are then eschewed. It is this tendency that supports the cycle of change and no change in education that we have already noted.

▸ Third, most educational research is expressed in a way that is not immediately accessible by teachers and even when it is of good quality, it is rarely presented in an implementable form.

▸ As a consequence, networking and professional learning become largely superficial activities because the discourse they are designed to engender has nothing substantive to focus on.

Ben Levin (2010, p. 1) has recently made a similar argument when commenting on the place of innovation and transformation in education reform:

> *We hear many calls today for the transformation of schooling; to reshape schools in some entirely new way, and for a greater role for innovation in improving schools ... [My] argument ... is that*

we should be cautious about embracing transformation and its handmaiden, innovation as the requirements for schooling. I take the view that the more promising avenue in terms of student outcomes ... would focus instead on improving existing school systems by focusing on better. This is not an argument against change, but springs from the belief that a focus on innovation and transformation could distract us from what is both possible and desirable in order to pursue goals that may be desirable but are not very possible.

Like Levin, I am not arguing against innovation or networking per se—neither of us are Luddites! Rather, we both seem to be advocating approaches to improvement that deepen and extend current best practice about what is known to work. Similarly, in terms of networking and professional learning, we advocate the utilisation of approaches that build capacity and extend evidence-based practice. To quote Levin (2010, p. 6) again:

Organizing schools so that we get much more of practices known to be effective and much less of practices known to be ineffective is highly likely to yield more results per unit of effort than is the search for further innovation or for transformation, both of which carry significant risks.

It is important to recognise that such approaches to improvement are characteristic of the practices that exist in successful schools. As Peter Matthews reminds us in his study of *Twelve outstanding secondary schools* (Ofsted 2009a, p. 28), 'Great schools maintain rigour and consistency while continuing to innovate and develop'. As David Hargreaves (2003b, p. 8) puts it: 'There will be no true transformation of education unless we have innovation networks that prosper in the creation and transfer of robust good practice'. The critical point here is that in embracing innovation, networking and professional learning, both school and system reform efforts need to be channelled in robust and rigorous ways to ensure that the transfer of practices that impact most directly on student achievement are at the heart of the matter.

So in exploring the myth surrounding innovation and networking and its contribution to school reform, this chapter will:

▶ engage in a more extensive discussion about the nature of innovation
▶ explore recent research on the utility of and conditions for effective networking
▶ evidence 'the elephant in the classroom' and the importance of professional learning
▶ elaborate on both deductive and inductive approaches to professional learning.

A perspective on innovation

When I first began my study of educational change, almost four decades ago, I was very impressed with Everett Rogers' theory of innovation. It not only had the ring of truth, but was also both elegant and practical. Rogers was a rural sociologist and reviewed over 500 research studies to develop his theory first published in his book *Diffusion of innovations* (Rogers 1962). Although none of Rogers' original research studies were from education, his theory stands the test of time and has particular relevance for school reform today. There are four aspects of his theory that relate to themes developed in this chapter. First, Rogers identified four key elements in diffusion research, summarised in Table 7.1.

Table 7.1 Rogers' four key elements in diffusion research as related to school reform

Key element	Rogers' definition	Relevance for school reform
1. Innovation	An idea, practice or object that is perceived as new by an individual or other unit of adoption.	A specific change or refinement of practice that has a positive impact on student learning.
2. Communication channels	The means by which messages get from one individual to another.	The school's narrative and process of professional learning.
3. Time	Rate of adoption is the relative speed with which an innovation is adopted by members of a social system.	How long the new practice takes to influence student learning.
4. Social system	A set of interrelated units that are engaged in joint problem-solving to accomplish a common goal.	The school or educational system that is using the innovation.

It is clear that the elements described above are relevant to the way in which educational ideas are adopted and implemented. What is particularly interesting, in terms of the myth that we are confronting in this chapter, is Rogers' definition of the characteristics of an innovation. This is the second aspect of his theory that has direct applicability to the current school reform context, in that each characteristic identified relates to an individual's decision to adopt or reject an innovation. These can be described as follows.

▶ **Relative advantage:** How much better the new practice is over existing ways of working.

▶ **Compatibility:** How relevant the new practice is to the work of the teacher.

▶ **Complexity or simplicity:** How difficult the new practice is to use. If it is not in the 'zone of proximal development' of the teaching staff, then it is unlikely to be used.

▶ **Trialability:** How easily an innovation can be experimented with, as it is adopted.

▶ **Observability:** An innovation that is visible will drive communication among an individual's peer or personal networks and create more reactions (either positive or negative).

The critical point is that Rogers is implying a deepening and extending of existing practice that relates to moral purpose and effectiveness, rather than the abandonment of current practice in the search for something exotic or completely new.

The third aspect of Rogers' theory is the identification of a series of five stages in the process of adopting an innovation. In his most recent formulation they are: knowledge, persuasion, decision, implementation and confirmation. Finally and famously, Rogers describes five categories of adopters of an innovation within a school or social system. The categories of adopters are: innovators, early adopters, early majority, late majority and laggards. They are often depicted as if following a sigmoid curve.

This brief review of some of Rogers' key ideas has an acute relevance to more contemporary discussions of innovation in school improvement. More recently, many have become excited over the potential of viral communication as an alternative approach to managing and implementing educational change. Viewing the process of educational change as akin to the spreading of a virus stands in stark contrast to the centre-periphery model of change that has been so dominant in the recent past and that underpins the myth being discussed in this chapter. The best-known exposition of this alternative theory of change is that of Malcolm Gladwell (2000) in his book *The tipping point*. He argues that every successful innovation that impacts upon society has a 'tipping point' where the change transforms itself exponentially from enjoying a limited local or sectional interest to become a mass phenomenon. In detailing this process he identifies three laws of the 'tipping point'.

Gladwell's first law—the 'Law of the few'—requires concentrating resources on a few key actors. It says that 'Connectors'—who know lots of people, 'Mavens'—who accumulate knowledge and 'Salesmen'—who have the power of persuasion are responsible for starting word-of-mouth epidemics, which means that resources ought to be solely concentrated on those three groups. The second law relates to the 'Stickiness factor'. This says that there are specific ways of making a contagious message memorable; there are relatively simple changes in the presentation and structuring of information that can make a big difference in how much of an impact it makes. The third law is the 'Power of context', which says that human beings are a lot more sensitive to their environment than they may seem. That is why social change is so volatile and so often inexplicable. We are powerfully influenced by our surroundings, our immediate context and the personalities of those around us.

Gladwell argues that if there is volatility in the world, there is also a large measure of hopefulness as well. Merely by manipulating the size of a group, we can dramatically improve its receptivity to new ideas. By tinkering with the presentation of information, we can significantly improve its stickiness. Simply by finding and reaching those few special people who hold so much social power, we can shape the course of social epidemics. In the end, he says, tipping points are a reaffirmation of the potential for change and the power of intelligent action.

Despite a four-decade interval, there are obvious resonances between Rogers' theory and Gladwell's laws of the tipping point. Both direct us to the critical role of individuals as mediators in the process of innovation, the characteristics of innovation itself and how these factors relate to the systemic nature of successful innovation in practice. The major problem when applying these ideas to education is the lack of evidence on the proven effectiveness of practices. Levin (2010, p. 2) puts it this way:

> *Most systems do not have a system for judging ideas or making distinctions between those that are more likely to be effective and feasible ... The decision to adopt particular innovations seems to depend often on the views of an individual—perhaps a principal, a superintendent or a board member. Questions about the evidence behind the proposed policy or program tend not to be asked.*

This situation is, however, beginning to change. The What Works Clearinghouse in the USA, the Evidence for Policy and Practice Information and Co-ordinating Centre (EPPI-Centre) in England and the work of ACER in Australia are three examples of recent efforts to provide more guidance to school systems on what is known, and with what degree of confidence, about various practices and policies. John Hattie's book *Visible learning* (2009) is an invaluable source of such effective practices, presenting as it does a comparison of over 130 programs, strategies and interventions documented in the meta-analyses of 800 research studies in education. It is still a compendium, though, not a theory of action; and there is as yet no educational equivalent to the *Lancet* or clinical practice guidelines in medicine, as stated in the opening commentary of this chapter.

This discussion leads to four broad conclusions about innovation in school reform:

▶ First, we need high quality innovations, with proven effectiveness, that extend current practice and result in significant gains in student learning and achievement.

▶ Second, we need effective ways of enhancing professional learning focused on the collaborative development of practice, rather than on external accountability.

▶ Third, we need to increase the consistency of practice in reducing within-school variation, which according to PISA dwarfs between-school variation in the UK, USA and Australia.

▶ Fourth, we need to learn more about how to move the adoption of proven practices to scale.

A cautionary note about innovation in education needs to be added to the conclusions presented above. I was recently talking with a school principal about her future plans for personalised learning and was sadly unable to glean a clear idea of what she was intending to do. This led me to think again about what is involved in designing, developing and implementing innovation in classrooms and schools. The flow of action is something like this:

▶ Phrases such as 'personalised learning' only indicate an educational philosophy or direction of travel; they do not contain a guide to action for operational activity. For this to occur, one must identify a range of strategies that represent the school's interpretation of personalised learning, based on their own diagnosis and context.

▶ Once selected, these strategies should be given operational power through reference to external sources such as those cited above; there is no need to reinvent the wheel, as practical research-based specifications are now readily available.

▶ It is wrong to assume that the mere adoption of these practices will impact directly on student learning and that the innovation will therefore necessarily add value—the best of teachers realise this and customise practices through developing protocols that differentiate the use of innovative strategies to meet the needs of all students.

This is where innovation actually occurs in school reform. In most situations it is not the selection of a philosophical direction or the formulation of a new strategy. Rather, it is the development of protocols or artefacts that enable the customisation and fine-tuning of these practices to the learning of students that makes the real difference. This is what innovation is really about and, once developed, these artefacts can be shared, so moving this creativity to scale.

What is central to this argument, however, is a clear recognition that in moving innovation to scale, it is the focus on student learning and achievement that provides the driving force for both innovation and the networking of knowledge about what works in schools. This point is underlined by Matthew Horne (2008, p. 8) who argues that successful innovation must occur in at least four different dimensions: 'how students are taught and how they learn; how, when and why students are assessed; what knowledge and skills the students learn; how education is organised'. Beyond these high level themes which provide a point of focus for the conduct of innovation in education, it is also helpful to address the lessons learnt from schools about the processes of leading innovation in the context of school reform. These are usefully captured in Figure 7.1. The five components of leading curriculum innovation were identified through research with over 50 schools working on a project in England to develop a 21st century curriculum (Barnes & Smith 2007).

In considering the forms of support needed for impactful innovation in the terms outlined here, we now turn in the following section to a discussion of networking.

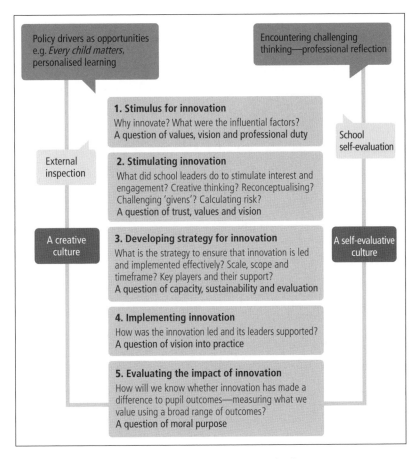

Figure 7.1 Leading curriculum innovation: the five components
(Reproduced from Barnes & Smith 2007, p. 4)

Networking for school and system improvement

As we move into a new phase based on inside–out ways of working, more creative and responsive structures are needed for supporting the work of schools and for moving effective practices to scale. Among these are the variety of networks and collaborative arrangements schools engage in to support a range of school improvement, professional development and innovative activities. Many argue that networks are the essential unit of organisation as we leave behind us the false dichotomy between top-down and bottom-up approaches to educational change (Hargreaves 2003a; Huberman 1995) and seek to find more effective ways of enabling widespread innovation in schools which genuinely add value at both the student and the system levels.

Unfortunately there are various interpretations of the word 'network'; it is a concept open to a high degree of conceptual pluralism. Although many claims have been made regarding the system level benefits of networking (Hadfield et al. 2006), as well as the positive impact of networks on improving teaching, learning and attainment (Bell, Cordingley & Mitchell 2006) and on leadership and leadership learning (Church et al. 2006), in reality, some networks can simply be 'clubs' for sharing 'good practice'. While this is not in itself a bad thing, particularly when structured to support effective knowledge transfer between education professionals, without an unrelenting focus on student learning and achievement such networks do little to add value to reform efforts at either school or system levels (Earl & Katz 2005; NCSL 2006c). As David Hargreaves (2003b, p. 8) suggests:

The process of networking, how you learn to collaborate and share, how you make sure that the transaction costs of networking are low enough for you to make real gains: all this matters, of course. But you must take care that you don't spend too much time on, and get lost in, the issues of process to the neglect of substance. The substance is, of course, exactly what you're networking for: what the outcomes of the networking will be, and how the network has made a real value-added difference to what goes on in schools and classrooms, to the benefit of students and their teachers.

If networks are genuinely to deliver the outcomes claimed for them, we require a far more robust definition of the term and a clearer specification of the processes involved. Let me therefore propose a definition of the type of network that has a chance of realising the aspirations the argument so far has for them.

Networks are purposeful social entities characterised by a commitment to quality, rigour, and a focus on standards and student learning. They are also an effective means of supporting innovation in times of change. In education, networks promote the dissemination of good practice, enhance the professional development of teachers, support capacity building in schools, mediate between centralised and decentralised structures and assist in the process of restructuring and re-culturing educational organisations and systems.

This definition and the following discussion are based on work undertaken for the second phase of the OECD *Schooling for tomorrow* program on educational innovation (OECD 2004), which examined innovation through networks, multi-site change and supporting initiatives. There is evidence from both research and practice that underpins the value added by networks defined in these terms, together with attempts to explicate the processes involved as illustrated in Figure 7.2. Based on the review of over 70 literature sources drawn from research and evaluation studies conducted throughout the life of England's *Networked learning communities* program (2002–2006), the model presented captures many of the key features in the definition of networks offered above. It also provides an insight into the specification of the networking processes involved which are defined in Figure 7.2 as the twelve building blocks of successful school networks.

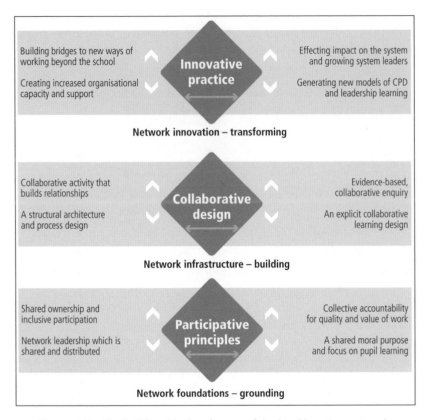

Figure 7.2 The building blocks of successful school learning networks (Reproduced from Carter & Paterson 2006, p. 2)

The qualities of networks implied by the definition and illustration above are not easily acquired. It is, however, worth the effort as networks can provide a means of facilitating local innovation and change as well as contributing to large-scale reform. They offer the potential for reinventing local support for schools, by promoting different forms of collaboration and multi-functional partnerships. The system emphasis is not to achieve control (which is impossible), but to harness the interactive capability of systemic forces (Fullan

2000). On the basis of this analysis, it is clear that networks have the potential to support educational innovation and change by:

‣ **keeping the focus** on the core purposes of schooling, in particular on student learning
‣ **enhancing the skill** of teachers, leaders and other educators as change agents, managing the change process and creating or sustaining discourse on teaching and learning
‣ **providing a focal point** for dissemination of practice, generalisability of innovation and the creation of 'action oriented' knowledge about effective educational practices
‣ **building capacity** for continuous improvement at a local level and in particular in creating professional learning communities, within and between schools
‣ **ensuring systems of integration** in the provision of pressure and support, e.g. helping professional learning communities incorporate pressure or support in a seamless way
‣ **acting as a link** between centralised and decentralised policy initiatives, in particular contributing to policy coherence horizontally and vertically.

Working within the same paradigm, David Hargreaves outlines an agenda for school reform based on innovation and networking in his monograph *Education epidemic* (2003a). The essential task, Hargreaves argues, is to create a climate in which it is possible for teachers to actively engage in innovation and to transfer validated innovations rapidly within their school and into other schools. This does not mean a return to 'letting a thousand flowers bloom', but a disciplined approach to innovation. This involves moving innovation in education to scale through 'front-line innovation conducted by leading-edge institutions and government-supported "pathfinders", which develop new ideas into original practices' (p. 39); and by 'transferred innovation' which closes the gap between the least and most effective schools (or subject departments). Hargreaves (2003a, p. 46) suggests that the achievement of such a 'lateral strategy' for transferred innovation requires four strategic components.

1. It must become clear what is meant by 'good' and 'best' practice among teachers.
2. There needs to be a method of locating good practice and sound innovations.
3. Innovations must be ones that bring real advantages to teachers.
4. Methods of transferring innovation effectively have to be devised.

We conclude this discussion on networking with two examples of successful networks in both England and Australia as a link forward to the following discussion on professional development as the essential transactions that occur within network structures.

Example in action: England

Networks as the unit of engagement: Derbyshire Local Authority (DfES 2005b, p. 24)

In open consultation with headteachers and governors, Derbyshire has developed a structure for supporting and challenging networks and clusters of schools:

▶   Advisory teams facilitate termly opportunities to share effective practice around locally-raised issues. Secondary schools and their primary partners receive annual funding for collaborative projects to improve transition across key stages.
▶   Learning is carefully evaluated and then disseminated through local cluster meetings. Planning for learning networks has been supported by a rigorous

programme of interactions with trained network mentors, ensuring a continuous focus on outcomes for children.

▶ School-based network champions, or 'Lead Developers', empowered by their headteachers, work with all staff and children in designing innovative strategies to raise standards through wider collaboration.

Example in action: Australia

The Darebin Schools Network: Northern Metropolitan Region, Victoria

This highly collaborative schools network, located in the City of Darebin in Melbourne's northern suburbs, is united in its efforts to improve the outcomes of all students, but it wasn't always so. The City of Darebin is the result of a mid-1990s forced merger between the gentrified and more affluent City of Northcote in the south and the poorer City of Preston. This north–south divide in socioeconomic status was reflected in a lack of engagement between schools in the two cities.

The advent of Achievement Improvement Zones (AIZ) and earlier work bringing principals together in collegiate groups to manage performance has brought schools together in ways that would have been unimaginable only a few years earlier. The Network was the largest group in the first phase of the AIZ and all schools established School Improvement Teams and funded, in conjunction with the region, teams of 'Learning Leaders' who were released from teaching to be trained and act as coaches in each school.

Although there is variability, data sets across the network have consistently improved over recent years. Data related to literacy, numeracy and Year 12 achievement have improved. Opinion data—student, teacher and parent— have improved every year, as have retention and attendance data.

Principals and teachers come together regularly to challenge and encourage each other and to engage in deep collaboration. The second phase of the AIZ work—curiosity and powerful learning—is being adopted with remarkable enthusiasm and reflects both the compelling nature of the theories of action contained in the curiosity work as well as the relentless focus of Darebin teachers and principals.

The elephant in the classroom and the importance of professional learning

During this discussion of innovation and networking we have been skirting around perhaps the most resilient challenge in school reform today. As described previously, 'the elephant in the classroom' is the lack of a professional practice that provides a language and a set of behaviours or processes to connect teaching to learning. This issue has already been addressed in Chapter Five in terms of its implications for meeting the challenge of personal change in teaching and the importance of working within the zones of proximal development of staff as well as students in the school. In the discussion that follows, the focus is on a more detailed consideration of how professional learning can be designed, developed and delivered in order to support the generation of shared professional practices.

The framework shown in Figure 7.3 links together the three critical elements required in any school-based system for professional learning. In discussing 'making it happen' with heads and teachers, the diagram has proved to be helpful in framing the challenge. The creation of a new culture of teaching and learning in school requires the integration of three distinct but complementary aspects of the organisation of the school.

1. Vision—These are the explicit commitments that the school makes to the approach to learning it wants for its students and the expectations that it has for their success. In terms of this book it is a reflection of the four theories of action that relate to the whole school.

2. Theories of action—These are the precise specifications of practice that when incorporated into the repertoires of teachers will accelerate student learning, skills development and achievement, and result in them becoming more successful learners.

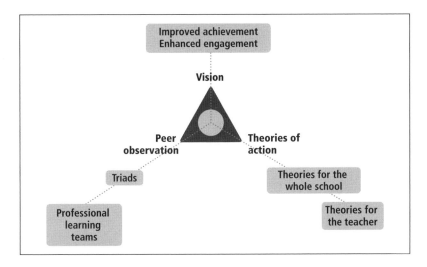

Figure 7.3 A framework for professional learning

3. Peer observation—This refers to the culture of professional learning created in the school, the scheduled time it makes available for the learning of staff and the forms of activity involved. Without regular timetabled opportunities for professional collaboration such as peer coaching or triads that are non-judgemental, it is unlikely that the teaching and learning culture of the school will change.

How the amalgamation of vision, structured professional learning opportunities and specifications of practice play out will also reflect the particular stage of development of the school. As confidence and competence increases so the professional enquiry becomes deeper and more learner or curiosity focused.

In the spirit of collaborative working, putting this framework into practice requires actions from teachers, the school and the local authority. The term 'local authority' is used here as a synonym for region, school district, academy chain or any other middle-tier organisation.

▶ **Teachers** will need to be prepared to expand their 'circles of competence' by embracing the theories of action and incorporating them into their professional repertoires. The real insight as we have seen is that teachers can maintain all their personal values and commitments, while at the same time seeing their practice as an instrument for expressing who they are as a professional.

▶ **Schools** will need to become increasingly self-conscious and specific about the expectations and entitlements of their students as learners. Simultaneously, they will need to allocate time to allow for powerful professional learning opportunities among their staff.

▶ **Local authorities** will need to develop the narrative around learning as well as carefully balancing challenge and support for schools as they progress on their journeys of school improvement.

There is a strong link here with Heifetz's (1994) prescient comment that professional learning opportunities are for many an 'adaptive challenge'. An adaptive challenge is a problem situation for which solutions lie outside current ways of operating. So adaptive challenges demand learning, as progress here requires new ways of thinking and operating. Mobilising people to meet adaptive challenges, as we shall see later in Chapter Eight, is at the heart of leadership practice. By way of a prelude to this discussion, it is helpful to consider here the link between Heifetz's theory of adaptive challenge and Keith Grint's (2005) typology of problems, power and authority shown in Figure 7.4. This framework has direct relevance to the professional learning needs of school leaders engaged in managing innovation to support school and system reform efforts.

This typology is generated from the relationship between the two axes shown 'with the vertical axis representing increasing uncertainty about the solution to the problem—in the behaviour of those in authority—and the horizontal axis representing the increasing need

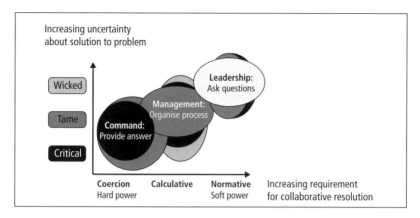

Figure 7.4 A typology of problems, power and authority
(Reproduced from Grint 2005, p. 1477)

for collaboration in resolving the problem' (Grint 2005, p. 1477). From this analysis it is possible to see that as problems become more complex and the degree of uncertainty increases, so does the need to move towards more collaborative practices in finding innovative solutions to 'wicked' problems. In responding effectively to the adaptive challenges implied by this progression, there is increasing emphasis on the need for leadership rather than management in tackling the complex problem solving required for effective innovation. This makes the case for both increased distribution of leadership and collaborative working in tackling the 'wicked' problems faced by educators at both school and system levels.

In the context of current school reform, ultimately, adaptive work requires us to tackle complex problems in collaborative ways. Selecting the most appropriate staff development activity is critical to success here. In terms of 'adaptive challenges' the critical element in all of these strategies is the provision of 'in classroom support' or 'peer coaching'. This is the essential ingredient that is common to all effective approaches to professional learning that have an impact on student learning. It is the facilitation of peer coaching that enables teachers to extend their repertoire of teaching skills and to transfer them to different classroom settings. The important point is that unless the coaching arrangement involves modelling, it appears to have little impact on teachers' behaviour. Peer coaching is most helpful when:

▶ curriculum, teaching and assessment are content of staff development
▶ workshops are designed to develop understanding and skill
▶ school-based groups use specific models to help attain 'transfer of training'
▶ peer coaching teams are relatively small e.g. between two and four members
▶ the entire staff including heads and deputies participate in training and practice
▶ formative study of student learning is embedded in the process.

In summary, the design of staff development that leads to enhanced levels of student achievement needs to be based on the following six principles (Hopkins 2007):

1. Make space and time for enhancing teacher enquiry and creating a 'professional practice'.
2. Utilise evidence from research and practice in developing a range of teaching models that impact on student learning.
3. Study the models' impact on student learning and use data formatively and habitually.
4. Invest in school-based processes, both deductive and inductive, for extending teachers' repertoires.
5. Link the classroom focus with whole-school development and embed pedagogic innovation within curriculum plans.
6. Use this emerging 'professional practice' as a basis for networking and system-wide capacity building.

We turn in the following section to a discussion of how these non-judgemental peer observation activities underpin the range of staff development strategies.

Deductive and inductive approaches to professional learning

One of the best-kept secrets in school and system reform is the range of staff development strategies available to facilitate more precise and deeper forms of professional learning. What is not sufficiently recognised is the potential to link the aims of staff development to increasingly more specific strategies that can deliver changes to teacher behaviour that will profoundly impact on student learning. Recently Bruce Joyce and Emily Calhoun (2010) have helpfully surveyed the field in their book *Models of professional development*. In this book they describe five contrasting families or models of professional learning. In summary, their five models are (Joyce & Calhoun 2010, pp. 12–13):

1. **Supporting the individual**—Although all of staff development intends to support individuals, some types focus on the individual as a person and provide avenues for people to grow according to their own lights.
2. **Personal/professional service**—Here, some teachers and administrators are designated to provide help to others. In some ways, this type of staff development has evolved from supervision, but some forms of coaching are new on the scene and are markedly different from the supervisory mode.
3. **Social construction of knowledge and action**—The school as an organisation is on stage, with the development of learning communities. This model can be very open-ended or take the form of disciplined action research.

4. **Curriculum/instructional initiatives**—Courses are prominent; developed ways of teaching or the dissemination of curriculums are the content of formal workshops.

5. **The infamous menus of brief workshops**—No treatise on staff development would be complete without contemplation of the currently most criticised and common way of organising people for study—the menus of brief workshops on designated staff development days. Despite the critiques, when properly executed this mode can be effective. Staff development organisers should not dismiss it out of hand.

This is a helpful taxonomy, particularly for those charged with organising staff development events. What it does not capture, however, in such an abbreviated description is the mode of enquiry adopted, or the necessity of non-judgemental collaboration emphasised at the end of the previous section. For these reasons, in our own work with schools we have adopted a slightly different approach. In our work we have identified two broad categories of strategies that have a proven track record in building professional learning cultures within schools. The two contrasting approaches are:

1. **Deductive**: where the staff work collectively to expand their repertoires of professional practice by using specifications of what is known about effective instruction.

2. **Inductive**: where staff and other invited colleagues work collectively and iteratively from the existing practice in the school to develop theories of action that discipline and deepen the instructional culture of all the teachers in the school.

Both approaches should end up at the same place and the choice often depends on where the school is starting from. For example, it may be more appropriate in a school that has a very weak instructional culture to use a deductive approach initially to master basic knowledge and skill, before moving into a more iterative approach. Similarly, a school with a more healthy instructional culture may start using the inductive approach, but fairly rapidly assimilate the range of specifications of models of teaching into the work (DEECD 2011).

The best-known strategy within the 'deductive mode' is the now established approach to coaching developed by Bruce Joyce and his colleagues (Joyce & Showers 2002; Joyce, Calhoun & Hopkins 1999). This research on staff development has identified a number of key training components which, when used in combination, have much greater power than when they are used alone. The major components of training are:

‣ presentation of theory or description of skill or strategy
‣ modelling or demonstration of skills or models of teaching
‣ practice in simulated and classroom settings
‣ structured and open-ended feedback providing information about performance
‣ coaching for application—hands-on, in-classroom assistance with the transfer of skills and strategies to the classroom.

The evidence cited by Joyce and Showers (2002) is compelling. As seen in Table 7.2, if we are looking for a shift in teaching behaviour that is powerful enough to impact on student learning, that is, 'transfer of training', the inclusion of coaching in the staff development design is absolutely essential. Sadly, over the years, most staff development strategies have focused solely on developing teacher knowledge rather than skill or transfer. This explains why there has been so little impact on classroom practice and student learning.

Table 7.2 Effect sizes for training outcomes by training components
(Reproduced from Joyce & Showers 1995, p. 112)

Training components and combinations	Training outcomes		
	Knowledge	Skill	Transfer of training
Information	0.63	0.35	0.00
Theory	0.15	0.50	0.00
Demonstration	1.65	0.26	0.00
Theory, demonstration	0.66	0.86	0.00
Theory, practice	1.15		0.00
Theory, demonstration, practice		0.72	0.00
Theory, demonstration, practice, feedback	1.31	1.18	0.39
Theory, demonstration, practice, feedback, coaching	2.71	1.25	1.68

It is also helpful to distinguish between the locations in which these various forms of staff development are best located—either in the 'workshop' or in the 'workplace' (Joyce & Calhoun 2010). The workshop, which is equivalent to the best practice in the traditional professional development course, is where teachers gain *understanding*, see *demonstrations* of the teaching strategy they may wish to acquire and have the opportunity to *practise* in a non-threatening environment. If the aim is to transfer those skills back into the workplace—the classroom and school—then merely attending the workshop is insufficient. The research evidence is very clear: skill acquisition and the ability to transfer vertically to a range of situations require 'on-the-job support'. This implies changes to the workplace and the way in which staff development is organised. In particular, this means the opportunity for immediate and sustained practice, collaboration and peer coaching and studying development and implementation. The paradox is that changes to the workplace cannot be achieved without, in most cases, drastic alterations in the ways in which schools are organised. Yet the transfer of teaching skills from professional development sessions to classrooms settings will not occur without them.

The best-known current approach in the 'inductive mode' is instructional rounds; the application of the 'rounds' approach to medical training to the work in classrooms that is currently being popularised by Richard Elmore (City et al. 2009). Essentially this is training in the workplace rather than the lecture theatre and involves, in Elmore's words, 'learning the work by doing the work'. It also engages participants in practising the two essential skills of the professional—diagnosis and treatment. In educational terms, these might be phrased as 'What are the necessary educational goals for this student?' and 'How can we bring to bear the most powerful curriculum and instructional strategies to achieve them?'

Instructional rounds imply a four-step process: identifying a problem of practice, observing, debriefing and focusing on the next level of work. The approach is based around the use of networks of teachers and leaders who have agreed to schedule significant and systematic time to explore the practice of teaching and learning in a school. The process works something like this (City et al. 2009).

1. The network convenes in a school for a rounds visit hosted by a member or members of the network (principal, head teacher or teachers, regional or local authority officers). The visit starts with an introduction to the school, its history and aspirations.
2. The network divides into smaller groups that visit a rotation of at least six classrooms for approximately twenty minutes. In each classroom, network participants collect descriptive evidence related to the teaching and learning focus. The emphasis is unrelentingly on description, rather than judgement or evaluation. Given existing norms, most participants find being in the descriptive mode initially quite challenging.

3. After completing the classroom observations, the entire group assembles in a common location to work through a process of description, analysis and prediction. The group analyses the evidence for patterns and looks at how what they have seen explains (or does not explain) the observable student performance in the school. From this, they develop a series of constructs that provide a logical and analytical description of what they have observed and then develop appropriate 'theories of action' for each construct.

4. Finally, the group discusses the next level of work and makes recommendations for the school and system to make progress on student learning and teaching practice. No comments are made about the behaviours of individual teachers; the focus is on describing the practice and how it can be enhanced. The resulting theories of action and suggestions are shared with all.

The purpose of this discussion is two-fold: the first, to emphasise that the essential ingredient of educational innovation and networking is peer-to-peer collaboration among teachers; and the second, that different strategies are required for different objectives and contexts. This is all in pursuit of the goal of more precise teaching strategies that can impact positively on student learning.

Coda

As was said at the outset, this myth is a tricky one. Who can seriously argue against innovation and networking? This is not the intention here. The purpose of raising this myth is to emphasise that superficial approaches to innovation, networking and professional learning will have little positive effect on student learning. For changes in teacher behaviour to impact positively on student performance, more robust strategies of the type described in this chapter need to be employed.

We have discussed in some detail the authentic nature of innovation and the intricacies of professional learning. It may be helpful in concluding and supporting the exploding of this myth to say a little more about networks. This is because networks are the critical structures that allow authentic forms of innovation and professional learning to flourish.

First, it is important to consider in more detail both the conditions necessary to support effective networks and the role of networks in supporting innovation. All the evidence suggests that there are a number of key conditions that need to be in place if networks are to realise their potential as agents of educational innovation. These include:

▶ **consistency of values and focus.** It is important that networks have a common purpose, that the values of the network are 'owned' by those involved and that these embrace an unrelenting focus on the learning and achievement of students

▶ **clarity of structure.** Effective networks are well-organised with clear operating procedures to ensure broad-based participation is achieved within and between schools, preferably with a whole-organisation or systemic focus

▶ **knowledge creation, utilisation and transfer.** Effective networks create and disseminate knowledge to support improvement and innovation. This needs to be evidence-based, focused on classroom processes and to facilitate teacher learning

▶ **rewards related to learning.** Effective networks invest in people and their sense of belonging in the network—rewards are best related to supporting professional development and the encouragement of teacher and student learning

▶ **dispersed leadership and empowerment.** Effective networks have skilful people who collaborate and work well together—network members have effective teamwork skills that include a focus on dispersed leadership and empowerment

▶ **adequate resources.** Networks need to be adequately resourced, but it is not necessarily the quantum of resource that is important; more crucially there needs to be flexibility in the way in which it is deployed for network purposes.

It is evident that in the context of supporting innovation, one can discern the beginnings of a 'typology of networks'. At the basic level, networks facilitate the sharing of good practice; at the highest level they can act as agents of system renewal. The emerging typology of networks along this continuum looks something like this.

▶ At its most basic level, a network could be regarded as simply groups of teachers joining together for a common curriculum purpose and for the sharing of good practice.
▶ At a more ambitious level, networks could involve groups of teachers and schools joining together for the purposes of school improvement with the explicit aim of not just sharing practice, but of enhancing teaching, learning and student achievement throughout a school or group of schools.
▶ Over and above this, networks could also not just serve the purpose of knowledge transfer and school improvement, but also involve groups of stakeholders joining together for the implementation of specific policies locally and possibly nationally.
▶ A further extension of this way of working is found when groups of networks (within and outside education) link together for system improvement in terms of social justice and inclusion.
▶ Finally, there is the potential for groups of networks to work together, not just on a social justice agenda, but also to act explicitly as agents for system renewal and transformation.

This typology not only provides a way of categorising networks, but also demonstrates how they have an explicit role to play in systemic change. Although this statement is true, as is the realisation that it is the network structure that allows innovation and professional learning to prosper, it is leadership that moulds these structures and aspirations to context. It is to a consideration of educational leadership that we turn in the following chapter.

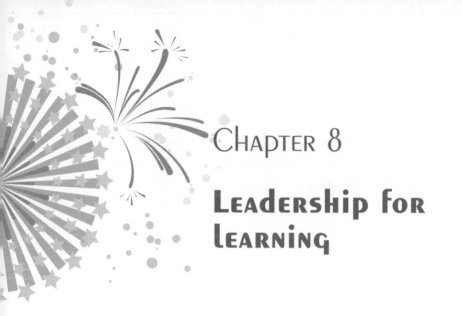

Chapter 8

Leadership for Learning

The myth of the contribution of charismatic leadership to school reform

At first glance this is not much of a myth. Most would agree that the image of the adrenaline-fuelled (and this is not a gender specific term) leader, riding a white horse across the plains on their way to committing another random act of kindness, is at best a 20th century metaphor for leadership. It is Jim Collins (2001) in his book *Good to great* who deserves the credit for originally debunking this myth. Although Collins' research focused on companies rather than schools, there are some fascinating comparisons in terms of what 'great' companies are like and how they became great. It is instructive to relate these two descriptions of great companies to those outstanding schools one is familiar with. Collins (2001, pp. 194, 195) wrote:

> *Enduring great companies don't exist merely to deliver returns to shareholders. Indeed, in a truly great company, profits and cash flow become like blood and water to a healthy body. They are absolutely essential for life, but they are not the very point of life.*

And

> *Enduring great companies preserve their core values and purpose while their business strategies and operating practices endlessly adapt to a changing world. This is the magical combination of 'preserve the core and stimulate progress'.*

The image of schooling conjured up by these quotations is one of a school and classroom culture of high expectations where students realise their potential as a consequence of the types of pedagogic and curriculum strategies described in this book. What is more germane for our purposes here is the type of leadership necessary to enable a school to become great. Collins calls this 'Level 5' leadership.

> *The term 'Level 5' refers to a five-level hierarchy of qualities. Level 1 relates to individual capability, level 2 to team skills, level 3 to managerial competence and level 4 to leadership as traditionally conceived. Level 5 leaders possess the skills of levels 1 to 4 but also have an 'extra dimension': a paradoxical blend of personal humility plus professional will. They are somewhat self-effacing individuals who deflect adulation yet who have an almost stoic resolve to do absolutely whatever it takes to make the company great, channeling their ego needs away from themselves and into the larger goal of building a great company. (*Good to Great *by Jim Collins © 2001)*

Collins elaborates:

> *It's not that Level 5 leaders have no ego or self-interest. Indeed, they are incredibly ambitious—but their ambition is first and foremost for the institution, not themselves. (2001, p. 21)*

These attributes for school leaders have recently been validated in internationally based research, such as the two-volume OECD (Pont, Nusche & Hopkins 2008; Pont, Nusche & Moorman 2008) study *Improving school leadership* and the McKinsey (Barber et al. 2010) study *Capturing the leadership premium: how the world's top school systems are building leadership for the future.*

The OECD study asks rhetorically, 'School leadership: why does it matter?' and answers thus.

▸ At the school level, leadership can improve teaching and learning by setting objectives and influencing classroom practice.
▸ At the local level, school leadership can improve equal opportunities by collaborating with other schools and local communities.
▸ At the system level, school leadership is essential for successful education reform.

The McKinsey (Barber et al. 2010, p. 8) research highlights a common set of beliefs, attitudes and personal attributes that effective leaders possess. They are:

▸ *focused on student achievement and put children ahead of personal or political interests*
▸ *resilient and persistent in goals, but adaptable to context and people*
▸ *willing to develop a deep understanding of people and context*
▸ *willing to take risks and challenge accepted beliefs and behaviours*
▸ *self-aware and able to learn*
▸ *optimistic and enthusiastic.*

Despite this confluence of thinking, a paradox still lurks here. It is that under certain conditions, particularly when a school or system is in crisis and performing badly, then prescriptive forms of top-down leadership are still necessary while the pre-conditions for effectiveness are put into place. This chapter will explore this paradox in some detail, in particular how leadership can promote student learning at the same time as building a sustainable work culture in the school. Specifically, the discussion focuses on:

▶ developing a model of leadership
▶ understanding how leadership affects learning
▶ establishing school improvement teams
▶ confronting the 'killer' theory of action.

Towards a model of leadership

In exploring the nature of Level 5 leadership and its application to education as well as the paradox noted above, it is useful to begin with some history. In our recent review of the research on school and system improvement (Hopkins, Harris et al. 2011) we noted that although 'principal as instructional leader' was one of Edmonds' (1979) 'five correlates' of school effectiveness, it has taken considerable time for the approach to become accepted and understood. Murphy (1991) for example, suggested that the thinking about leadership falls into a number of phases: the focus on trait theories of leadership; the focus on what it is that leaders actually do; developing awareness that task-related and people-centred behaviours may be interpreted quite differently; and situational approaches to leadership. All these represented a movement towards the notion of leadership as transformational, having the potential to alter the cultural context in which people work, and, importantly, the potential for school leaders to 'drive' increases in student achievements. At the dawn of the 21st century, however, it became clear that the 'transformational' approach to leadership may have been necessary, but was an insufficient condition for measurable school improvement. It lacked a specific orientation towards student learning that is the critical feature of the approach to school improvement taken in this book.

For this reason the complementary historical notion of 'instructional leadership' has become increasingly attractive. Ken Leithwood and colleagues (Leithwood, Jantzi & Mascall 1999, p. 8) have led this renaissance. They initially defined instructional leadership as an approach that emphasises 'the behaviours of teachers as they engage in activities directly affecting the growth of students'. Under commission from the Wallace Foundation, Leithwood with his colleagues (Leithwood et al. 2004) provided one of the clearest definitions of those leadership practices most closely associated with enhanced levels of student outcomes. These are:

▶ **setting direction** to enable every learner to reach their potential, and to translate this vision into whole-school curriculum, consistency and high expectations
▶ **managing teaching and learning** to ensure that there is a high degree of consistency and innovation in teaching practices to enable personalised learning for all students
▶ **developing people** to enable students to become active learners and to create schools as professional learning communities for teachers
▶ **developing the organisation** to create evidence-based schools and effective organisations, and to be involved in networks collaborating to build curriculum diversity, professional support and extended services.

A subsequent series of international studies, besides the OECD and McKinsey research already noted, have confirmed and to an extent deepened these conclusions. For example, research sponsored by the Wallace Foundation has taken our collective understanding further in terms of the link between leadership and student outcomes, with distributed leadership and professional community playing important roles (Louis et al. 2010). Robinson, Hohepa and Lloyd's (2009) international best evidence synthesis showed that leaders promoting and participating in teachers' professional development have at least twice the effect-size of any other aspect of leadership in terms of the link with student outcomes. Hallinger's (2010) publication *Leadership for learning* reviewed thirty years of empirical research on the impact of leadership on student learning and also confirms these trends. The *School leadership and pupil outcomes research project* research study described in the following section of this chapter has provided empirical detail to support these perspectives, which are summarised in the two 'strong claims' pamphlets (Day et al. 2010; Leithwood et al. 2007).

Leithwood's work has given us a much clearer idea of the behaviours and activities engaged in by those leaders who are most effective in raising the standards of learning and achievement of their students. But even though this increasing clarity is necessary, it is not sufficient. We have already noted the personal and professional challenges faced by educators when engaged in pedagogic change and appreciated that such change in repertoire cannot be achieved by exhortation, fear or charismatic approaches. We have also already noted (in Chapter Seven) some of the professional learning strategies necessary for expanding professional repertoire, but this also requires creating a work culture conducive to such changes occurring. This approach to leadership is concerned with responding to the adaptive challenge of system change (Hopkins 2007).

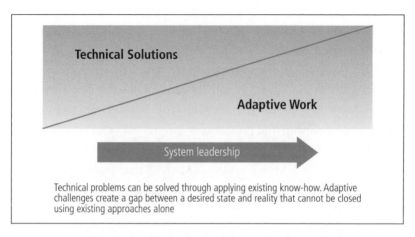

Figure 8.1 System leadership as adaptive work
(Reproduced from Hopkins 2007, p. 157)

It was Ron Heifetz (1994) who focused attention on the concept of an adaptive challenge as a problem situation for which solutions lie outside current ways of operating. This is in stark contrast to a technical problem for which the know-how already exists. This distinction has resonance for educational reform. Put simply, resolving a technical problem is a management issue; tackling adaptive challenges however, requires leadership and, as we have seen previously (Grint 2005), increasing levels of collaboration. Often we try to solve technical problems with adaptive processes or, more commonly, force technical solutions onto adaptive problems. Figure 8.1 captures this distinction, emphasising the importance of capacity building and illustrating how this issue underpins the policy conundrum of making the transition from prescription to professionalism (Hopkins 2007).

Mobilising people to meet adaptive challenges is at the heart of leadership practice. In the short term, leadership helps people meet an immediate challenge. In the medium to long term, leadership generates capacity to enable people to meet an ongoing stream of adaptive challenges. Ultimately, adaptive work requires us to reflect on the moral purpose by which we seek to thrive, and demands diagnostic enquiry into the realities we face that threaten the realisation of those purposes (Heifetz 2003).

In developing the model of leadership consistent with this book's approach, a number of themes already discussed are coming together. In particular: the focus on moral purpose and systemic reform; the importance of learning and teaching in the pursuit of student achievement; the need to embrace the challenge of personal and professional change; and the emphasis on capacity building and sustainability in inside–out working. Collectively, these lead to the definition of a more comprehensive form of leadership—system leadership (Higham et al. 2009; Hopkins 2007; Pont, Nusche & Moorman 2008).

As the system leadership movement develops, we will find a new model of leadership flowing inductively from the actions of our best educational leaders, which is described in more detail in the final chapter. In *Every school a great school* (Hopkins 2007), I made an initial attempt to capture the main elements of this emerging practice that are standing the test of time. It is seen in Figure 8.2. What is distinctive about the model is that the individual elements build on each other to present a theory of action for leadership in the new educational context.

The model exhibits an inside–out logic in which leaders, driven by a moral purpose related to the enhancement of student learning, seek to empower teachers and others to make schools a critical force for improving communities. It is premised on the argument made in this book that sustainable educational development requires educational leaders who are willing to shoulder broader leadership roles; they care about and work for the success of other schools as well as their own.

It begins in the centre with the recognition that such forms of leadership are imbued with moral purpose in the way defined earlier.

Without that, there would not be the passion to proceed or the encouragement for others to follow. Though necessary, this is not sufficient, as has already been seen—it is clear from the practice of our best system leaders that there is a characteristic set of behaviours and skills that they share. As illustrated in the next ring of the diagram these are of two types. First, system leaders engage in 'personal development', usually informally, through benchmarking themselves against their peers and developing their skill base in response to the context they find themselves working in. Secondly, all the system leaders we have studied (Higham et al. 2009) have a strategic capability; they are able to translate their vision or moral purpose into operational principles that have tangible outcomes (Hopkins 2007).

As is denoted in the third ring of the model, the moral purpose, personal qualities and strategic capacity of the system leader find focus on three domains of the school—managing the teaching and learning process, developing people and developing the organisation. As we have seen, these three aspects of system leadership have a strong empirical base. To summarise very briefly, system leaders engage deeply with the organisation of teaching, learning, curriculum and assessment in order to personalise learning for all their students, reduce within-school variation and support curriculum choice. In order to do this they develop their schools as personal and professional learning communities, with relationships built across and beyond each school to provide a range of learning experiences and professional development opportunities.

Although there is a growing number of outstanding leaders who exemplify these qualities and determinations, they are not necessarily 'system leaders'. A system leader not only needs these aspirations and capabilities but also, as seen in the outer ring of the model, strives for equity and inclusion through acting on context and culture and through giving their communities a sense of worth and empowerment.

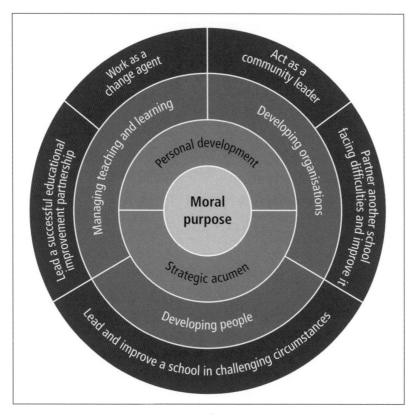

Figure 8.2 An emerging model of system leadership
(Reproduced from Hopkins 2007, p. 166)

They realise that in order to change the larger system they have to engage with it in a meaningful way (Hopkins 2007). The detail of these emerging roles is discussed in more detail in Chapter Ten.

The purpose of this section has been to chart the emergence of an approach to leadership driven by moral purpose that can be increasingly clearly defined in terms of concepts, capacities, roles and strategy. It is clear that Collins' term 'humble leadership' is the embodiment of system leadership that has a moral purpose beyond the school and the antithesis of the old charismatic or heroic models now outdated. All of this provides more evidence for exploding the myth of charismatic leadership. What is so exciting about the potential of system leadership as a movement is that the practices it employs will, as we will see, grow out of the future demands of system leaders. So, in moving system leadership to scale, we will in the rest of this chapter pay attention to the within-school system leadership role and then in Chapter Ten explore its more systemic character.

How leadership affects learning

In elaborating on the model presented in the previous section, there is a need to explore in more detail the link between leadership and learning. Such a discussion could take many books in itself. So to give a sense of the intricacies involved, this section draws on a research project I was recently involved in—the *School leadership and pupil outcomes research project*—that was led by Chris Day (Day et al. 2010, 2011). The key question addressed by the research was 'What forms of leadership can cope with the increasing list of challenges facing school leadership and still be able to continue to raise the standards of learning and achievement of students?' This was the conundrum that we attempted to resolve in our book *Successful school leadership* (Day et al. 2011). Elsewhere we have summarised our research into this question as *Ten strong claims about successful school leadership* (Day et al. 2010). As is seen below, these claims built on our previous review *Seven strong claims about successful school leadership* (Leithwood et al. 2007), but have been elaborated and deepened as a result of the more recent research.

The ten claims summarised here provide a succinct encapsulation of those values and strategies that enable such a resilient approach to leadership to prevail. In one sentence, these school leaders improve pupil outcomes through who they are—their values, virtues, dispositions, attributes and competences—as well as what they do in terms of the strategies they select and how they adapt their leadership practices to their unique context. This research lends even more support to the anti-charismatic leadership thesis.

Claim 1: Head teachers are the main source of leadership in their schools

Head teachers are perceived to be the main source of leadership by key school staff. Their educational values, reflective strategies and leadership practices shape the internal processes and pedagogies that result in improved pupil outcomes. The leadership of the head has a direct effect on teachers' expectations and standards. This includes the way they think about, plan and conduct their teaching and learning practices, their self-efficacy, commitment and sense of wellbeing and their organisational loyalty and trust—all of which indirectly influence pupil outcomes. Leaders in improving schools diagnose individual and organisational needs and place the needs of pupils first. (Day et al. 2010, p. 3)

Claim 2: There are eight key dimensions of successful leadership

These are centred on student learning, wellbeing and achievement. Successful leaders:

▶ define their values and vision to raise expectations, set direction and build trust
▶ reshape the conditions for teaching and learning
▶ restructure parts of the organisation and redesign leadership roles and responsibilities
▶ enrich the curriculum
▶ enhance teacher quality
▶ enhance the quality of teaching and learning
▶ build collaboration internally
▶ build strong relationships outside the school community. (p. 4)

Claim 3: Head teachers' values are key components in their success

The most successful school leaders are open-minded and ready to learn from others. They are flexible rather than dogmatic within a system of core values. They are persistent in their high expectations of others and they are emotionally resilient and optimistic. Such traits help explain why successful leaders facing daunting conditions are often able to push forwards against the odds. Care and trust feature highly in achievement-focused cultures that aim to improve student outcomes and introducing a whole-school approach to pupil behaviour management is considered a positive step towards improving student outcomes. (p. 7)

Claim 4: Successful heads use the same basic leadership practices, but there is no single model for achieving success

The most effective heads or principals work intuitively and from experience, tailoring their leadership strategies to their particular school context. Their ability to respond to their context and to recognise, acknowledge, understand and attend to the needs and motivations of others defines their level of success. Heads use a combination of leadership strategies according to: their judgements about the conditions for teaching and learning in the school; the confidence, experience and competence of their staff; the behaviour, aspirations and attainment levels of pupils; and the experience of the heads themselves. (p. 8)

Claim 5: Differences in context affect the nature, direction and pace of leadership actions

Schools that improved from a 'low start' experienced the most changes in pupil behaviour, attendance, motivation and engagement. Successful heads in disadvantaged contexts make greater efforts to effect improvement across a range of areas—especially pupil behaviour, motivation and engagement and school culture—because they know that improvements in only one or two areas are unlikely to be enough to secure sustained gains in pupil outcomes. (p. 9)

Claim 6: Head teachers contribute to student learning and achievement through a combination and accumulation of strategies and actions

Highly effective and improving schools tend to reduce within-school variation by building common goals and being consistent in their approach. Although most school-level variables have small effects on pupil outcomes when examined independently, the combination of their impact tends to be stronger. Pupil learning and achievement are affected by a combination of leadership strategies which, when taken together, address school culture and staff development and focus on enhancing the processes of teaching and learning. (p. 10)

Claim 7: There are three broad phases of leadership success

In the early phase, heads prioritised: improving the physical environment of the school to create more positive, supportive conditions for teaching and learning, and for teachers and pupils; setting, communicating and implementing school-wide standards for pupil behaviour; and restructuring the senior leadership team, its roles and responsibilities. There was also a focus on implementing performance management systems for all staff. This had the effect of distributing leadership more and led to the development of a set of organisational values. In the middle phase, heads prioritised the wider distribution of leadership roles and responsibilities and more regular and focused use of data to inform decision-making about pupil progress and achievement. In the later phase, heads' key strategies related to personalising and enriching the curriculum, as well as wider distribution of leadership. (p. 12)

Claim 8: Head teachers grow and secure success by layering leadership strategies and actions

Effective heads make judgements according to their context about the timing, selection, relevance, application and continuation of strategies that create the right conditions for effective teaching, learning and pupil achievement within and across broad development phases. So although some strategies did not continue, others grew in importance and formed significant foundations on which further strategies could be built. It was clear that, in later phases, a range of strategic actions were being implemented simultaneously. Some had a higher priority than others, but it was the combination of actions— along with gradual broadening and deepening of strategies—that enabled the later strategies to succeed and made it possible for the head's leadership to have such a powerful impact on pupil outcomes. (p. 15)

Claim 9: Successful heads distribute leadership progressively

There is a connection between the increased distribution of leadership roles and responsibilities and the improvement of pupil outcomes. The distribution of leadership roles and responsibilities was a developing feature in all schools and presented a pattern of progressive and selective leadership distribution over time, determined by four factors:

▶ the head's judgement of what was right for the school at different phases of its development
▶ the head's judgement of the readiness and ability of staff to lead
▶ the extent to which trust had been established
▶ the head's own training, experience and capabilities. (pp. 16–17)

Claim 10: The successful distribution of leadership depends on the establishment of trust

Trust is essential for the progressive and effective distribution of leadership. It is closely associated with a positive school ethos, improved conditions for teaching and learning, an enhanced sense of teacher classroom autonomy and sustained improvement in pupil behaviour, engagement and outcomes. The distribution of leadership over time by heads was a clear expression of the importance they placed on gaining others' trust and extending trust to them. For these heads, effective distributed leadership depended upon five key factors of trust:

▶   values and attitudes
▶   disposition to trust
▶   trustworthiness
▶   repeated acts of trust
▶   building and reinforcing individual relational and organisation trust. (p. 17)

***

So in summary, to return to the starting theme of how leadership affects learning, it would appear that it is the cognitive, emotional and practical capacities of school leaders that enables them both to achieve effectiveness in terms of enhanced student learning and to meet the increasing range of challenges in a significantly more demanding and complex context. It is also clear from the testimony of the head teachers involved in the *Successful school leadership* research that as their schools move towards excellence they wish to share these successful practices with other schools. The move towards distributed leadership is partially to support their increasing efforts to collaborate with other schools. In many ways, distributed and system leadership need to be seen as the opposite sides of the same coin. This theme of collaboration and increased systemic involvement provides the focus of the discussion presented in Chapter Ten.

Establishing school improvement teams

As we have seen from the discussion presented in Chapter Two, the concepts of development and maintenance are crucial to an understanding of how capacity is built and sustained in school improvement. One of the underpinning characteristics of sustainable school improvement is the separation of maintenance activities from development work. Structurally, the formal roles and responsibilities, the committee configurations and the decision-making processes of schools have evolved in relation to organisational hierarchies designed to support efficiency, stability and functional effectiveness. This is *maintenance.* Put another way, staff are appointed to roles which involve the management of units that tend to incorporate a standard set of functions, which often provide perpetual membership of committee structures, all of which relate predominantly to management and maintenance aspects of the school. Schools then tend to overburden this system by asking it also to take on *development* roles for which it was never designed. As an aside, the same structures create vertical communication systems, but virtually prevent lateral communication or lateral learning. Sadly, different organisational units within a school rarely exchange practices or learn from one another; in some schools that we know, they rarely even talk to one another! As was seen in Figure 2.1 in Chapter Two, the establishing of a school improvement team provides the organisational framework for resolving the tensions in schools caused by the conflicting demands of maintenance and development.

Typically, the school improvement team is cross-hierarchical and could be as small as three to six in comparatively small schools, to between six and ten in large schools. Though one of the team is likely to be the head or principal, it is important to establish groups that are genuinely representative of the range of perspectives and ideas available in the school—it should, ideally, then, be cross-hierarchical, cross-institutional, have a mix of ages, experience, gender, length of time at the school and so on. School improvement team members should also not come together in any already existing group within the school, such as the senior management team or a heads of department group, so that the problem of 'pooled rationalisations' is minimised. The school improvement group is responsible for managing school improvement efforts on a day-to-day basis within the school. They are supported through a core training program, through networking with school improvement teams from other schools and by external consultancy support and facilitation.

The school improvement group is essentially a 'temporary membership system' focused specifically upon enquiry and development. This temporary membership system brings together teachers (and support staff) from a variety of departments and year groups within the school, with a range of ages or experience and from a cross-section of roles to work together in a status-free, collaborative learning context. One teacher has described it as 'the educational equivalent of a research and development group', and the traditional school as 'analogous to a company in which everyone works on the production line, without any research and development function'. The result is stagnation, and that is how many schools have been in the past. The establishment of a school improvement team creates the research and development capacity, while also retaining the existing structures required for organisational stability and efficiency. It also unlocks staff potential often stifled within formal structures and opens up new collaborations.

It goes without saying that all levels of staff are involved, including newly qualified teachers, support staff and, in an increasing number of schools, students. Each partnership is entirely free of status positions within the more formal organisational structure of the school and offers leadership opportunities to a variety of individuals. Some partnerships might be involved with significant whole-school issues, while others may be engaged in focused classroom research activity, both related initially to the 'theories of action'. The scale of the intended impact is less significant than the quality of the knowledge deriving from the enquiry. A piece of classroom research, for example, can have equally powerful whole-school impact if the knowledge is sufficiently significant and widely owned. Finally, in the same way that the school improvement team is mutually supportive of one another, the school community (the wider staff and the institutional support of senior management and governing body) makes a number of tacit commitments, too.

▶ To support each partnership in whatever way possible—time, resources, visits to centres of good practice, the adoption of recommendations, etc.
▶ To agree to remain informed about the progress of each area of enquiry in order to maintain collective ownership of the directions being travelled.
▶ To support the implementation of new practices, new structures or new ways of working.
▶ To be open to the research process by contributing ideas, responding to research instruments, opening up classrooms for observation or offering professional support in whatever way required.
▶ To engage in workshop activity within full staff meetings, staff days or other school meetings in order to contribute to the ongoing knowledge creation and learning process.

Our experience of working with school improvement teams over the years suggests that they need time to become fully operational. The notion of development structures is quite exotic to many school leaders and potential team members and time and experience is needed to fully understand the implications of the role and become confident in practising the new behaviours. My colleague Mel West puts it like this (West 2000, pp. 55):

> It also seems ... that the stages of development through which cadre groups move can be associated not only with 'typical' behaviours for each stage, but also with the way they view the 'task' ... and the way they conceive solutions.

The three phases of this cycle of development are summarised in Table 8.1.

Table 8.1 Three-phase cycle of development (Adapted from West 2000)

Phase 1: uncertainty about focus	Phase 2: clearer about focus	Phase 3: change or renewal of the cadre group
▶ Cadre feeling its way (What is a cadre?) ▶ What is school improvement? ▶ What is the role of the cadre group? ▶ How can the cadre work best together as a group? ▶ Initial reliance on established ways of working	▶ Using existing structures in new ways, e.g. department meetings with single item research agendas ▶ New ways of working ▶ Greater openness within the cadre group, e.g. voice of main scale teacher	▶ Research and development establishing its own rhythm—school development planning becomes more organic ▶ New structures and roles emerge, e.g. head of department as facilitator of research

▶

Table 8.1 (continued)

Phase 1: uncertainty about focus	Phase 2: clearer about focus	Phase 3: change or renewal of the cadre group
▶ Initial reliance on existing structures ▶ Initial reliance on key personnel or leaders within the cadre ▶ Start to collect data and share it ▶ Uncertainty about the theory ▶ Where is it all going? It's hard to make things happen	▶ Better at making meaning from data ▶ Beginning to shift from staff development mode to school improvement mode ▶ The theory makes sense ▶ Seeing the connections; learning how to implement	▶ Establishment of research culture within the school with evidence-based risk taking ▶ Involvement of students as researchers—from data-source to partners in dialogue ▶ Collection of data, making meaning and supporting research outcomes ▶ The school generates its own theory ▶ The implementation becomes growth

This summary of how a school improvement team evolves is provisional, but it does give a clear indication of how a structure for distributed leadership that relates to instructional, adaptive and system leadership is established. It also illustrates how the team evolves over time, gradually expanding its leadership capacity and increasing its understanding about organisational learning, the learning of the school improvement team members and other teachers and the learning of students.

Confronting the 'killer' theory of action

The model of leadership proposed in this chapter is grounded in the concepts of both 'instructional' and 'adaptive' leadership. These are forms of leadership that are antithetical to the myth of charismatic leadership insofar as they focus on moral purpose, the quality of teaching and learning and through this ensure that students achieve their academic potential, as well as acquiring the skills and dispositions necessary for becoming successful contributing citizens of our global world. In light of this, the discussion that follows focuses upon those aspects of leadership that are necessary for ensuring a reliable linkage between leadership, student achievement and sustainability.

The ongoing enquiry into classroom, school and system improvement employing the 'instructional rounds' process has, as already described in Chapter Five, provided a powerful means of enhancing the pedagogic leadership capacity of school leaders. An accidental but welcome outcome of that endeavour has been the identification of the 'Ten Theories of Action' that, when taken together, not only enhance the learning outcomes of students, but also their learning capability—in a word their 'curiosity' (NMR 2011). As we saw in Chapter Five, these ten theories of action fall into two groups: those that pertain to the whole school level, that enable teachers to do their work; and those that relate to the teacher level, that enable them to create more effective and enquiring learning environments for their students. The four whole-school theories of action as previously stated are:

1. When schools and teachers *set high expectations and develop authentic relationships* then students' confidence and commitment to education increases and the school's ethos and culture deepens.
2. When teacher-directed instruction becomes more *enquiry focused* then the level of student achievement and curiosity increases.
3. By consistently adopting *protocols for teaching*, student behaviour, engagement and learning is enhanced.
4. By consistently adopting *protocols for learning*, student capacity to learn, skill level and confidence is enhanced.

As the enquiry has developed (Caerphilly County Borough Council 2012; NMR 2011) it has become clear that the second of the school-level theories of action outlined above is not only the most powerful, but also the most difficult to implement. In a slightly expanded form it is:

When there is a whole-school commitment to infusing teacher-directed instruction with a spirit of enquiry, then the level of student engagement and achievement increases. This is the foundation stone for not only high quality teaching, but also the development of curiosity.

Although most of the schools we had been working with had identified a set of theories of action related to teacher behaviours to focus on and had introduced professional learning opportunities for teachers to develop them, this did not mean that the whole-school 'spirit of enquiry' also became realised. Achieving this is a major leadership challenge. In trying to resolve this conundrum, five interlinking and sequential conditions were identified that seem to be in place when schools realise this desiderata. Although most schools were implementing some of the theories of action (condition 2) through professional learning approaches (condition 3), in many cases this only resulted in superficial and variable impact. It was only when there was narrative (condition 1) and consistency (condition 4) that the change in culture (condition 5) embracing the spirit of enquiry was reliably achieved. The sequence from 1 to 5 provides a script that leaders can follow.

When working at scale we found it necessary to develop frameworks that not only assist school leaders through this process, but also allow them to more precisely monitor the impact of implementation. In the brief description of the five conditions outlined here, there is also reference to the monitoring frameworks that can be used to realise the spirit of enquiry, so ensuring that the 'killer' theory of action is effectively addressed and successfully implemented and sustained at whole-school level.

1. The story of the curiosity journey is introduced

A clear reform narrative for student learning is developed and consistently applied over time, with an urgency that translates the vision of curiosity into clear principles for action. This narrative is the task of leadership to develop. It is based on detailed and strategic planning, is couched in inclusive and understandable language and links moral purpose to action in practical and concrete ways. Above all, it highlights the connection between curiosity, enquiry, problem solving and collaboration as the necessary ingredients of a teaching and learning culture that results not just in high standards, but also in student empowerment.

Monitoring framework

The school's position on the performance cycle from 'awful to adequate', 'adequate to good' and 'good to great', as indicated in Table 8.2, is used as a basis for developing the narrative.

Table 8.2 Contrasting school improvement journey and selected improvement dimensions

School journeys ➜ Improvement dimension ⬇	Awful to adequate	Adequate to good	Good to great
Environment	Orderly	Learning	Self-directed
Teaching practice	Consistency	Sharing best practice	Models of learning; tools for teaching
Curriculum	Literacy and numeracy basics	Literacy and numeracy across curriculum	Cross-curricular enquiry projects

▶

Table 8.2 (continued)

School journeys ➡ Improvement dimension ⬇	Awful to adequate	Adequate to good	Good to great
Assessment	Teacher/school ownership of student progress	Assessment of learning	Students set own targets and monitor progress
Data	Establish systems for data use	Monitor student progress through data	Formative and student use of data
Leadership	Developing leadership capacity	Distributed leadership	System leadership

2. Key pedagogic strategies are selected

High leverage theories of action related to student learning are selected and implemented strategically and operationally. High leverage relates to the ability of the theory of action to not only have virtually immediate impact on the teaching and learning practices of the school, but also to lay the foundation for future action. Over time this will also influence the ways in which the narrative of the curriculum within the school evolves, from simply covering content to a series of sequential and integrated problem-solving activities.

Monitoring framework

The three-year planning framework illustrated in Figure 8.3, and adapted from Figure 3.7 in Chapter Three, provides a means of building the narrative and also ensuring that priorities are selected that will not only produce short-term gains, but also lay the foundation for the next phase of the work.

3. Professional learning is placed at the heart of the process

In schools where staff development implies going on a course, and classroom observation is both hierarchical and evaluative, putting professional learning at the heart of the process marks a distinctive and necessary break with tradition. It is only forms of professional learning that emphasise non-judgemental peer observation disciplined by clear protocols that develop professional practices that have a predictable impact of student achievement. Replacing normative approaches to performance management is also a characteristic of high achieving schools and the hallmark of inside–out working.

Monitoring framework

The Joyce and Showers coaching model (2002) overviewed in Table 8.3, is used to ensure that the appropriate phases and sequencing of professional learning activities are in place.

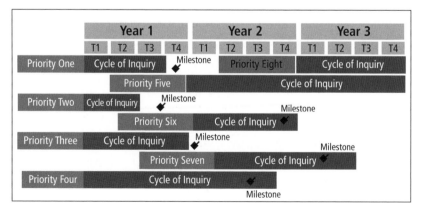

Figure 8.3 A school improvement planning framework

Table 8.3 Joyce and Showers' training components

Training components	
Theory	Explain and justify the new approach
Demonstration	Show/model how it can be done in practice
Practice	Teachers practise in non-threatening situations
Feedback	Teachers receive feedback from their triad (professional learning team)
Coaching	Supports teachers to improve their practice

4. Consistency across the whole school is seen as paramount

Leadership works self-consciously to ensure that over time the vision of curiosity and spirit of enquiry is pervasive, more precise, carefully monitored and supported by robust and highly reliable school structures. The 'loose-coupling' (to use Karl Weick's term) so characteristic of underperforming and coasting schools is incrementally tightened (Weick 1985). Although this is essential in reducing within-school variation, a word of caution needs to be added here. While top-down approaches are useful in schools that are dysfunctional and underperforming, autocratic or charismatic forms of leadership need to be used judiciously with schools on the inside–out journey.

Monitoring framework

The Hall and Hord (1987) 'Levels of use' framework is used to identify the levels of implementation required to impact directly on student learning.

Table 8.4 The levels of use indicators

Levels of use	Associated behaviours
0 Non-use	No interest shown in the innovation; no action taken
1 Orientation	Begins to gather information about the innovation
2 Preparation	Begins to plan ways to implement the innovation
3 Mechanical	Concerned about mechanics of implementation
4a Routine	Comfortable with innovation and implements it as taught
4b Refinement	Begins to explore ways for continuous improvement
5 Integration	Integrates innovation with other initiatives; does not view it as an add-on; collaborates with others
6 Renewal	Explores new and different ways to implement innovation

5. Cultures are changed and developed

A culture of disciplined action and a professional ethos that values curiosity and enquiry is embedded and deepened over time as a consequence of the impact of the work structures implied by the previous four conditions. As Andy Hargreaves (1994, p. 256) once wrote:

It is not possible to establish productive school cultures without prior changes being effected in school structures that increase opportunities for meaningful working relationships and collegial support among teachers. The importance of restructuring may be less in terms of its direct impact on curriculum, assessment, ability grouping and the like ... than in terms of how it creates improved opportunities for teachers to work together on a continuing basis.

Monitoring framework

An adapted version of David Hargreaves' and his colleagues' culture game (Hargreaves 1999) is used to monitor the development and cohesiveness of the school's culture over time.

So it is the interaction of the first four conditions that results in the fifth—a culture of teaching and learning in the school that prizes the spirit of enquiry, which results in high standards and deeper levels of learning. It should be increasingly clear that the mechanistic and instrumental approaches to school improvement associated with charismatic leadership and management are totally unable to deliver the high standards, the adaptive learning and the sustainability that are the hallmarks of outstanding schools and systems. It is the skill of

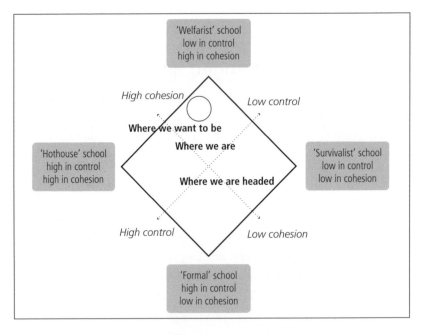

Figure 8.4 The 'culture game'
(Adapted from Hargreaves 1999, p. 51)

leadership—that develops and nurtures the narrative, embraces and sequences the theory of actions, creates the professional learning opportunities and allows the tightening of the loose-coupling—that ultimately ensures consistency. It is the interaction of these conditions that together produce the cultural change that sustains the enquiry and keeps on giving.

Coda

The purpose of this chapter has been to explode the myth of charismatic leadership and to propose an alternative approach. This has been done through proposing a model for system leadership, exploring more deeply the link between leadership and learning and proposing the school improvement team as a means of distributing leadership as well as building capacity. A set of strategies that leadership can employ to establish and sustain the enquiry-oriented school was then described. It has also been acknowledged that in certain circumstances, in particular at low performing schools, some form of top-down leadership is needed for a limited period.

In reflecting on this discussion, it is clear that the form of leadership proposed in this chapter is qualitatively different from charismatic and other approaches insofar as it is driven by a moral purpose. Although we have already discussed the concept of moral purpose in Chapter One let us conclude by focusing on how it relates more specifically to leadership.

In October 2006 I convened a group of 100 principals from 14 vastly different countries (the G100) at the National Academy of Education Administration (NAEA) in Beijing, China to discuss the transformation of and innovation in the world's education systems. During the final session of the workshop the whole group collaborated in preparing a communiqué about their conclusions (Hopkins 2008, pp. 130–131). The final paragraphs read thus:

> *[We need to] ensure that moral purpose is at the fore of all educational debates with our parents, our students, our teachers, our partners, our policy makers and our wider community ... We define moral purpose as a compelling drive to do right for and by students, serving them through professional behaviours that raise the bar of achievement and narrow the gap between the advantaged and the disadvantaged and through doing so demonstrate an intent to learn with and from each other as we live together in this world.*

That such a diverse—in terms of context, yet homogenous, in terms of values—group of head teachers could unanimously say that speaks volumes about the moral purpose that drives our outstanding heads, both nationally and globally. Moral purpose for these heads is not high-blown idealism; it is simply the commitment to provide a high quality education for all students regardless of background; to ensure that the conditions are in place to enable every student to reach their potential. This moral purpose is usually reflected in a small number of tangible, but ambitious objectives for student learning and achievement that are being vigorously pursued. Through setting such a goal and establishing the processes to achieve it, they are confident that they will secure a step-change in the quality of education for their students. If these are the goals, then the means of achieving them are the values, behaviours and strategies described on the preceding pages.

Finally, it is important to remember that ultimately the challenge of leadership, particularly within a systemic context, has great moral depth to it. It addresses directly the learning needs of students, the professional growth of teachers and enhances the role of the school as an agent of social change. As we have seen, moral purpose in education is best defined as a resolute refusal to accept context as a determinant of academic and social success. Acting on context and not accepting poverty and social background as necessary determinants of success in schooling is at the heart of the systemic approach to school transformation. This is the message the heads we have been describing in these pages have been at pains to tell us.

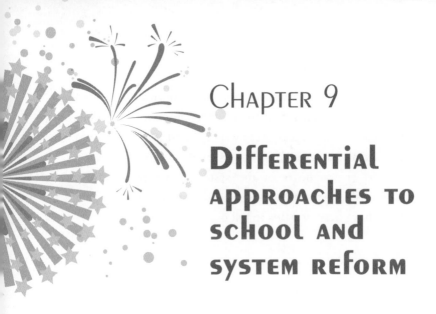

Chapter 9

Differential approaches to school and system reform

The myth that 'one size fits all' in implementing school reform

Although most would agree that this myth is self-evidently true, ironically it is the one with the most power to derail even the best-intentioned school improvement effort. Because of the top-down and instrumentalist approach so dominant in most school reform, as a global community we have succumbed by-and-large to a single solution approach—this reading scheme, this theory of learning or the latest textbook. This is another version of the faddism noted in Chapter Seven. By way of contrast, inside–out school improvement works from careful diagnosis followed by customisation of strategy to context. Without a degree of professional precision and reflexivity to context, it is understandable why pre-packaged solutions, however good and well intentioned, end up having a limited effect on student learning.

In our recent review (Hopkins, Harris et al. 2011) we noted enthusiastically that the field of school and system reform is beginning to recognise and take this issue seriously. Two examples make the point. In his paper 'Choosing the wrong drivers for whole system reform' Michael Fullan (2011) describes how certain popular policy options are implemented, but without any serious consideration of context. We will return to his analysis later in this chapter, but the following quotes give a flavour of the argument (Fullan 2011).

> A 'wrong driver' is a deliberate policy force that has little chance of achieving the desired result, while a 'right driver' is one that ends up achieving better measurable results for students. (p. 3)

> The glue that binds the effective drivers together is the underlying attitude, philosophy, and theory of action. The mindset that works for whole system reform is the one that inevitably generates individual and collective motivation and corresponding skills to transform the system. (p. 5)

Similarly, but from the other end of the argument, Pasi Sahlberg (2011) in his bestselling book *Finnish lessons* explains the success of the Finnish educational system, not in terms of the adoption of a range of external strategies and policies, but more in terms of carefully reflective, customised and culturally relevant approaches. Listen to Pasi speak and he talks about the Finnish paradox that 'less is more' with the following implications: teach less, learn more; test less, learn more; and ensure more equity through growing diversity. This is not a universal panacea and it certainly does not apply to all systems, but is an intelligent response to the cultural context of Finland. The Finns themselves sensibly prefer to combine knowledge of what works, together with a view as to how the Finnish system itself will continue to evolve.

    All of this points to the importance of taking seriously the concept of 'differential approaches' to school and system reform. This idea was first introduced in our paper 'Understanding the school's capacity for development: growth states and strategies' (Hopkins, Harris & Jackson 1997) and further elaborated in the two other books that form part of this trilogy, *School improvement for real* (Hopkins 2001) and *Every school a great school* (Hopkins 2007). For this reason the repetition of these ideas will be brief and the words of others will be used to expand the original concept, especially as they apply to system reform. For example, the recent authoritative McKinsey report *How the world's most improved school systems keep getting better* (Mourshed et al. 2010) emphasises the importance of contextually and culturally relevant improvement strategies. Although this work will be discussed in more detail later in this chapter, it is worth heeding their advice here:

> *Each particular stage of the school system improvement journey is associated with a unique set of interventions. Our research suggests all improving systems implement similar sets of interventions to move from one particular performance level to the next, irrespective of culture, geography, politics, or history … This suggests that systems would do well to learn from those at a similar stage of the journey, rather than from those that are at significantly different levels of performance. It also shows that systems cannot continue to improve by simply doing more of what brought them past success. (p. 3)*

In exploding the myth that 'one size fits all' in implementing school reform, this chapter explores the idea of differential approaches to reform at both school and system levels. The argument presented in the chapter is quite complex, so in an attempt to simplify matters, the first two sections deal specifically with school reform and the third and fourth tackle issues to do with the system. The discussion presented in the following pages aims to achieve this by:

- describing a default model of school improvement
- elaborating on the three phases of school improvement for inside–out working
- introducing the four phases of system reform as defined by the McKinsey research
- reflecting on the cross-cutting themes and cautions essential for successful system reform.

A default model of school improvement

The framework for school improvement introduced in Chapter One and developed in Chapter Two has provided the foundation for the improvement strategy based on inside–out working described in this book. This approach eschews both top-down and 'à la carte' approaches in favour of a whole-school improvement strategy designed to address the learning needs of all students in a particular school. Consistency and high expectations are the lubricants for such integrated whole-school strategies. Some thought also needs to be given to how the school organises itself to become what is commonly being called 'a professional learning community' (Bolam et al. 2005; Stoll 2007; Stoll & Louis 2007). This, as we have seen, involves teachers not just planning together, but also observing each other and gathering formative data on the impact of various strategies on student learning. School improvement from the inside–out occurs where individual program elements combine to create a comprehensive strategy that is both systemic and purposeful. It is necessary here to set out the basic generic approach that is amenable to adaptation to context, before describing the differential approaches to school improvement.

The school improvement strategy described below was developed as part of the *Improving the quality of education for all* (Hopkins 2002) approach outlined in Chapter Two. The model not only focuses on improving student behaviour, learning and attainment, but also pays attention to teacher and school development. Although the approach was originally developed some twenty years ago, it has been refined over time and adapted to changing circumstances. The reason it has so much applicability to inside–out working is that it is based on a belief that to advance achievement for all students it is necessary to address not only the learning of individual teachers, but also the organisational capacity of the school. In other words, without an emphasis on capacity, a school will be unable to sustain continuous improvement efforts that result in student attainment. As is seen in Figure 9.1, the approach has two major components—the 'capacity building dimension' and the 'strategic dimension'.

The capacity building dimension relates to the conditions at both school and classroom levels. Through sustained work on the conditions for development, or, as earlier, management arrangements, the school enhances its capacity for managing change. The strategic dimension reflects the ability of the school to plan sensibly for improvement

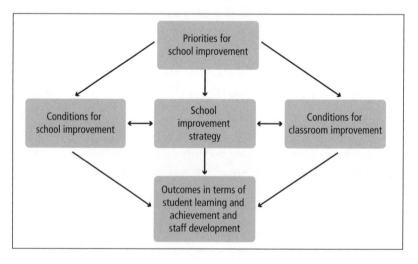

Figure 9.1 A strategic school improvement framework

efforts. Most schools are by now familiar with the need to establish a clear and practical focus for their improvement efforts. In this sense, the choice about priorities for development represents the school's interpretation of the current reform agenda. The final element in the framework is school culture. A key assumption is that school improvement strategies will lead to cultural change in schools through modifications to their internal conditions. It is this cultural change that sustains progressive deepening of teaching and learning strategies, which leads to enhanced outcomes for students.

It is in these ways that the most successful schools pursue their improvement efforts. While focusing on the learning needs of students in the context of systemic and environmental demands, they also recognise that school structures must reflect both these demands, as well as offering a suitable vehicle for the future development of the school. In this sense the structure of the school provides the skeleton that supports cultural growth, rather than the framework that constrains it. This three-stage school improvement process has at its core an unrelenting focus on learning and attainment. Given this central focus, the school improvement strategy encompasses classroom practice, particularly the expansion of teachers' pedagogic repertoire, and the building of capacity at the school level, especially the redesign of staff development. While this is not a 'quick fix' approach, many of the activities involved will bring short- as well as medium-term gains. The three stages are: establishing the process; going whole-school; and sustaining momentum.

Stage one: Establishing the process

This stage involves:

▶ commitment to the school improvement approach
▶ selection of a school improvement team
▶ enquiring into the strengths and weaknesses of the school

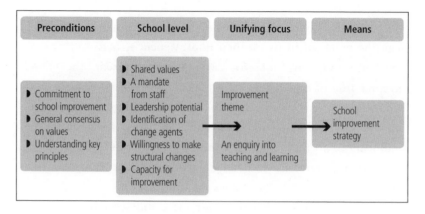

Figure 9.2 Preparing for school improvement
(Reproduced from Hopkins 2007, p. 127)

 designing the whole-school program
 seeding the whole-school approach.

This flow of activity is illustrated in Figure 9.2.

Stage two: Going whole-school

This cycle of activity usually lasts between two terms and up to a year. The activities in this phase are:

 initial whole-school training day(s)
 establishing the curriculum and teaching focus
 establishing learning teams
 initial cycle of enquiry
 sharing initial success and impact on student learning from the 'curriculum tour'.

The flow of activity during this phase of the process is illustrated in Figure 9.3.

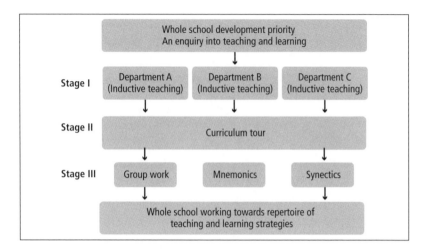

Figure 9.3 Going whole-school (Reproduced from Hopkins 2007, p. 128)

Stage three: Sustaining momentum

It is in this phase that the capacity for change at school and classroom level becomes more secure. Learning teams become an established way of working and there is an expansion of the range of teaching strategies used throughout the curriculum. This activity includes:

▶ establishing further cycles of enquiry
▶ building teacher learning into the process
▶ sharpening the focus on student learning
▶ finding ways of sharing success and building networks
▶ reflecting on the culture of the school and department.

When these ways of working are embedded, then not only will student attainment have risen, but also the school will have established itself as an effective learning organisation.

Figure 9.4 illustrates the range of activities that contribute to a capacity for learning within a school and how a number of the

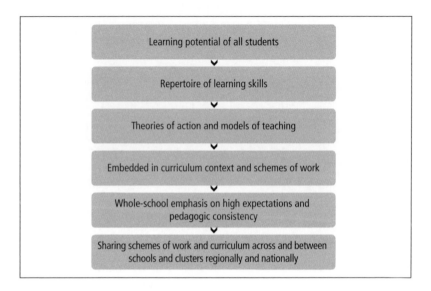

Figure 9.4 The logic of school improvement
(Reproduced from Hopkins 2007, p. 160)

elements of school improvement come together in practice. It begins from two assumptions. The first is that all students have a potential for learning that is not fully exploited. The second is that students' learning capability refers to their ability to access that potential through increasing their range of learning skills (Hopkins 2007).

This potential is best realised and learning capability enhanced through the range of theories of action and teaching and learning models that teachers use with their students. The teaching and learning strategies are not 'free floating', but embedded in the schemes of work and curriculum content that teachers use to structure the learning in their lessons. These schemes of work also have the potential to be shared between schools and be available for wider dissemination.

Finally, this way of working assumes a whole-school dimension through the establishment of a staff development infrastructure, an emphasis on high expectations and the careful attention to the consistency of teaching and the discussion of pedagogy that pervades the cultures of these schools. Although this is a generic framework it still contributes to exploding the myth in two ways. First, the myth survives because many assume that such a generic framework is applicable to all contexts; it is necessary, but not sufficient because second, the framework needs adapting to the particular phase of the performance cycle that the school is in. This is the focus of the following section.

The three phases of school improvement

There is now significant evidence to support and illuminate such approaches to differential school improvement. In the *Improving schools* study (Gray et al. 1999) we explored how schools became effective over time and identified three different 'routes to improvement'.

1. **Tactics**—A tactical response to improvement included: monitoring performance, targeting students, introducing extra classes for certain groups of students, changing examination boards, etc. Such a combination of tactics was powerful enough to raise the performance of low achieving schools towards average levels of performance, but no further. The data suggested a plateau effect after at best a couple of years.

2. **Strategies**—Schools who acted strategically employed tactical responses, but with two major differences. The first was that they were all engaged in coordinated and purposeful responses to the challenge of school improvement. Second, the focus of their work was explicitly at the classroom or learning level to ensure consistency of practice across the school. What differentiated these schools was that they were clearly interested in the dynamics of student learning and classroom practice.

3. **Capacities**—These schools collectively understood the causes of positive change and the areas of resistance in the school. They

knew when change was happening, understood the reasons why and were able to find ways to sustain positive change into the medium and long term. Above all, they developed a willingness to go beyond the incremental approach to restructuring and genuinely saw school improvement as a way of life.

The clear implication of this research is that there is a developmental sequence in school improvement narratives that needs certain building blocks to be in place before further progress can be made. As we have already seen in Chapter Eight this suggestion finds support in more recent research that identifies a clear iterative process in most successful school improvement efforts. This idea was expressed in Figure 8.4. There were two dimensions to the matrix outlined in that diagram—the phase of the school improvement journey and the improvement dimension. In terms of this analysis, three phases of the school improvement journey were identified—'awful to adequate', 'adequate to good' and 'good to great'. The implication is that different strategies and combinations of strategies are necessary at different phases of the process. So a clear and accurate diagnosis of where the school is at on the performance cycle is necessary in defining appropriate strategies for change. The point here is four-fold.

▶ First is that all the components need to be worked on at the same time.
▶ Second, together they combine to create a distinctive school–work culture and address both a substantive focus on teaching and learning as well as capacity building.
▶ Third, as progress is being made, the move from one phase to another reflects a deepening of work on each dimension.
▶ Fourth, three phases of improvement are being described here, but there could be an argument for extending this to a fourth phase in order to give greater opportunity for differentiation.

Ongoing work with schools has led to a series of guidelines for action at each phase of the school improvement journey.

Phase one: Awful to adequate

By definition, schools in this phase cannot improve themselves. They are 'stuck' or some would say 'failing' schools that need a high level of external support. Within these schools a number of early interventions and changes need to be made which have a direct focus upon basic organisational issues. These would include (Hopkins et al. 1997):

▶ **change at leadership level.** It is too sweeping to say that the heads or principals of failing schools do not have the capacity to be effective school leaders. It is, though, certain that they do not have the capacity to resurrect *that* school, and therefore are potentially a part of the problem. New leadership opportunities will need to be created for different staff, using new models, to achieve new goals

▶ **provision of early, intensive outside support.** Schools in a failing situation are likely to be isolated and in a state of cultural stasis. They are unlikely to have the potential for constructive self-analysis or evaluation, and will need support from outside to provide knowledge about school improvement strategies and models of ways of working

▶ **surveying staff and student opinion; gathering and disaggregating data on student achievement.** The collection of data will help find out why the school is unsuccessful, and where to direct efforts for greatest improvement. Data need to be gathered at whole-school and classroom level, as well as from students. This potentially gives the school community ownership of the improvement agenda

▶ **a short-term focus on easy change targets, e.g. the environment, attendance, uniform.** Changes to the school environment, attendance and uniform will be short-term changes, but can result in tangible gains. Following a period of low morale, such visible

changes will demonstrate that things are to be different in the
school. These changes should reflect the core values that the new
leadership is articulating

▶ **a focus on managing learning behaviour, not on behaviour
management.** This means creating the conditions where learners
can learn most effectively. Strategies for managing learning
behaviour would inevitably include a focus upon praise and
positive reinforcement, rather than punishment and discipline,
throughout the school

▶ **intensive work on re-skilling staff in a specific repertoire of
teaching and learning styles.** In the first instance, the focus for
staff development could be quite simple, for example, seating
arrangements, classroom organisation, the phasing of lessons or
active use of resources. Staff could explore these skills in teams in
order to create new partnerships that may have been detrimental
to school development in the past.

Phase two: Adequate to good

Schools in this phase need to refine their developmental priorities and
focus upon specific teaching and learning issues and build capacity
within the school to support this work. Developmental strategies for
this type of school include:

▶ **changing leadership strategies.** This change incorporates both
leadership styles and range. Restructuring will be necessary in
order to diversify leadership opportunities and unlock static
structures and systems. This enables the process of management
to become more dynamic and to be geared towards increasing the
capacity for change

▶ **lengthening the lesson unit.** Some curriculum restructuring occurs
to support the re-skilling of teachers. Time is given to focus on a
wider repertoire of teaching and learning styles and on the

development of learning behaviours. The longer the time unit, the more time staff will have to plan together and practise different teaching approaches

▶ **targeting particular students at certain thresholds across the ability range.** If achievement is to matter, then underachievement at all levels should be targeted. Data about performance will provide opportunities to generate dialogue with staff and with students—in groups and individually, by gender and by ability

▶ **talking to pupils about their aspirations; giving their achievement meaning.** Schools are good at internally assessing pupil effort and achievement, but less skilled at assessing potential and it is in this gap that the potential for improvement lies. So formal mechanisms of rewarding all types of pupil achievement are important and should be built in to any school restructuring program

▶ **harnessing the energy and optimism of new staff.** Morale will inevitably be low, but new members of staff who have accepted jobs at the school within the last year or two will have done so with optimism and hope for what they might achieve. These staff can be used to re-energise others, and can become a catalyst for change

▶ **generating an ongoing dialogue about values.** The values and beliefs, of both the profession and the school, need to be articulated and re-affirmed. All staff members need to be clear about the value dimension in their everyday work. All professional decisions will have their roots in the values and beliefs of the school community—and they need to be shared and debated.

Phase three: Good to great

It is imperative that those schools that are effective remain so. Consequently, in this third phase there is a need for specific strategies that ensure the school remains a 'moving' school that continues to enhance pupil performance. These strategies include:

▶ **articulating values, developing narrative and disseminating eloquence.** 'In effective schools, school leaders disseminate eloquence' (Weick 1985). It is a school leader's role to articulate the school's values and to reinforce them at every opportunity. These values need to be embedded and shared by staff, parents and pupils

▶ **raising expectations and defining achievement; creating an achievement orientation.** Schools need to be explicit, eloquent and prolific in their definition of achievement. Such a process will ignite the enthusiasm of staff and generate motivation among students. It is important to give pupils and the wider community ownership of the school's achievements, involving them in regular celebrations of the school's success

▶ **involving and empowering students in the focus on learning; developing a student charter.** It is important that students feel involved and empowered in the process of learning. By providing their constructive feedback and views about how their learning can be improved in the individual classroom, within the department and within the school, students are contributing to the improvement process

▶ **using networking and system leadership to develop leadership skills, team-building and teaching and learning.** A learning school will seek out best practice elsewhere, share their own practices and initiate networks. The development of system leadership can offer alternative curricular practices and new ways of teaching and learning. Staff become skilled in these new processes by working alongside others in and beyond the school

▶ **generating a common language around learning and achievement.** Developing common understandings about learning and achievement is important. Members of staff who have a shared language concerning learning and achievement, say, through the use of the theories of action, are more likely to work together and to be committed to understanding and improving the processes of teaching and learning

▶ **giving teachers space to experiment, share and celebrate successes.** Effective schools encourage experimentation and risk-taking with the knowledge that real learning lies in understanding the failures rather than the successes. All schools, at whatever stage in their development, should also take joy in every demonstration of success and aim to orchestrate optimism and celebration of achievement at all levels.

There are two relatively new features to the analysis so far. The first is the emphasis on narrative and its impact on both strategy and culture. It is the nature of narrative that makes it integrative and cumulative, presenting a series of complex and interacting initiatives within a unifying story around the image of a journey. This is 'strategic' insofar as it links a wide variety of initiatives and projects with a forward-looking perspective and 'cultural' insofar as it speaks to both the individual and the collective contribution. The second feature is the emphasis on 'systems' and the transferability and sustainability of best practice. System reform depends, not just on correlating growth state and improvement strategy, but critically on excellent practice being developed, shared, demonstrated and adopted across and between systems as well as schools. This is the proposition discussed in the following section.

The four phases of system reform

We now turn the spotlight from differential strategies for school reform to those that have systemic impact. Here the knowledge base is less certain (as was noted in Chapter One), as it is a topic that has only recently received serious consideration. It was the publication of the PISA results since 2001 that has provided an impetus for such work and has demonstrated that whole systems can accelerate (as well as regress) their performance over relatively short periods of time. In terms of moral purpose, systemic reform is crucial given the commitment to the progress of all students irrespective of their background. Following the early administrations of PISA, Andreas Schleicher (2009), who runs the PISA program for the OECD, began to draw clear conclusions about the characteristics of those systems whose students achieved well above the OECD average, as well as reducing the range of performance of the total population. On the basis of this evidence Schleicher claimed that both excellence and equity are achievable. The factors that he identified were:

▸ systematic and equitable funding
▸ universal standards—mirrored in the views of students, parents and school principals
▸ school autonomy
▸ a mix of accountability systems—both internal and external
▸ continuous monitoring of standards and quick interventions to address failure
▸ creating the appropriate environment to achieve the standards set
▸ focus on the curriculum and introduce skills required for the 21st century
▸ networking and innovation.

Although at one level very helpful, such a list has limited utility in giving policy makers systems-context-specific advice about what policies and strategies to adopt at what stage of development. This line of thinking has been given a greater degree of prominence and precision at the system level by the recent publication of the McKinsey report *How the world's most improved school systems keep getting better* (Mourshed et al. 2010). This study is the most ambitious attempt so far to examine the improvement trajectories of educational systems. Based on their performance across a range of international benchmarking studies, twenty systems were identified as either 'sustained improvers' or 'promising starts'. From an examination of this sample, four stages of improvement or 'stage-dependent intervention clusters' were identified. In line with this narrative, there were also a number of actions that the authors stated apply equally across each of the phases. These were related to ensuring a coherent policy framework, and are similar to the list already produced by Andreas Schleicher. They are:

▶ curriculum and standards
▶ establishing and using data systems
▶ assessing students
▶ building technical skill and appropriate reward structures.

Of more interest to this discussion are the four phases of improvement that Mourshed and colleagues identified as being stage-dependent intervention clusters. These they termed:

1. 'Poor to fair'—focused on ensuring basic standards.
2. 'Fair to good'—focused on consolidating system foundations.
3. 'Good to great'—focused on professionalising teaching and leadership.
4. 'Great to excellent'—focused on system-led innovation.

What follows is a summary of the key actions identified by the McKinsey authors (Mourshed et al. 2010) in each of these phases.

Phase one: Poor to fair

The systems in this group were those who had made promising starts, such as those in Chile from 2001 and 2005 and the Western Cape and Ghana from 2003 onwards. System improvement journeys in this phase focused on achieving basic literacy and numeracy by emphasising three themes:

1. **Providing scaffolding and motivation for low skill teachers and principals**
   - *Scripted lessons:* the system creates instructional objectives, lesson plans and learning materials for daily lessons to enable teachers to focus on executing lessons and reduce expectation for devising lessons.
   - *Coaching on curriculum:* the system creates a field-force of coaches to visit schools and work with teachers in class on effectively delivering the curriculum.
   - *Incentives for high performance:* the system gives rewards (monetary and prestige) to schools and teachers who achieve high improvement in student outcomes against targets.
   - *School visits by centre:* the system's central leaders or administrators visit schools to observe, meet and motivate staff and discuss performance.
   - *Instructional time on task:* the system increases student instructional time.

2. **Getting all schools to a minimum quality standard**
   - *Targets, data and assessments:* the system sets minimum proficiency targets for schools and students, frequent student learning assessments (linked to lesson objectives, every 3 to 4 weeks) and data processes to monitor progress.
   - *Infrastructure:* the system improves school facilities and resources to a minimum threshold adequate for attendance and learning.
   - *Textbooks and learning resources:* the system provides textbooks and learning resources to every student.
   - *Supporting low performing schools:* the system funds targeted support for low performing schools.

3. Getting students in seats
   ‣ *Expand seats:* the system increases school seats to achieve universal access.
   ‣ *Fulfil students' basic needs:* the school provides for student basic needs to ensure that more students attend school and that absenteeism declines.

Phase two: Fair to good

The countries is this group include both those who are making promising starts and also current 'sustained improvers' who are now at, or close to, the top rank, but went through this phase earlier in their development (e.g. Hong Kong between 1983 and 1988 and Singapore during a similar time period). This evidence demonstrated that system improvement, like school improvement, is not an 'à la carte' process, but involves sequential stages that build on each other. Improvement journeys in this phase emphasise getting the system foundations in place, focusing on three key strategies that build on those outlined in the previous phase. They are:

1. Data and accountability foundation
   ‣ *Transparency and accountability:* the system establishes student assessments and school inspections to create reliable data on performance and to hold schools accountable for improvement.
   ‣ *Improvement areas:* the system uses this data to identify and tackle specific areas with lagging performance, e.g. subjects, grades, gender.
2. Financial and organisational foundation
   ‣ *Organisation structure:* the system takes steps to make the school network shape and governance manageable, and to delineate decision rights accordingly.

> *Financial structure:* the system establishes an efficient and equitable funding allocation mechanism for schools.

3. Pedagogical foundation

> *Learning model:* the system selects a learning model consistent with raising student capabilities and designs the necessary supporting materials for this new model, e.g. standards, curriculum, textbooks.

Phase three: Good to great

It is interesting to note that the McKinsey report (Mourshed et al. 2010) includes in this stage systems which have contrasting trajectories: Poland which made a great start from 2003 onwards and may well progress further; England between 1995 and 2005 which made great progress also, but now seems to have stalled; and Singapore which went through this phase between 1988 and 1998 and has continued to make sustained progress. Improvement journeys in this phase emphasise shaping the professional. To be successful in this phase, systems need to have the elements of previous phases embedded, before progress here can be predicted. The three components of this phase are:

1. Raising the calibre of entering teachers and principals
> *Recruiting:* the system raises the entry bar for new teacher candidates.
> *Preparation and induction:* the system raises pre-service training quality and certification requirements.
2. Raising the calibre of existing teachers and principals
> *Professional development:* the system raises professional development requirements and provides more opportunities for self-, peer- and centre-led learning.
> *Coaching on practice:* instructional coaches work with teachers to strengthen their skills in areas such as lesson planning, student data analysis and in-class pedagogy.

> *Career pathways:* the system creates teacher and leadership specialisations through career pathways, raising expectations with each successive pathway rung and increasing pay accordingly.
3. School-based decision-making
> *Self-evaluation:* the system cultivates ownership in schools for improvement through introducing self-evaluation for schools and making performance data more available.
> *Flexibility:* the system gives schools the flexibility to pursue specialised programs appropriate to their students and increasingly decentralises pedagogical rights.

Phase four: Great to excellent

The countries or systems that McKinsey (Mourshed et al. 2010) identified as currently being in this group include Hong Kong, Ontario and Singapore. As we have seen, these are systems that have given careful and sustained thought to achieving both excellence and equity as well as working on system reform in a sustained and progressive way for some time. To ensure that there is maximum system capacity at the point of delivery, improvement journeys in this final phase emphasise learning through peers and innovation. In line with the argument of this book, this phase might not be entered into by all systems and certainly not those who espouse top-down or outside–in ways of working. By definition, these strategies cannot unleash greatness; they just ensure that all schools regress to the mean. The three broad strategies here are:

1. Cultivating peer-led learning for teachers and principals
> *Learning communities:* the system facilitates school-based learning communities to create peer-led support and accountability to each other.
> *Flexibility:* the system provides effective educators with greater pedagogical autonomy.

> *Rotations:* the system rotates educators throughout the system in order to spread learning and varied styles of mentorship.

2. Creating additional support mechanisms for professionals
   > *Leverage:* the system provides administrative staff in schools so that teachers and principals can focus on pedagogy and leadership rather than administrative tasks.

3. System-sponsored innovation across schools
   > *Stakeholder innovation:* the system sponsors and identifies examples of innovative practices in schools (teaching and learning practice, parent/community involvement practices, etc.) and then develops strategies to share them across all schools.

We still have a long way to go before systems improvement literature based on the research on system effectiveness reaches the level of maturity of that associated with school improvement and effectiveness. The analysis described in this section does, however, take us a good step forward in providing helpful contextual advice for policy makers and system leaders. We consider in the following section some broader issues that need to be taken into account when applying this research knowledge in practice.

Cross-cutting themes and cautions

There is no doubt that summaries, such as the one presented above based on McKinsey's (Mourshed et al. 2010) groundbreaking analysis of system improvement, are very attractive. They should not, however, be regarded as panaceas, no matter how beguiling; such prescriptions need to be treated with at least two points of caution. The first cautionary note relates to the naive habit of 'policy borrowing' and the second relates to the process of adaption and implementation.

The dangers of policy borrowing have already been alluded to in Chapter Six. An extreme yet far too common example of this is the case of Finland. Finland has scored highly on every PISA test so far and as a consequence has become the focus of much educational tourism. So much so, that there are now specialist educational travel agents in Finland and the government is putting a charge on educational visits as a means of increasing national revenues. As David Hargreaves (2012, p. 8) has noted in his recent think piece *A self-improving school system in international context*:

> *This ... has not prevented many countries from borrowing selectively from Finland to boost their levels of student achievement, and it is true that there is no hard evidence that such borrowing will not work. But the borrowing is usually highly selective. In England politicians have taken to the idea that all teachers should have a Master's, but quietly ignore, for example, the fact that the Finns do not have a national curriculum, that formal schooling starts at age seven, and that there are no compulsory tests or examinations until higher secondary school. Little attention is paid to ... Finnish culture.*

As we noted in our own cross-case analysis of PISA (OECD 2011a, p. 229), *Strong performers and successful reformers in education*:

> *Any exploration of the individual country trajectories towards high educational performance must account for each country's unique history and economic evolution, recognising that countries hold different values, different assets and different liabilities in their educational systems, and employ different strategies to gain world-class results.*

I have been explaining this paradox to myself by using the diagram presented in Figure 9.5. It suggests that the effect of any country's educational system is not only a combination of deliberate policies and strategies, but also a reflection of the cultural and social capital it

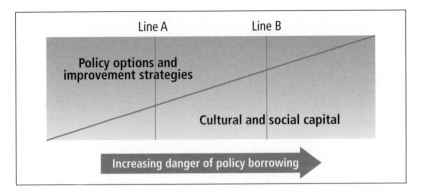

Figure 9.5 Policy borrowing and cultural determinism

possesses. Policy borrowing becomes increasingly dangerous when looking at systems with high levels of the latter. One should not, for example, underestimate the influence of the mother's role and the collective responsibility for educational success in high-performing systems such as Japan, South Korea and Singapore. Line B illustrates this position. Line A, on the other hand, represents an educational strategy such as specific classroom practices that transfer well from context to context.

In reflecting on this issue, it is worth quoting David Hargreaves again (2012, p. 25):

> There may be real gains from looking around the world for some educational policies and practices that might benefit our schools. But a transformation of schooling that is self-generating and sustainable requires that attention be paid to the deep cultural capital that underpins the life of individual schools, of partnerships and alliances, and of the school system as a whole. This is the key lesson we learn from China and East Asia, one by which we can develop our version, based on our own well-established native roots of extended moral purpose and distributed system leadership.

So the key point here is the danger of promiscuous policy borrowing. This is for two reasons: first, that many of the highest performing countries owe their position to the effect of rich and at times idiosyncratic levels of social and intellectual capital, which is not easily replicated; and second, as we have seen throughout this book, strategies required to move systems from 'great to excellent' are very different from those that are needed in making the shift from 'poor to fair'.

The second note of caution relates to the process of adoption and implementation. Even the carefully defined and intelligent stage-dependent clusters of the McKinsey analysis require sensitive adaptation to context. The McKinsey authors (Mourshed et al. 2010) paid great attention to this. It is therefore helpful to draw on their work briefly again here. They propose three key concepts— contextualising, sustaining and ignition:

1. **Contextualising system reform:** The McKinsey authors (Mourshed et al. 2010, pp. 70–71) emphasise that successful improving systems carefully tailor their intervention clusters at each performance stage to their context and note sensibly that interventions are unlikely to achieve their full impact without that. Contextualising is aimed at gaining the support of stakeholder groups and in particular involves making decisions about when the system should mandate an action or when it should make compliance voluntary. They suggest that context has two main forms. The first is current system performance—the particular point a school is on the system improvement journey, or which stage-dependent phase it is in. The second refers to the influence of history, culture, values, system structure, politics, etc. on improvement interventions. The McKinsey authors found that leaders use an array of strategies to accommodate the contextual realities in which they operate. Although they do not state this

directly, it is clear from their data that progress along the 'mandate to voluntary' continuum reflects the phase at which the system is operating. In other words, mandating compliance is more usual during the early stages of the improvement journey; in moving from 'good to great' and then from 'great to excellent', such top-down approaches increasingly become counter-productive.

2. **Sustaining system reform:** For a system's improvement journey to be sustained over the long-term, the improvements have to be integrated into the very fabric of the system pedagogy. McKinsey (Mourshed et al. 2010, p. 21) identified three ways that improving systems do this: by establishing collaborative practices; by developing a meditating layer between the schools and the centre; and by architecting tomorrow's leadership. Each of these aspects of sustaining improvement is an interconnected and integral part of the system pedagogy.

3. **Igniting system reform:** School systems that have successfully ignited reforms and sustained their momentum have all relied on at least one of three events to get them started: they have taken advantage of a political or economic crisis, they have commissioned a high profile report critical of the system's performance or they have appointed a new energetic and visionary political or strategic leader. The role of new leadership is a common and particularly important pattern in igniting school system reforms (Mourshed et al. 2010, pp. 99–103). These leaders take advantage of being new, but stay a longer time than usual. They also follow a common 'playbook' of practices, described as follows:

▶ decide on what is 'non-negotiable'
▶ install capable and like-minded people in the most critical positions
▶ engage with stakeholders
▶ secure the resources for what is non-negotiable
▶ get 'early wins' on the board quickly.

This discussion adds once again to the precision with which we can use the research on system effectiveness to formulate policy and assist with system improvement. There is no doubt that our knowledge in this area will increase exponentially over the next few years.

Coda

This chapter has presented a sustained and comprehensive argument against the myth that 'one size fits all' in school and system reform. Three points need to be reiterated. The first is that this analysis applies equally to individual schools or groups of schools, as it does to national or local governments and systems. The second point is that, unfortunately, most of the time single strategies or policy initiatives tend to be worked on discretely, rather than as a set of complementary and mutually supportive policies as proposed here. Third and critically, the set of strategies that have been selected need to be precisely aligned to the growth-state or performance phase of the school or system.

What is needed is a heuristic framework to help systems and schools to reflect on how best to balance these various strategies in a comprehensive approach to educational improvement. Figure 9.6 provides an example of such a framework. It seeks to identify three key elements of a coherent approach to school change. The framework also suggests how these three elements may interact and impact on the learning and achievement of students.

This concept was initially developed by Michael Barber (2005) based on Thomas Friedman's (1999) analogy of a nation's economy being compared to a computer system. There is the hardware—the infrastructure, funding and physical resources as well as human and intellectual capital. There is also the software—the interaction between the school and the student, the process of teaching and

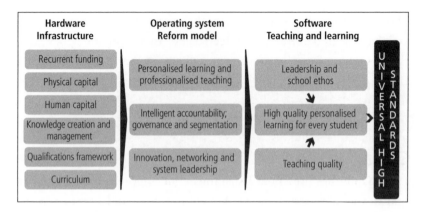

Figure 9.6 A coherent system design framework
(Adapted from Hopkins 2007, p. 176)

learning infused by the leadership of the school. In between the two, there is the operating system, or the strategy for change the school or system chooses (or not) to employ to develop itself as a whole. The operating system in the diagram refers to that proposed in *Every school a great school* (Hopkins 2007).

Many schools, as well as ministries of education worldwide, assume that there is a direct link between the hardware and the software—as long as the resources are in place then student learning will be satisfactory. This is rarely the case and the reason is simple. We need an improvement strategy, or in McKinsey's terms, a 'stage-dependent intervention cluster' to link inputs to outputs as, without it, student and school outcomes will remain unpredictable. With it, schools will be more likely to translate their resources more directly into better learning environments and, therefore, enhanced learning outcomes for their children (Hopkins 2007).

The same argument goes for local and national governments and systems. The existence of such a framework allows for a more intelligent debate over the policies adopted by different countries in terms of all three elements—the hardware, the software and the operating system and their integrated impact on standards of learning and achievement.

A similar logic also applies to Fullan's (2011) 'wrong drivers' referred to at the start of the chapter. Of course, Fullan's drivers may be wrong for one of two reasons, or both. They may be wrong because they are wrong, or wrong because they are inappropriate to the stage the school or system is at. As Fullan (2011, p. 5) comments:

> *In the rush to move forward, leaders, especially from countries that have not been progressing, tend to choose the wrong drivers. Such ineffective drivers fundamentally miss the target. There are four main 'wrong driver' culprits ...*
>
> 1. *accountability: using test results, and teacher appraisal, to reward or punish teachers and schools, versus capacity building;*
> 2. *individual teacher and leadership quality: promoting individual, vs group solutions;*
> 3. *technology: investing in and assuming that the wonders of the digital world will carry the day vs instruction;*
> 4. *fragmented strategies vs integrated or systemic strategies.*

Fullan's wrong drivers of course remind us of some of the myths already exploded in this book. In many ways the structure and argument of this book also reflects the framework above. Earlier, we discussed aspects of various national policies that provide the hardware or infrastructure for system improvement. The 'drivers', especially those related to the learning and teaching aspects, reflect the software aspects of the diagram. The concepts of system leadership, accountability and networking relate to the operating system. The key issue to remember is that operating systems are not immutable; they need to be continually refined to reflect their context. The policy frameworks related to system leadership discussed in the following chapter are a good example of how strategies or 'operating systems' evolve and build on each other as the system as a whole develops.

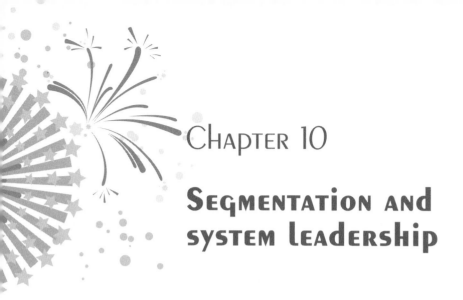

Chapter 10

Segmentation and system leadership

The myth that market forces drive educational excellence

The educational policy direction in many developed countries is changing quite dramatically at the present time. There is currently a rapid shift away from the government-managed educational changes of the 1990s and 2000s to far more decentralised systems based on principles such as 'autonomy', 'choice' and market forces. In many systems, reasons and forces other than educational are driving this trend. The biggest driver is the meltdown in global economic systems since 2008 and the resulting desire from many governments for the 'small state'. These irresistible forces are also coupled with a genuine belief by many that there is a need to unleash the power of the profession that has been harnessed by too much control. One hears strong arguments to support such a case, but it is foolish to think that by simply dismantling existing system structures and giving unfettered freedoms to schools will by itself raise standards. This is the myth. As we have already seen on p. 30, the McKinsey study (Barber et al. 2010,

p. 8) clearly states that, 'Differences in what leaders do are not directly related to the level of autonomy they are given'. It is clear from international benchmarking studies of school performance and the evidence of this book that:

▶ decentralisation by itself increases variation and reduces overall system performance. There is a consequent need for some 'mediating level' within the system to connect the centre to schools and schools to each other
▶ leadership is the crucial factor both in school transformation and system renewal, so investment particularly in principal and leadership training is essential
▶ the quality of teaching is the best determinant of student performance, so that any reform framework must address the 'fine motor behaviours' of teachers in the classroom. Top-down approaches have proven ineffective in delivering such authentic professional change
▶ outstanding educational systems find ways of learning from their best and strategically use the diversity within the system to good advantage
▶ the unrestricted reliance on market forces as an educational change strategy inevitably distorts and duplicates provision and militates against the achievement of those students from the poorest backgrounds.

So although deregulation and market forces may be the myth, this is by no means an argument for retaining the status quo. It is also clear from the argument presented in previous chapters that sustained educational excellence requires the creation of a new educational landscape, elements of which have already been described in the preceding pages.

David Hargreaves (2010, 2011, 2012) in a series of recent think pieces has been putting much intellectual energy into imagining what such a new landscape would consist of and in doing so has developed the concept of a self-improving system of schools (SISS). Hargreaves (2010, p. 5) comments:

> *At its core, the notion of a SISS assumes that much (not all) of the responsibility for school improvement is moved from both central and local government and their agencies to the schools. An obvious forerunner in England is local management of schools (LMS), the delegation of financial responsibilities to schools in the 1980s, which is generally regarded as a world-leading success story. However, a SISS is not merely the sum total of self-improving schools. The system element in a SISS consists of clusters of schools accepting responsibility for self-improvement for the cluster as a whole. A SISS embodies a collective responsibility in a way that neither school improvement nor LMS has ever done. In effect this involves the creation of a new intermediary body between the individual school and the local authorities, which are usually seen as the middle tier between central government and the individual school.*
>
> *The architecture of a SISS rests on four main building blocks:*
>
> ▶ *capitalising on the benefits of clusters of schools*
> ▶ *adopting a local solutions approach*
> ▶ *stimulating co-construction between schools*
> ▶ *expanding the concept of system leadership*

The equivalent of Local Management of Schools (LMS) is probably the 'self-managing school' in Australia and 'charter schools' in the USA. So the myth being exploded in this chapter is that market forces work in sustaining educational excellence. In doing this, a contrary proposal is developed around more lateral and self-sustaining ways of working that move beyond networking and collaboration, towards systemic capacity building. These ideas are explored in the chapter that follows by:

▶ refining the concept of system leadership
▶ introducing the idea of segmentation as a critical element in the new educational landscape
▶ arguing that the 'teaching' or 'laboratory' school concept is critical to building capacity for system reform
▶ illustrating a policy framework for achieving tri-level reform.

The chapter concludes with a reflection on how the ten myths when viewed positively, coalesce to form a model for school and system reform.

System leadership

Key to the creation of an educational landscape built on more lateral and inside–out ways of working is the role of the system leader. The concept of 'system leadership' is one that has recently caught the educational imagination. In *Systems thinkers in action*, Michael Fullan (2004b, p. 9) argued that:

> *A new kind of leadership is necessary to break through the status quo. Systematic forces, sometimes called inertia, have the upper hand in preventing system shifts. Therefore, it will take powerful, proactive forces to change the existing system (to change context). This can be done directly and indirectly through systems thinking in action. These new theoreticians are leaders who work intensely in their own schools, or national agencies, and at the same time*

connect with and participate in the bigger picture. To change organizations and systems will require leaders to get experience in linking other parts of the system. These leaders in turn must help develop other leaders with similar characteristics.

This quotation contains three implicit assumptions. The first is that if we are ever to achieve sustainable education change it must be led by those close to the school; the second is that this must have a systemic focus and the third is that system leadership is still an emerging practice (Hopkins & Higham 2010). Although system leadership is emerging as a professional practice, it is a concept that is located in a rich theoretical and research context. The key insight here has been summarised well by Kofman and Senge (1993, p. 27) when they state that the:

defining characteristic of a system is that it cannot be understood as a function of its isolated components … the system doesn't depend on what each part is doing but on how each part is interacting with the rest.

There is a strong thread across here to Heifetz's (1994) concept of 'adaptive leadership' discussed in Chapter Eight. It is clear that system leaders will need to work adaptively to lead people and organisations beyond restrictive boundaries, perceived wisdoms and entrenched cultures where they exist as obstacles to improvement.

Our own research on system leadership (Higham, Hopkins & Matthews 2009; Hopkins 2007; Hopkins & Higham 2007) led to the identification of the following taxonomy of roles. Although derived inductively from the work of thousands of heads in England in the mid 2000s, on the basis of our experience these roles seem to have a global relevance. They are:

▶ Develop and *lead a successful educational improvement partnership* across local communities to support welfare and potential.

▶ Choose to *lead and improve a school in extremely challenging circumstances.*

▶ *Partner another school facing difficulties and improve it*—this category includes executive heads and leaders of more informal improvement arrangements.

▶ Act as *curriculum and pedagogic innovators* who develop and then transfer best practice across the system.

▶ Work as *change agents* or *expert leaders* such as in England, e.g. National Leaders of Education, and erstwhile school improvement partners and consultant leaders.

The role that has attracted most popular attention is that of working with another school to improve the outcomes of the other. Sir Paul Grant (2011), head teacher of Robert Clack School in the East of London, describes how he supported an acting head teacher rather than 'taking over' the school. His plans for improvement included:

▶ diagnosis of the key practices that needed to develop

▶ clarity on teaching and learning and behaviour systems

▶ a visit to witness the behaviour management, assemblies and teaching and learning in action, so as to give an insight into what was possible in very similar circumstances

▶ the export and refinement of these systems from one school into the other, employing key staff to deliver, in particular, immediate improvements in behaviour.

The school improved rapidly and was operating at national standards within an 18-month period. Sir Paul also noted benefits for his own school including increased confidence among the leadership in knowing what needed to be done to get a school out of special measures. The flip side, as Sir Paul noted, was that personal reputations and the school's resources were put to the test: failure was not an option! Thus while system leaders work across schools, this in itself is not a sufficient criterion. As we note in *System leadership in practice* (Higham, Hopkins & Matthews 2009) most school leaders are involved in some form of collaboration or networking. What differentiates system leaders is that they:

▶ actively improve student learning (for every child) within the schools they work with including narrowing the gap(s) as well as increasing attainment overall

▶ develop the leadership of learning in other schools—combining high expectations with an understanding of a range of best practice in teaching and learning and an ability to transfer this to other schools

▶ change school (and local level) systems and structures to make certain that improvement can be sustained, e.g. wider responsibility; social cohesion.

Although the English practices of system leadership are some of the most developed in this field, this is a growing international phenomenon. The OECD study authors (Pont, Nusche & Hopkins 2008, p. 259) point out that:

Throughout OECD countries, there is a great deal of school leadership co-operation and collaboration going around. Practitioners do not work alone, and many benefit from a variaty of networks. Approaches to co-operation range from informal networking to new management structures ... in all countries participating in the OECD Improving School Leadership activity, there are some arrangements for co-operation between schools. School leaders are the key to these and are also strongly influenced by them.

Taken together, then, the research, informed comment and government policy suggests that the concept of system leadership is an idea whose time has come, and is now potentially a global movement. As we noted elsewhere (Hopkins & Higham 2007) it is seen to have the potential to provide:

▶ **a wider resource for school improvement**—making more of our most successful leaders by encouraging and enabling them to identify and transfer best practice, reduce the risk of innovation and change in other schools and develop and lead partnerships that improve and diversify educational pathways for students within and across localities

▶ **an effective and authentic response to low attaining schools**—our most successful heads hold the potential to impact on schools that are in special measures or in serious weaknesses, by working to develop and mobilise leadership capacity in the pursuit of whole school improvement

▶ **a potential to resolve challenges in the longer term**—such as the declining demographic supply of well-qualified school leaders, falling student rolls and hence increasingly non-viable schools, and yet ongoing pressures to sustain educational provision in all localities

▶ **a means of achieving moral purpose and social justice**—by using our most capable leaders to help deliver a national system in which every child has the opportunity to achieve their full potential.

One must also remember that system leadership, as Fullan originally pointed out, is not simply confined to the role of the head teacher or principal. To ensure system-wide sustained improvement it needs to be expressed, as we shall in the rest of this chapter, on at least three levels—at the school level, the local level and the system level.

Segmentation and the new educational landscape

The argument should by now be clear. Top-down and outside–in approaches produce structures, policy options and ways of working that are instrumental and regress performance to the mean. They generate bureaucratic forms of organisation that, although efficient and probably necessary, in the early phases of a change process, also have a dark side. Max Weber, whose classic studies on bureaucracy are still insightful, warns that they pose a threat to individual freedoms and that ongoing bureaucratisation leads to a 'polar night of icy darkness', in which increasing rationalisation of human life traps individuals in the 'iron cage' of bureaucratic, rule-based, rational control (cited in Baehr 2001). So dominant have been bureaucratic forms of administration in our public services and notably in education that they now often appear to be the norm and, as a consequence, they place a ceiling on the move of a system from good to great. As Michael Barber (Barber, Moffit & Kihn 2011) has pointed out, one can mandate the move from awful to adequate and fair to good, but as one progresses one needs to 'unleash greatness'. Bureaucracies are not very good at doing that!

That is why as we try to develop more robust forms of inside–out ways of working we need to design and create a new educational landscape. This is not easy work and the forces of convention and entropy are very strong. Glimpses of this new landscape have been evidenced on the preceding pages of this book. A number of our leading educational thinkers, such as David Hargreaves (2010, 2011, 2012) in his think pieces referred to above, Andy Hargreaves and Dennis Shirley (2009) writing from the USA in their *Fourth way* publication and Brian Caldwell (2011) in much of his recent work in Australia, are helping to define the territory. A complete picture is still to emerge and this book is a modest contribution to this goal. The direction of travel, however, is clear and Charles Leadbeater (2012) has expressed it as well as anyone:

> *New forms of co-operation will be needed at every level of our lives, from the global challenges of financial instability, climate change and resource depletion, to the growing recognition that most of what matters most to us—love, care, friendship, respect, trust—come from relationships. All of which leads to a simple prediction: the societies that succeed in the decades to come will be fair and relatively non-hierarchical because they will be better at co-operation than those that are divided and unequal.*

So although the development of a new educational landscape is still work in progress, it is very necessary work indeed. In order to give a more concrete idea of what is needed, the following two examples from my recent work in England and Australia are offered.

Segmentation and system leadership in England

In *Every school a great school* (Hopkins 2007), I introduced the concept of segmentation as a strategy for system improvement based on inside–out ways of working. It is important to realise however, that this aspiration of system transformation being facilitated by the degree of segmentation existing in the system only holds when certain conditions are in place. There are two crucial aspects to this: first, that

Table 10.1 The segmentation of secondary schools in England

Type of school	Key strategies (responsive to context and need)
1. Leading schools	▶ Become leading practitioners ▶ Formal federation with lower-performing schools
2. Succeeding, self-improving schools	▶ Regular local networking for school leaders ▶ Between-school curriculum development
3. Succeeding schools with internal variations	▶ Consistency interventions such as Assessment for Learning ▶ Subject specialist support to particular departments
4. Underperforming schools	▶ Linked school support for underperforming departments ▶ Underperforming pupil catch-up programs
5. Low attaining schools	▶ Formal support in federation structure ▶ Consultancy in core subjects and best practice
6. Failing schools	▶ Intensive support program ▶ New provider such as an academy

there is increased clarity on the nature of intervention and support for schools at each phase of the performance cycle; and second, that schools at each phase are clear as to the most productive ways in which to collaborate in order to capitalise on the diversity within the system. The example that I gave was the segmentation of the secondary school system in England, where a total of 3313 secondary schools were analysed according to their effectiveness in terms of student achievement at age 16. Six categories of schools emerged from this analysis and a summary of the approach suggested for each is set out in Table 10.1.

In order to be successful, however, this segmentation approach to system transformation requires a fair degree of boldness in setting system level expectations and conditions. There are four implications in particular that have to be grappled with (Hopkins 2007).

1. All failing and underperforming (and potentially low achieving) schools should have a leading school that works with them in either a formal grouping federation (where the leading school principal or head assumes overall control and accountability) or a more informal partnership.

2. Schools should take greater responsibility for neighbouring schools, so that the move towards networking encourages groups of schools to form collaborative arrangements outside of local control. Encouraging local schools to work together will build capacity for continuous improvement at local level.

3. The incentives for greater system responsibility should include significantly enhanced funding for students most at risk in order to counter the predictive character of poverty. Beyond incentivising local collaboratives, the potential effects for large-scale long-term reform include a more even distribution of 'at risk' students and associated increases in standards and a significant reduction in 'sink schools' even where 'at risk' students are concentrated.

4. A rationalisation of national and local agency functions and roles to allow the higher degree of national and regional coordination for this increasingly devolved system. At present there are too many national and local organisations acting in a competitive, uncoordinated and capricious way.

Networked autonomy in Victoria, Australia

The current educational context in the state of Victoria mirrors these global trends well. In his speech of 28 November, Minister Martin Dixon (Dixon 2011) outlined his vision for the next phase of the development of the Victorian public school system describing the 2010s as the 'phase of autonomy'. In this speech the Minister added greater texture to his concept of autonomy by sketching out the principles upon which autonomy is to be based: student outcomes, order and inclusion, innovation and internationalising education. These are laudable ambitions as befits Victoria's status as a world-class education system. The key question now, however, is how to deliver on these goals at a time when system capacity is being significantly reduced.

This is not an argument to retain existing structures, but to find an alternative and authentic way to deliver Victoria's educational ambition within a new budgetary and structural regime. The task is to build a delivery system based on what is known about the best performing school systems. The proposition is a system based on networked autonomy. Such a set of principles would allow schools in Victoria to use networked autonomy to:

▶ more fully express their moral purpose of enabling every student to reach their potential
▶ ensure that every teacher has the maximum time to teach and to develop their professional competence
▶ maximise resource allocation to ensure that this happens
▶ explore the full potential of the inside–out school development strategy
▶ enable leadership to work more effectively with the system and generate sustainable networks that deepen the impact on student learning
▶ move from external to professional forms of accountability.

What would this system architecture look like for Victoria? The following three-point proposition or theory of action is based on best available knowledge of current structural and budgetary changes occurring in Victoria at time of writing.

1. The restructured and downsized regional offices would have most of their existing functions moved to the centre and have as their main function the facilitation of networked autonomy.

2. This would require the creation of a market for educational services, which is the norm in a number of other systems that are following the same direction of travel as Victoria. The problem is that, in many jurisdictions, the quality of service provision is both highly variable and distorted by the profit motive. The proposal here is that the remit of the Bastow Institute (currently the provider of the State's leadership and professional development programs) be adapted to meet the demands of networked autonomy.

3. Central to this new system of networked autonomy is a small number of providers who can provide more strategic and specific support to principals, schools and networks. This requires the ability to work in a practical way with principals and teachers on the key leadership, professional learning, data and pedagogic strategies necessary to enable schools to move to the next level of work and performance.

So in summary it can be seen that there is a high degree of consistency between the characteristics of high-performing educational systems and the aspiration of Minister Dixon's (2011) speech. This analysis also suggests a system architecture realisable within current parameters that is capable of delivering on these goals. On the basis of the international evidence, if implemented, such a delivery system will ensure that Victoria will continue to be a global leader in education.

Building capacity for system reform: teaching or laboratory schools

One of the ways that systems are increasingly building capacity for more lateral and inside–out ways of working is through developing a systemic approach to 'teaching schools'. Increasingly, educational systems are identifying substantive roles for schools in the training of teaching that go beyond the provision of conventional practicum placements. In England, teaching schools are a recent policy initiative; the Professional Development School in North America is a more established example and in Victoria, Australia, the School Centres for Teaching Excellence is a current innovation. Commenting on the new model of national teaching schools in England, David Hargreaves (2011, p. 5) says:

> The new teaching schools, based on the concept of the teaching hospital, are to be a critical element in a more self-improving school system. By 2014–15 there will be some 500 teaching schools that will:
>
> ▶ train new entrants to the profession with other partners, including universities
> ▶ lead peer-to-peer learning and professional development, including the designation and deployment of the new specialist leaders of education (SLEs)
> ▶ identify and nurture leadership potential
> ▶ lead an alliance of other schools and partners to improve the quality of teaching and learning
> ▶ form a national network to support the schools in innovation and knowledge transfer
> ▶ be at the heart of a different strategy of school improvement that puts responsibility on the profession and schools.

All of these approaches build in some way on the 'laboratory school' concept originally developed in the USA. These schools are ones where collaborations or partnerships have been established between schools, local agencies and university schools of education that focus on high quality education, the preparation of student teachers, continuing professional development for school staff and continuous inquiry into improving practice. These are medium-term relationships characterised by reciprocity and parity, and by commitments to shared beliefs about teaching and learning and issues of equity. In beginning to shape the laboratory school concept, it is worth considering the following four questions as a basis for program design that were stimulated by a think piece by Bruce Joyce (2012).

1. Clinical skills. What kinds of knowledge and skill should a new teacher possess?

The relevant research on teacher education and the best of international practice in teacher education, professional development and school improvement suggests that teacher education programs focus on the three objectives outlined below. The essence is that teacher candidates should learn to:

▶ develop an initial repertoire of teaching and learning strategies—the ability to use several of the best approaches to instruction that we possess at this time, those grounded in research and sound theory. Learning to use such strategies involves understanding their rationales, their perspectives on learning and the research underpinning them. For convenience, we call these the 'theories of action' that then lay the basis for the 'models of teaching'
▶ teach from an action research perspective—studying their teaching and its effects on student learning in the personal, social and academic domain in a formative, clinical mode
▶ work collaboratively with colleagues and others to find ways of improving the schools where they teach.

2. Program components. What are the essential components of teacher education programs?

Assuming the three objectives outlined above are essential, research and experience suggests that there are three core components that capture the key strands or dimensions of teacher education programs.

▶ Seminars on curriculum and instruction, the conduct of action research, formative assessment of student learning and collaborative school improvement. Readings, discussions, collaborative inquiry into research are combined. The seminars are designed around the group investigation model where the teacher candidates are organised to inquire into problems that lead them to the content of the strand and sub-strands.

▶ Following mastery of the 'Theories of Action' student teacher candidates will then be introduced to several basic models of teaching. It is helpful to begin with the cooperative or inductive inquiry models. The design of the component is the training model that includes the study of the rationale of each model, observation of demonstrations (most often presented through videos of actual teaching), the use of methods for analysing the teaching that is observed and preparation for practice with K–12 students.

▶ Practise teaching in schools, particularly practise with the models of teaching that are focused on in the seminar or training including organising students into learning communities and assessing student learning. Although it is traditional to place one student teacher with one cooperating teacher, there are good reasons to consider placing two or even four student teachers with an experienced teacher. The students can work together to learn teaching strategies, observe one another and analyse their practices, and they can also plan and teach together, including assessing student learning. Placed together, they are of more help to the experienced teacher at an earlier stage in the year and eventually can free the teacher to attend seminars and training sessions at the higher education institution.

3. Teacher learning. How do teachers learn new teaching and learning strategies?

The research on how new and experienced teachers learn leads to a clear paradigm—in order to become fully competent to use any model of teaching teachers need to:

> ◗ understand its rationale and how it works
> ◗ experience demonstrations of it, that is, a teacher demonstrates the model and its syntax with students—to be understood to the point where the teacher candidate can practise it and the major features are fully comprehended.

Next, the teacher candidate needs to practise the model many times and analyse the responses of students and what they learn during the teaching and learning sessions.

The process requires companionship with other learners—cooperating teachers, university faculty members and other students can be very supportive and provide much needed companionship as the teacher candidates learn to use the model effectively.

4. Alliances. How will schools work together effectively in a strategic and systemic alliance?

A key element in the capacity building function of laboratory or teaching schools is their ability to build alliances and networks on a regional and national basis. Their involvement in a segmented systemic approach described earlier is therefore crucial, but not unproblematic. As Hargreaves (2011, p. 5) again comments:

> *An area of concern and contention is the relationship between a teaching school, its alliance partners and other local schools. It is not intended that a teaching school should in every way be better or more advanced than its partners. Certainly it has to be an outstanding school in Ofsted terms, but its task, as in any strategic alliance, is to be the network's hub or the nodal school that offers strategic leadership, and co-ordinates, monitors and quality assures alliance activities and expertise.*
>
> *The role of the in-school coach or co-operating teacher is pivotal here also. Recruiting and training coaches to meet the*

demands of producing a 21st century workforce is an essential
feature within any model of teaching schools. In moving to scale,
all coaches should have Masters level or equivalent qualifications;
be developing the concept of a professional tutor within the
school; and together build a cadre of coaches across the system on
a regional basis.

As we seek to professionalise teaching, there is a need to recognise
that it is through teacher preparation programs that professional-level
knowledge and skill is acquired. In too many countries, teacher
education programs simply socialise the new teachers to current
normative practice. The best programs try to elevate teaching beyond
what is accepted, by equipping their graduates with the best we know
from research and experience and to use this as the basis for systemic
renewal and reform.

The influence of teacher education programs on system
improvement should not be underestimated—teacher education is
simultaneously the worst problem and the best solution in the quest
for school reform! As a consequence, the highest performing school
systems are investing heavily in innovative and productive approaches
to teacher preparation in order to address the key ingredient of school
improvement at source.

Alignment and tri-level reform

The final nail in the coffin of the myth of market forces and
deregulation in driving educational quality is found in the
characteristics of successful systemic improvement. There have been
countless examples and evidence in this book to illustrate that the
most successful school systems leave nothing to chance. As they
increasingly devolve responsibility to the front-line, they do it with
careful thought about both horizontal and vertical alignment and by

carefully selecting and sequencing complementary policies and strategies. The discussion in the previous chapter of what McKinsey (Mourshed et al. 2010) calls stage dependent clusters is good example of this. Michael Fullan and colleagues (2001) register a useful caution on this crucial issue.

> *Our argument in a nutshell is that to get large scale reform, you need to establish and coordinate ongoing accountability and capacity-building efforts at three levels—the schools, the district, and the state. (p. 6)*

> *The caution. Change in complex society will never be linear. So don't expect a tri-level coherent system that settles down once and for all ... But successive approximations are possible. Whatever level in the system you are at, work on the tri-level agenda. To be content with your own bailiwick is to make large scale, sustainable reform impossible. And indeed, to confine local reform to episodic spasms. (p. 23)*

The caution is well taken and to move from good to great, tri-level reform may be necessary but not sufficient. It has also to be combined with alignment across the system as well as between levels. Fullan refers to this form of capacity building as being 'indirect' and the most powerful. It is worth quoting him again (Fullan 2009a, p. 283).

> *By indirect capacity building, I mean the use of deliberate strategies designed to help peers to learn from each other—within schools, across schools and across districts. We call this lateral capacity building, and it is most powerful because educators are learning from their colleagues. The central leaders have a proactive role in funding and coordinating these activities. They seek best*

ideas wherever they can be found and use the 'wisdom of the crowd' to spread and assess their worth and impact.

It would require another book to fully explicate the complexities of this argument. Such a luxury is not available, so to illustrate what is meant here, I draw on an example from my recent work. The advice summarised below is based on work done for my home country of Wales. So for me it is a happy way to conclude this chapter. This work (Hopkins 2010a) was commissioned by the Association of Directors of Education in Wales (ADEW) for the Minister of Education, following Wales' dramatic decline in the PISA rankings. It serves as an example of how the principles espoused in the book can be put into practice in a system that is striving to improve. The 12 strategic proposals are as follows.

1. ADEW believes that the overall aim of any reform effort must be to **raise the standards of educational attainment to world-class levels** for our children and young people and to reduce the variation of performance between them. The recent publication of the PISA results suggests that we are not meeting either of these objectives. Urgent action is required to reverse this alarming trend and ADEW is committed to taking a leadership role in arresting and reversing what the Minister has described as a 'systemic failure'.
2. ADEW endorses the Minister's **three priorities of literacy, numeracy and reducing the gap.** In the spirit of intelligent accountability and in order to raise the bar and narrow the gap, three types of target in literacy and numeracy (at the end of each Key Stage) are proposed: a floor target, an aspirational target and a progress target.
3. Each local authority, through its consortia, will **'RAG-rate' each of their schools in relation to literacy and quality of teaching.** This exercise will produce three outcomes: the identification of those

schools that require immediate support; those local authorities that require additional support; and a set of educational issues for which additional programs and support materials are needed. Subsequent support will take the form of human, curricular and in some cases financial support.

4. The work on **establishing consortia** is well underway, system leaders are being identified in each consortia and there is a framework for a differentiated approach to school improvement to support and direct their work. There is much energy around training in professional learning communities, but this now needs to be aligned with the system's key priorities to ensure that high quality knowledge of what works is widely disseminated and implemented through them.

5. Support without knowledge of what works rarely results in the step change in learning and achievement that the students in our most challenging schools deserve. There is therefore a concomitant need to **expand the knowledge base on professional practice.** If teachers are to raise standards and reduce variation, then they need access to the very best knowledge whether from research or established practice.

6. The core purpose of **collaboration is to improve standards of attainment and wellbeing for students.** This will be achieved by making economies of scale and releasing efficiency savings. The process will enhance the accountability of schools, participating local authorities and consortia. The baseline target will be set nationally, but consortia will agree when each member authority will reach the aspirational target and will agree on challenging progress targets with member authorities.

7. This much can be achieved within relatively short timeframes. Much more, needs to be done though, to ensure that Wales becomes the high-performing educational system we wish it to be.

This can only occur with a **high degree of policy alignment and synergy,** where the whole is greater than the sum of its parts. This alignment needs to be both horizontal and vertical, and at all levels of the system.

8. There is an urgent need for the creation of an **intelligent accountability framework** in order to not just measure, but also to drive the educational achievement for the young people of Wales. ADEW believes that an appropriate balance between external accountability and internal assessment needs to be put in place, which can be adjusted according to school performance through differentiated strategies.

9. It is clear that the **quality of teaching in Wales is too variable.** ADEW is committed to working with partners to enhance the quality of teaching through the following four suggested strategies: enhancing the quality of new entrants to the profession; focusing continuing professional development (CPD) on professional practice; expanding the knowledge base on professional practice; and using performance management to enhance professional practice.

10. There are **outstanding leaders** in Welsh schools, but the quality is too variable. ADEW believes that there needs to be a sustained focus on leadership and in particular the identification of the basic leadership practices, a staff college, extending the system leader role and the establishing of teaching schools. These are all features of systems that sustain high levels of performance.

11. Although not calling for a thorough review of the **curriculum,** ADEW believes that an immediate focus on rapid increases in literacy and numeracy performance, a concomitant grip on learning and thinking skills, an emphasis on the involvement of parents and families and a range of entitlements at the end of Key Stage 3 are all required.

12. ADEW is convinced that school-age education in Wales is at a crossroads. **The recent PISA results are a wake-up call.** Without urgent and drastic action, results will continue to stagnate and decline. ADEW is committed to the agenda outlined above, but knows that it would be all the more effective if this work were undertaken in collaboration with other actors in the system to achieve it.

It is probably a little self-indulgent to use an example of one's own advice from one's own country at the end of a book like this! However, having reviewed similar exhortations I have written recently for a number of other different systems, the proposals, once context has been accounted for, remain very similar. All emphasise the importance of alignment and tri-level reform and comment on the myth of market forces as the driver for educational excellence.

Coda

Although the artifice of 'exploding the myths' is a helpful device in structuring a book like this, such an approach has two potential downsides. The first is that the narrative will appear unduly negative and second, that the argument will become fragmented, by reflecting problems with individual myths rather than presenting a coherent and integrated theory of action. I hope that this is not the case here, as I have taken some care to present a positive response to each of the myths and to build the case for a holistic approach to school and system reform based on inside–out ways of working. It is worthwhile, however, in this final coda of the book to illustrate how this heuristic device adds value to what we know about achieving school and system reform.

Discussion of the myths stems from a deep frustration that despite what we collectively know about school and system reform, the potential contained in this knowledge is not systematically realised. This is because, as Fullan says, 'the wrong drivers are chosen' and often occurs because of ineptness, misunderstanding or cultural and bureaucratic hegemony. So as Machiavelli presciently commented, 'It seems to me better to follow the real truth of things than an imaginary view of them.' This is what I have attempted to do in this book, and the overarching narrative goes something like this:

1. We know much about school and system reform—this was summarised in the coda at the end of Chapter One.
2. Unfortunately, this knowledge is often misused and an illusion or myth is generated that leads in unproductive directions and consequently has little impact on the learning and achievement of students.
3. In order to fulfil our moral purpose we must correct the myths and present 'the real truth of things'.
4. We need then to couch them as theories of action within an overall strategy for school and system reform.

It is hoped that tasks one to three have been accomplished in the preceding pages; now is the time to address task four. A summary of the argument is presented in Table 10.2. The first column, 'knowledge', represents the summary of what is known about school and system reform that is found in the coda at the end of Chapter One. In the second column these ten points are linked to the 'myths' that provide the focus for each chapter. Finally, the third column contains a theory of action that provides a positive response to both the knowledge base and the associated myth.

Table 10.2 Knowledge, myths and theories of action for school and system reform

Knowledge	Myth	Theory of action
Moral purpose as the achievement and learning of all students	The myth that achievement cannot be realised at scale for all students	When schools and systems are driven by moral purpose then all students are more likely to fulfil their potential
Enhancement of the quality of teaching, rather than structural change	The myth of school autonomy and the reality of change	When the focus of policy is on the quality of teaching rather than structural change, then student achievement will increase
Teacher selection policies that ensure that only the very best become teachers	The myth that poverty is a determinant of student and school performance	When schools and teachers are of high quality, poverty is no longer a determinant of educational success
Standards of professional practice	The myth that it is the curriculum rather than the learning that counts	When the focus is on powerful learning, then students will both attain more and develop their cognitive and social skills
Sustained professional learning opportunities	The myth that teaching is either an art or a science	When teachers acquire a richer repertoire of pedagogic practice then students' learning will deepen.
Formative, ongoing and transparent data	The myth that external accountability results in sustained school reform	When data is used to monitor, feedback and enhance student performance, then students' progress will more quickly accelerate

Table 10.2 (continued)

Knowledge	Myth	Theory of action
Going deeper and early intervention	The myth that innovation and networking always add value to school reform	When teachers and schools go deeper in their search for improvement (rather than adopting fads) then the student learning experience also deepens and outcomes improve
Instructional and system leadership	The myth of the contribution of charismatic leadership to school reform	When leadership is instructionally focused and widely distributed, then both teachers and students are able to fully capitalise on their capacity to learn and achieve
Inequities in student performance	The myth that 'one size fits all' in implementing school reform	When teachers and leaders employ more precise strategies for teaching, learning and improvement, the whole system benefits
System level structures	The myth that market forces drive educational excellence	When the system as a whole takes student learning seriously then moral purpose is achieved

This is a far more productive way of viewing the myths. It provides an action framework for moving from what we know, by addressing the barriers that prevent us realising that potential, to theories of action that give more strategic precision to the achievement of our moral purpose. The overarching or meta-theory of action is something like this:

When all the distinct but interrelated parts of what we know about school and system improvement are aligned and working together, then all students and schools (as well as the system as a whole) will realise their individual and collective potential.

A visual representation of the relationship between the theories of action is shown in Figure 10.1.

So this is the culmination of our narrative. It has been a long and at times intricate journey, because there are so many moving parts to link together and to make sense of. It is also a reflection of the relative immaturity of the current thinking in our field and our current theories of action about system reform. We should not, however, be disheartened. We have learnt much over the past ten years or so, as these pages have demonstrated, about making our school systems better places for the next generation of global citizens to learn. But there is still much to do and the next generation deserve, and require

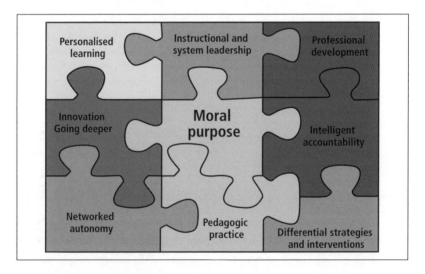

Figure 10.1 An action framework for school and system improvement built on what we know, the myths and theories of action

us to do, our very best work. As I search for a conclusion, I hear ringing in my ears the words of Ernest Becker (1985, p. xix) that I first read nearly 30 years ago and which still inspire me today. In the preface to his posthumous book, *Escape from evil*, he wrote about the necessity to 'get some kind of grip on the accumulation of thought' because if we do not, we will 'continue to wallow helplessly, to starve amidst plenty'. In a modest way this is what I have attempted to do by *Exploding the Myths of School Reform* in this book.

Bibliography

Abell, RG 1977, *Own your own life*, Bantam Books, New York.

Alington, AF 1961, *Drama and education*, Blackwell, Oxford.

Anderson, LW & Krathwohl, DR (eds) 2001, *A taxonomy for learning, teaching and assessing: a revision of Bloom's Taxonomy of educational objectives*, complete edition, Longman, New York.

Aristotle, *The Nichomachean ethics*, book II.

Arnstein, S 1969, 'A ladder of citizen participation in the USA', *Journal of the American Institute of Planners*, vol. 35, no. 4, pp. 216–24.

Assessment Reform Group 2002, *Assessment for learning: 10 principles. Research-based principles to guide classroom practice*, AGR, London.

Baehr, P 2001, 'The "Iron Cage" and the "Shell as Hard as Steel": Parsons, Weber and the stahlhartes Gehäuse metaphor in *The Protestant Ethic and the Spirit of Capitalism*', *History and Theory*, vol. 40, no. 2, pp. 153–69.

Ballantyne, P, Jackson, D & Temperley, J with Lieberman, A 2006, *System leadership in action: networks as the proving ground for system leaders*, National College for School Leadership, Nottingham.

Barber, M 2004, 'The virtue of accountability: system redesign, inspection, and incentives in the era of informed professionalism', *Journal of Education*, vol. 185, no. 1, pp. 7–38.

Barber, M 2005, 'A 21st century self-evaluation framework. Annex 3 in *Journeys of discovery: the search for success by design*', Keynote speech in the National Center on Education and the Economy Annual Conference, Florida.

Barber, M 2008, *An instruction to deliver*, Methuen, London.

Barber, M 2009, 'From system effectiveness to system improvement', in A Hargreaves and M Fullan (eds), *Change wars*, Solution Tree, Indiana.

Barber, M, Moffit A & Kihn, P 2011, *Deliverology 101: a field guide for educational leaders*, Corwin, Thousand Oaks, California.

Barber, M & Mourshed, M 2007, *How the world's best performing school systems come out on top*, McKinsey & Company, London.

Barber, M, Whelan, F & Clark, M 2010, *Capturing the leadership premium: how the world's top school systems are building leadership capacity for the future*, McKinsey & Company, London.

Barnes, I & Smith, P 2007, *Leading curriculum innovation: learning from research*, National College for School Leadership, Nottingham & Qualifications and Curriculum Authority, London.

Becker, E 1985, *Escape from evil*, Simon & Schuster, New York.

Bell, M, Cordingley, P & Mitchell, H 2006, *The impact of networks on pupils, practitioners, organisations and the communities they serve*, National College for School Leadership, Nottingham.

Bentley, T & Miller, R 2006, 'Personalisation: getting the questions right', *Schooling for tomorrow: personalising education*, OECD, Paris.

Berne, E 1961, *Transactional analysis in psychotherapy*, Condor Books, New York.

Berne, E 1964, *Games people play: the psychology of human relationships*, Grove Press, New York.

Berne, E 1973, *What do you say after you say hello? The psychology of human destiny*, Bantam Books, New York.

Black, P 1998, *Testing: friend or foe? The theory and practice of assessment and testing*, Falmer Press, London.

Black, P & Wiliam, D 1998, *Inside the black box*, Kings College, London.

Blanchard, J 2002, *Teaching and targets: self-evaluation and school improvement*, RoutledgeFalmer, London.

Bolam, R, McMahon, A, Stoll, L, Thomas, S, Wallace, M, Hawkey, K & Greenwood, A 2005, *Creating and sustaining effective professional learning communities*, Department for Education and Skills Research Brief RB637, University of Bristol.

Bollen, R & Hopkins, D 1987, *School based review: towards a praxis*, Acco, Leuven.

Broadfoot, P & Murphy, R 1995, *Effective assessment and the improvement of education*, Falmer Press, London.

Brown, A & Holmes, D 2004, 'There ain't no dark 'til something shines', in *Towards Ubuntu: a learning journey to Capetown*, National College for School Leadership, Bedfordshire, pp. 20–3.

Caerphilly County Borough Council, 2012, *Caerphilly skills strategy: theories of action for leading learning*, CCBC, Caerphilly, Wales.

Caldwell, BJ & Centre for Strategic Education 2011, *System leadership for innovation in education*, CSE, East Melbourne.

Carroll, L 1998 (1872), *Alice's adventures in Wonderland & Through the looking glass*, Penguin Classics, London.

Carter, K & Franey, T 2006, 'Leading beyond the school: exploring the boundaries of the system', in *School leadership: how leaders succeed in challenging times*, National College for School Leadership, Nottingham.

Carter, K with Paterson, F 2006, *Understanding learning networks*, National College for School Leadership, Nottingham.

Carter, K & Sharpe, T (eds) 2007, *Leading curriculum innovation in practice*, National College for School Leadership, Nottingham & Qualifications and Curriculum Authority, London, http://www.nationalcollege.org.uk/downl oad?id=17255&filename=leading-curriculum-innovation-in-practice.pdf

Childress, S 2009, 'Six lessons for pursuing excellence and equity at scale', *Phi Delta Kappan*, vol. 10, no. 3, pp. 13–18.

Church, M, Crowe, V, Plummer, G & Worral, N 2006, *What does network practice tell us about the impact of networking and collaboration?*, National College for School Leadership, Nottingham.

City, EA, Elmore, RF, Fiarman, SE & Teitel, L 2009, *Instructional rounds in education: a network approach to improving teaching and learning*, Harvard Education Press, Cambridge, Massachusetts.

Clarke, S 2008, *Active learning through formative assessment*, Hodder Education, London.

Claxton, G 2002, *Building learning power: helping young people become better learners*, TLO, Bristol.

Claxton, G 2007, 'Expanding young people's capacity to learn', *British Journal of Educational Studies*, vol. 55, no. 2, pp. 115–34.

Collins, J 2001, *Good to great: why some companies make the leap and others don't*, HarperBusiness, New York.

Coleman, JS, Campbell, E, Hobson, C, McPartland, J, Mood, A, Weinfeld, F & York, R 1966, *Equality of Educational Opportunity*, US Government Printing Office, Washington, DC.

Dann, R 2002, *Promoting assessment as learning: improving the learning process*, RoutledgeFalmer, London.

Day, C, Sammons, P, Hopkins, D, Harris, A, Leithwood, K, Qing G, Brown, E & Ahtaridou, E 2011, *Successful school leadership: linking with learning and achievement*, Open University Press, Maidenhead, Berkshire.

Day, C, Sammons, P, Leithwood, K, Hopkins, D, Qing G & Brown, E 2010, *Ten strong claims about successful school leadership*, National College for School Leadership, Nottingham.

Department for Children, Schools and Families 2007, *The children's plan: building brighter futures*, DCSF Publications, London.

Department for Education and Employment & Qualifications and Curriculum Authority 1999a, *Flexibility in the secondary curriculum*, DfEE & QCA, London.

Department for Education and Employment & Qualifications and Curriculum Authority 1999b, *The national curriculum: handbook for primary teachers in England*, Her Majesty's Stationery Office, London.

Bibliography

Department for Education and Skills 2003, *Excellence and enjoyment: a strategy for primary schools*, DfES, London.

Department for Education and Skills 2004a, *Excellence and enjoyment: learning and teaching in the primary years*, DfES, London.

Department for Education and Skills 2004b, *Improving performance through self-evaluation*, DfES, London.

Department for Education and Skills 2004c, *A national conversation about personalised learning*, DfES Publications, Nottingham.

Department for Education and Skills 2004d, *A new relationship with schools*, DfES, London.

Department for Education and Skills 2005a, *Secondary national strategy for school improvement: tracking for success*, DfES Publications, Norwich.

Department for Education and Skills 2005b, *Spreading innovation across local authorities: realising the potential of school-based networks*, DfES Publications, Nottingham.

Department for Education and Skills 2006, *Making good progress: how can we help every pupil to make good progress at school?*, DfES Publications, Nottingham.

Department of Education and Early Childhood Development 2008, *Strengthening student support services: a discussion paper for consultation*, Student Wellbeing and Support Division, Office for Government School Education, DEECD, Melbourne, <http://www.education.vic.gov.au/healthwellbeing/support/ssso.htm>.

Department of Education and Early Childhood Development 2011, *Powerful learning: taking educational reform to scale*, paper no. 20, prepared by D Hopkins, March, Education Policy and Research Division, Office for Policy, Research and Innovation, DEECD, Melbourne.

Department of Education and Training 2003, Blueprint for government schools: future directions for education in the Victorian government school system, Communications Division, East Melbourne, http://www.education.vic.gov.au/about/publications/policy/blueprint.htm

Dixon, MF 2011, *Victoria as a learning community: extended special lecture, Melbourne Graduate School of Education*, 28 November, Department of Education and Early Childhood Development, Melbourne.

Doyle, W 1983, 'Academic work', *Review of Educational Research*, vol. 53, no. 2, pp. 159–99.

Dusay, JM 1976, 'Transactional analysis', in E Berne (ed.), *A layman's guide to psychiatry and psychoanalysis*, Ballantine Books, New York, p. 311.

Earl, L & Katz, S 2005, *What makes a network a learning network?*, National College for School Leadership, Bedfordshire.

Edmonds, R 1979, 'Effective schools for the urban poor', *Educational Leadership*, vol. 37, no. 1, pp. 15–27

Elias, MJ, Kress, JS & Hunter, L 2006, 'Emotional intelligence and the crisis in schools', in J Ciarrochi, JP Forgas & JD Mayer (eds), *Emotional intelligence in everyday life*, Psychology Press, Hove and New York, pp. 166–86.

Elmore, RF 2004, *School reform from the inside out*, Harvard Education Press, Cambridge, Massachusetts.

Elmore, R 2007, *Educational improvement in Victoria*, unpublished internal communication.

Estyn 2002, *Excellent schools: a vision for schools in Wales in the 21st century*, Estyn, Cardiff.

Fielding, M 2004, 'Transformative approaches to student voice: theoretical underpinnings, recalcitrant realities', *British Educational Research Journal*, vol. 30, no. 2, pp. 295–311.

Fischer Family Trust 2007, *Guidance notes: using the FFT database and online reports*, Fischer Family Trust, October, Cowbridge, www.fischertrust.org/downloads/dap/Training/A_school_guide_to_using_FFT_databases_and_online_reports.pdf

Fisher, A & Moss, N 2012, 'Adventure learning teaching styles: synectics', PowerPoint presentation, Dallam School, Milnthorpe, Cumbria.

Franey, T 2012, 'Best practice in primary', workshops delivered for OSIRIS Educational in Manchester, Birmingham and London, July.

Friedman, T 1999, *The lexus and the olive tree: understanding globalization*, Anchor Books, New York.

Friedman, TL 2006, *The world is flat: the globalised world in the twenty-first century*, Penguin Books, London.

Fullan, M 1985, 'Change processes and strategies at the local level', *The Elementary School Journal*, vol. 85, no. 3, pp. 391–421.

Fullan, M 1991, *The new meaning of educational change*, Cassell, London.

Fullan, M 1992, *Successful school improvement*, Open University Press, Buckingham.

Fullan, M 2000, 'The return of large scale reform', *Journal of Educational Change*, vol. 1, no. 1, pp. 1–23.

Fullan, M 2003, *The moral imperative of school leadership*, Corwin Press, Thousand Oaks, California.

Fullan, M 2004a, *Leadership and sustainability: system thinkers in action*, Sage, London.

Fullan, M 2004b, *System thinkers in action: moving beyond the standards plateau*, DfES Innovation Unit, London, in partnership with NCSL, Nottingham, www.standards.dfes.gov.uk/innovation-unit

Fullan, M 2005, 'Leadership and sustainability', in National College for School Leadership, *What are we learning about ... LEA involvement in school networks?*, NCSL, Nottingham.

Fullan, M 2007, *The new meaning of educational change*, 4th edn, Teachers College Press, New York.

Fullan, M 2009a, 'Have theory, will travel: a theory of action for system change', in A Hargreaves & M Fullan (eds), *Change wars*, Solution Tree Press, Indiana, pp. 275–85.

Fullan, M 2009b, 'Large scale reform comes of age', *Journal of Educational Change*, vol. 10, no. 2, pp. 101–13.

Fullan, M 2011, 'Choosing the wrong drivers for whole system reform', *CSE Seminar Series* paper no. 204, May, Centre for Strategic Education, East Melbourne.

Fullan, M, Hill, P & Crévola, C 2006, *Breakthrough*, Corwin Press, California and Sage, London.

Fullan, M & Miles, MB 1992, 'Getting reform right: what works and what doesn't', *Phi Delta Kappan*, vol. 73, no. 10, pp. 745–52.

Fullan, M, Rolheiser, C, Mascall, B & Edge, K 2001, 'Accomplishing large scale reform: a tri-level proposition', unpublished paper, Ontario Institute for Studies in Education, University of Toronto, http://www.michaelfullan.ca/media/13396045990.pdf

Future Skills Wales 2003, *Generic skills survey summary report*, FSW, Caerphilly.

Gardner, H 1999, *Intelligence reframed. Multiple intelligences for the 21st century*, Basic Books, New York.

Gayford, M 2011, *A bigger message: conversations with David Hockney*, Thames & Hudson, London.

Geneen, HS & Bowers, B 1997, *The synergy myth and other ailments of business today*, St Martin's Press, New York.

Gilbert, C 2006, *2020 Vision: report of the Teaching and Learning in 2020 Review Group*, Department for Education Services Publications, Nottingham.

Gipps, C 1994, *Beyond testing*, Falmer Press, Washington DC.

Gladwell, M 2000, *The tipping point: how little things can make a big difference*, Little, Brown, London.

Glass, GV, McGaw, B & Smith, ML 1981, *Meta-analysis in social research*, Sage, Beverly Hills.

Goleman, D 1996, *Emotional intelligence: why it can matter more than IQ*, Bloomsbury Publishing, London.

Good, T & Brophy, J 2008, *Looking in classrooms*, 10th edn, Allyn and Bacon, Boston, Massachusetts.

Grant, P 2011, 'Leadership for school and system improvement: the case of Robert Clack School', invited keynote address to the International Forum on Creative School Management, Seoul, South Korea, 23 September.

Gray, J, Hopkins, D, Reynolds, D, Wilcox, B, Farrell, S & Jesson, D 1999, *Improving schools: performance and potential*, Open University Press, Buckingham.

Grint, K 2005, 'Problems, problems, problems: the social construction of "leadership"', *Human Relations*, vol. 58, no. 11, pp. 1467–94.

Hadfield, M, Jopling, M, Noden, C, O'Leary, D & Stott, A 2006, *What does the existing knowledge base tell us about the impact of networking and collaboration?*, National College for School Leadership, Nottingham.

Hall, GE & Hord, SM 1987, *Change in schools: facilitating the process*, State University of New York Press, Albany.

Hallinger, P 2010, 'Leadership for learning: what have we learned from 30 years of empirical research?', *CSE Seminar Series* paper no. 196, July, Centre for Strategic Education, East Melbourne.

Halpin, AW & Troyna, B 1995, 'The politics of policy bookwriting', *Comparative Education*, vol. 31, pp. 303–10.

Hargreaves, A 1994, *Changing teachers, changing times*, OISE Press, Toronto.

Hargreaves, D 1999, 'Helping practitioners explore their school's culture', in J Prosser (ed.) *School culture*, pp. 48–65, Paul Chapman Publishing, London.

Hargreaves, A, Earl, L & Schmidt, M 2002, 'Perspectives on alternative assessment reform', *American Educational Research Journal*, vol. 39, no. 1, pp. 69–95.

Hargreaves, A, Halász, G & Pont, B 2007, *School leadership for systemic improvement in Finland*, Organisation for Economic Co-operation and Development, Paris.

Hargreaves, A & Shirley, D 2009, *The fourth way*, Corwin, Thousand Oaks, California.

Hargreaves, DH 2003a, *Educational epidemic: transforming secondary schools through innovation networks*, Demos, London, http://www.demos.co.uk/publications/educationepidemic

Hargreaves, DH 2003b, transcript of presentation to first Networked Learning Communities Conference, Nottingham.

Hargreaves, DH 2006, *A new shape for schooling?*, Specialist Schools and Academies Trust, London.

Hargreaves, DH 2010, *Creating a self-improving school system*, National College for School Leadership, Nottingham.

Hargreaves, DH 2011, *Leading a self-improving school system*, National College for School Leadership, Nottingham.

Hargreaves, DH 2012, *A self-improving school system in international context*, National College for School Leadership, Nottingham.

Hargreaves, DH & Hopkins, D 1991, *The empowered school: the management and practice of development planning*, School development series, ed. D Hopkins & D Reynolds, Continuum, London.

Hargreaves, DH, Hopkins, D, Leask, M, Connolly, J & Robinson, P 1989, *Planning for school development*, Department of Education and Science, London.

Hargreaves, E 2003, *Assessment for learning? Thinking outside the (black) box*, Institute of Education, London University, http://eprints.ioe.ac.uk/2518/1/Hargreaves2005Assessement213.pdf

Hart, R 1992, 'Children's participation: from tokenism to citizenship', *Innocenti Essays*, no. 4, UNICEF International Child Development Centre, Florence.

Hattie, J 2009, *Visible learning: a synthesis of over 800 meta-analyses relating to achievement*, Routledge, Oxon.

Heifetz, R 1994, *Leadership without easy answers*, Belknap Press, Cambridge, Massachusetts.

Heifetz, R 2003, *Adaptive work in the adaptive state*, Demos, London.

Her Majesty's Inspectorate for Education 2001, *Core skills in Scottish further education colleges: an aspect report for SFEFC*, HMIE, Livingston, Scotland.

Higham, R, Hopkins, D & Matthews, P 2009, *System leadership in practice*, Open University Press, McGraw Hill Education, Berkshire.

Hill, PW 2010, 'Large-scale assessment for accountability purposes', in A Hargreaves, A Lieberman, M Fullan & D Hopkins (eds), *Second international handbook of educational change*, Springer Science+Business Media, London, pp. 415–32.

Hopkins, D (ed.) 1987a, *Improving the quality of schooling*, Falmer Press, Lewes.

Hopkins, D 1987b, *Knowledge information skills and the curriculum*, The British Library, London.

Hopkins, D (ed.) 1988, *Doing school-based review*, Acco, Leuven.

Hopkins, D 1990, 'The International School Improvement Project (ISIP) and effective schooling: towards a synthesis', *School Organisation*, vol. 10, no. 2–3, pp. 179–94.

Hopkins, D 1998, 'Development planning for pupil achievement', *School Leadership and Management*, vol. 18, no. 3, pp. 409–24.

Hopkins, D 2000, 'Powerful learning, powerful teaching and powerful schools', *Journal of Educational Change*, vol. 1, pp. 135–54.

Hopkins, D 2001, *School improvement for real*, RoutledgeFalmer, London.

Hopkins, D 2002, *Improving the quality of education for all: a handbook of staff development activities*, 2nd edn, David Fulton, London.

Hopkins, D 2005, 'Every school a great school', IARTV seminar series, paper no. 146, August, Incorporated Association of Registered Teachers of Victoria, Jolimont.

Hopkins, D 2006, 'Quality assurance and large scale reform: lessons for Chile'. Synthesis report from the international seminar on regulatory models and quality assurance systems, December, Santiago, http://www.davidhopkins.co.uk/articles/chilesynthesisreport.pdf

Hopkins, D 2007, *Every school a great school*, Open University Press, McGraw Hill Education, Berkshire.

Hopkins, D (ed.) 2008, *Transformation and innovation: system leaders in the global age*, Specialist Schools and Academies Trust, London.

Hopkins, D 2009a, *The emergence of system leadership*, National College for School Leadership, Nottingham.

Hopkins, D 2009b, 'Realising the potential of system reform', in H Daniels, H Lauder & J Porter (eds), *Knowledge, values and educational policy: a critical perspective*, Critical perspectives on education, Routledge, Oxon, pp. 202–17.

Hopkins, D 2010a, 'ADEW strategic proposal', working paper prepared for the Association of Directors of Education in Wales, Newport, December.

Hopkins, D 2010b, 'Every school a great school: realising the potential of a system leadership', in A Hargreaves, A Lieberman, M Fullan & D Hopkins (eds), *Second international handbook of educational change*, Springer Science+Business Media, London, pp. 741–64.

Hopkins, D 2010c, 'Personalized learning in school age education', in P Peterson, E Baker & B McGaw (eds), *International encyclopedia of education*, 3rd edn, Elsevier Science, Amsterdam, pp. 227–32.

Hopkins, D 2012, *The adventure learning schools handbook*, Adventure Learning Schools, Cumbria, http://adventurelearningschools.org/assets/files/ALS_prosp(low).pdf

Hopkins, D, Ainscow, M & West, M 1994, *School improvement in an era of change*, Cassell, London.

Hopkins, D & Harris, A 2000, *Creating the conditions for teaching and learning*, David Fulton, London.

Hopkins, D, Harris, A & Jackson, D 1997, 'Understanding the school's capacity for development: growth states and strategies', *School Leadership and Management*, vol. 17, no. 3, pp. 401–11.

Hopkins, D & Higham, R 2007, 'System leadership: mapping the landscape', *School Leadership and Management*, vol. 27, no. 2, pp. 147–66.

Hopkins, D & Higham, R 2010, 'System leadership', in P Peterson, E Baker & B McGaw (eds), *International encyclopedia of education*, 3rd edn, Elsevier Science, Amsterdam, pp. 78–84.

Hopkins, D & MacGilchrist, B 1998, 'Development planning for pupil achievement', *School Leadership and Management*, vol. 18, no. 3, pp. 409–24.

Hopkins, D, Munro, J & Craig, W 2011, *Powerful learning: a strategy for systemic educational improvement*, ACER Press, Camberwell.

Hopkins, D & Reynolds, D 2001, 'The past, present and future of school improvement: towards the third age', *British Educational Research Journal*, vol. 27, no. 4, pp. 459–75.

Hopkins, D & Stern, D 1996, 'Quality teachers, quality schools: international perspectives and policy implications', *Teaching and Teacher Education*, vol. 12, no. 5, pp. 501–17.

Hopkins, D, Harris, A, Stoll, L & Mackay, T 2011, 'School and system improvement: state of the art review', keynote presentation prepared for the 24th International Congress of School Effectiveness and School Improvement, Limassol, Cyprus, 6 January, http://www.icsei.net/icsei2011/State_of_the_art/State_of_the_art_Session_C.pdf.

Hopkins, D, West, M & Ainscow, M 1996, *Improving the quality of education for all*, David Fulton, London.

Horne, M 2008, *Honest brokers: brokering innovation in public services*, The Innovation Unit, London.

Huberman, M 1995, 'Networks that alter teaching: conceptualizations, exchanges and experiments', *Teachers and Teaching: theory and practice*, vol. 1, no. 2 pp. 193–211.

Huberman, M & Miles, M 1984, *Innovation up close*, Plenum, New York.

Johnson, RT & Johnson, DW 1994, 'An overview of co-operative learning', in J Thousand, A Villa and A Nevin (eds), *Creativity and collaborative learning*, Brookes Press, Baltimore.

Joyce, B 2012, 'Notes on the design of teacher education programs', paper prepared for a symposium on teacher education in India, Saint Simons Island, Georgia, January.

Joyce, BR & Calhoun, EF 2010, *Models of professional development: a celebration of educators*, Corwin Press, Thousand Oaks, California.

Joyce, BR, Calhoun, EF & Hopkins, D 1999, *The new structure of school improvement*, Open University Press, Buckingham.

Joyce, BR, Calhoun, EF & Hopkins, D 2009, *Models of learning: tools for teaching*, 3rd edn, Open University Press, Buckingham.

Joyce, BR & Showers, B 1995, *Student achievement through staff development*, 2nd edn, Longman, White Plains, New York.

Joyce, BR & Showers, B 2002, *Student achievement through staff development*, 3rd edn, ASCD, Alexandria, Virginia.

Joyce, BR & Weil, M 1996, *Models of teaching*, 5th edn, Prentice Hall, Englewood Cliffs, New Jersey.

Klenowski, V 2011, 'Assessment for learning in the accountability era: Queensland, Australia', *Studies in Educational Evaluation*, vol. 37, no. 1, pp. 78–83.

Kofman, F & Senge, P 1993, 'Communities of commitment: the heart of learning organizations', *Organizational Dynamics*, vol. 22, no. 2, pp. 5–23.

Kolb, DA 1984, *Experiential learning*, Prentice Hall, Englewood Cliffs, New Jersey.

Leadbeater, C 2005, 'Focusing on the big things', in *Leading personalised learning in schools: helping individuals grow*, National College for School Leadership, Nottingham.

Leadbeater, C 2012, 'No, we are not selfish: co-operation is at the heart of our existence', *Guardian*, 7 March, http://www.guardian.co.uk/commentisfree/2012/mar/07/selfish-cooperation-existence

Leithwood, K, Day, C, Sammons, P, Hopkins, D & Harris, A 2007, *Seven strong claims about successful school leadership*, National College for School Leadership, Nottingham.

Leithwood, K, Jantzi, D & Mascall, B 1999, 'Large scale reform: what works?', unpublished manuscript, Ontario Institute for Studies in Education, University of Toronto.

Leithwood, K, Seashore Louis, K, Anderson, S & Wahlstrom, K 2004, *How leadership influences student learning: a review of research for the learning from leadership project*, Wallace Foundation, New York.

Levin, B 2010, 'Innovation, transformation and improvement in school reform', paper prepared for *School effectiveness and school improvement*, http://o.b5z.net/i/u/10063916/h/Leadership%20Network%20Sessions/Innovation_book_chapter.pdf

Levy, F & Murnane, R 2004, *The new division of labor*, Princeton University Press, New York.

Louis, KS, Leithwood, K, Wahlstrom, KL & Anderson, SE 2010, *Investigating the links to improved student learning: final report of research finding*, University of Minnesota, Minneapolis & Ontario Institute for Studies in Education, University of Toronto.

MacBeath, J 2006, *School inspection and self-evaluation: working with the new relationship*, RoutledgeFalmer, London.

MacGilchrist, B, Mortimore, P, Savage, J & Beresford, C 1995, *Planning matters*, Paul Chapman, London.

MacGilchrist, B, Myers, K & Reed, J 1997, *The intelligent school*, Paul Chapman, London.

Miles, MB 1975, 'Planned change and organisational health', in JV Baldrige and T Deal (eds), *Managing change in educational organisations*, McCutchen, Berkeley, California.

Miles, MB 1986, 'Research findings on the stages of school improvement', mimeo, Center for Policy Research, New York.

Miles, MB 1987, 'Practical guidelines for school administrators', paper presented at American Educational Research Association, April, Centre for Policy Research, New York.

Miles, MB, Saxl, ER & Lieberman, A 1988, 'What skills do educational change agents need? An empirical view', *Curriculum Inquiry*, vol. 18, no. 2, pp. 157–93.

Miliband, D 2004, *Personalised learning: building a new relationship with schools*, Department for Education and Skills, London.

Mortimore, P 1991, 'School effectiveness research: which way at the crossroads?', *School Effectiveness and School Improvement: An International Journal of Research, Policy and Practice*, vol. 2, no. 3, pp. 213–29.

Mourshed, M, Chijioke, C & Barber, M 2010, *How the world's most improved school systems keep getting better*, McKinsey and Company, London.

Murphy, J 1991, *Restructuring schools: capturing and assessing the phenomena*, Teachers College Press, New York.

Murphy, J 1992, 'School effectiveness and school restructuring: contributions to educational improvement', *School Effectiveness and School Improvement*, vol. 3, no. 2, pp. 90–109.

National College for School Leadership 2006a, *Narrowing the gap: reducing within-school variation in pupil outcomes*, NCSL, Nottingham.

National College for School Leadership 2006b, *Spreading innovation across local authorities: networking and collaboration*, National College for School Leadership, Nottingham.

National College for School Leadership 2006c, *What are we learning about ... establishing a network of schools?*, NCSL, Bedfordshire.

Northern Metropolitan Region 2009, *Powerful learning: Northern Metropolitan Region school improvement strategy*, Department of Education and Early Childhood Development, East Melbourne.

Northern Metropolitan Region 2011, *Curiosity and powerful learning: Northern Metropolitan Region school improvement strategy*, Department of Education and Early Childhood Development, East Melbourne.

The Office for Standards in Education 2006a, *Best practice in self-evaluation: a survey of schools, colleges and local authorities*, Ofsted, London.

The Office for Standards in Education 2006b *Improving performance through school self-evaluation and improvement planning*, DfES & Ofsted, London.

The Office for Standards in Education 2006c, *The logical chain: continuing professional development in effective schools*, Ofsted, London.

The Office for Standards in Education 2009a, *Twelve outstanding secondary schools: excelling against the odds*, report prepared by P Matthews, Ofsted, London.

The Office for Standards in Education 2009b, *Twenty outstanding primary schools: excelling against the odds*, report prepared by P Matthews, Ofsted, Manchester.

The Office for Standards in Education 2011, *Self-evaluation: guidance for inspectors*, Ofsted, London.

Organisation for Economic Co-operation and Development 2004, *Learning for tomorrow's world*, OECD, London.

Organisation for Economic Co-operation and Development 2005, *Formative assessment: improving learning in secondary classrooms*, OECD, Paris.

Organisation for Economic Co-operation and Development 2010, *PISA 2009 results: what makes a school successful? Resources, policies and practices*, vol. IV, OECD, Paris.

Organisation for Economic Co-operation and Development 2011a, *Strong performers and successful reformers in education: lessons from PISA for the United States*, OECD, Paris.

Organisation for Economic Co-operation and Development 2011b, *PISA 2009 at a glance*, OECD, Paris.

Plato, *The republic*.

Plowden, B 1967, *The Plowden report: children and their primary schools*, Her Majesty's Stationery Office, London.

Pont, B & Hopkins, D 2008, 'Approaches to system leadership: lessons learned and policy pointers', in B Pont, D Nusche & D Hopkins, *Improving school leadership, volume 2: case studies on system leadership*, OECD, Paris, pp. 253–74.

Pont, B, Nusche, D & Hopkins, D 2008, *Improving school leadership, volume 2: case studies on system leadership*, Paris: OECD.

Pont, B, Nusche, D & Moorman, H 2008, *Improving school leadership, volume 1: policy and practice*, Paris: OECD.

Porritt, J, Hopkins, D, Birney, A & Reed, J 2009, *Every child's future: leading the way*, National College for Leadership of Schools and Children's Services, Nottingham.

Powell, J 2010, *The new Machiavelli: how to wield power in the modern world*, Vintage Books, London.

PR Newswire 2001, *The danger of 'celebrity' CEOs*, PR Newswire, 15 November, New York, http://www.thefreelibrary.com/The+Danger+of+%27Celebrity%27+CEOs.-a080075307

Purkey, SC & Smith, MS 1983, 'Effective schools: a review', *The Elementary School Journal*, vol. 4, pp. 427–52.

Robinson, V, Hohepa, M & Lloyd, C 2009, *School leadership and student outcomes: identifying what works and why, best evidence synthesis programme*, New Zealand Ministry of Education, Wellington.

Rogers, C 1977, *Carl Rogers on personal power*, Delacorte Press, New York.

Rogers, EM 1962, *Diffusion of innovations*, Free Press, New York.

Rudd, T, Colligan, F & Naik, R 2006, *Learner voice: a handbook form Futurelab*, Futurelab, Bristol, http://archive.futurelab.org.uk/resources/documents/handbooks/learner_voice.pdf

Rudduck, J & Flutter, J 2004, *How to improve your school: giving pupils a voice*, Continuum Press, London.

Rutter, M, Maugham, B, Mortimore, P & Ouston, J 1979, *Fifteen thousand hours*, Open Books Publishing, Somerset.

Sahlberg, P 2011, *Finnish lessons: what can the world learn from educational change in Finland?*, Teachers College Press, New York.

Schleicher, A 2009, 'International benchmarking as a lever for policy reform', in A Hargreaves & M Fullan (eds), *Change wars*, Solution Tree Press, Indiana, pp. 97–116.

Schmuck, RA & Runkel, PJ 1985, *The handbook of organizational development in schools*, 3rd edn, Palo Alto, California.

School Research Evaluation and Measurement Services (SREAMS) 2011, *Student Performance Analyser* home page, Orchard Downs, Red Hill, http://www.sreams.com.au

The Scottish Government 2008, *Curriculum for excellence: building the curriculum 3. A framework for learning and teaching*, Edinburgh.

The Scottish Government 2009, *Curriculum for excellence: building the curriculum 4. Skills for learning, skills for life and skills for work*, Edinburgh.

Secondary Heads Association 2003, *Towards intelligent accountability for schools*, SHA Cymru policy paper 1, SHA, Leicester, December, http://sha.org.uk/Mainwebsite/resources/document/sha%20cymru%20policy%20paper%201%20towards%20intelligent%20accountability%20final%20priced.pdf

Simms, E 2006, *Deep learning*, Specialist Schools and Academies Trust, London.

Slavin, RE & Madden, NA 1999, *Disseminating success for all: lessons for policy and practice*, report no. 30, Center for Research on the Education of Students Placed At Risk (CRESPAR), Baltimore, Maryland.

Stenhouse, L 1975, *An introduction to curriculum research and development*, Heinemann, London.

Stewart, L & Joines, V 1987, *TA today: a new introduction to transactional analysis*, Lifespace Publishing, Nottingham.

Stewart, W 2012, 'Think you've implemented Assessment for Learning?', *Times Educational Supplement* magazine, 13 July, http://www.tes.co.uk/article.aspx?storycode=6261847

Stoll, L & Louis, KS (eds) 2007, 'Professional learning communities: elaborating new approaches' in *Professional learning communities: divergence, depth and dilemmas*, Open University Press, McGraw Hill Education, Berkshire.

Stoll, L 2007, 'Professional learning communities: messages for system leadership and succession planning', in K Carter and T Sharpe (eds), *Stepping up, stepping out: learning about leadership in perspective*, National College for School Leadership, Nottingham.

Stoppard, T 1982, *The real thing*, Faber and Faber, London.

Stringfield, S 2009, *Bold plans for school restructuring: the new American schools designs*, Lawrence Erlbaum, Mahwah, New Jersey.

Stringfield, S & Nunnery, J 2010, 'Whole school designs for enhancing student achievement', in P Peterson, E Baker & B McGaw (eds), *International encyclopedia of education*, 3rd edn, Elsevier Science, Amsterdam, pp. 303–9.

Teddlie, C & Reynolds, D 2000, *The international handbook of school effectiveness research*, Falmer Press, London.

Tunstall, P & Gipps, C 1995, *Teacher feedback to young children informative assessment*, paper presented at the International Association for Educational Assessment Conference, Montreal, Canada, June.

Turner, M 1996, *The literary mind: the origins of thought and language*, Oxford University Press, Oxford.

Vacher, K 2007, 'Deep leadership: the redesigning of education' in K Carter & T Sharpe (eds), *Stepping up, stepping out: learning about leadership in perspective*, National College for School Leadership, Nottingham, pp. 7–8.

Vygotsky, LS 1962, *Thought and language*, MIT Press, Cambridge, Massachusetts.

Watkins, C 2001, 'Learning about learning enhances performance', *Research Matters*, no. 13, Institute of Education School Improvement Network.

Watterson, J & Caldwell, B 2011, 'System alignment as a key strategy in building capacity for school transformation', *Journal of Educational Administration*, vol. 49, no. 6, pp. 637–52.

Weick, KE 1985, 'Sources of order in underorganized systems: themes in recent organizational theory', in YS Lincoln (ed.), *Organizational theory and inquiry*, Sage, Beverly Hills.

Welsh Assembly Government 2008, *Skills framework for 3–19-year-olds in Wales*, Department for Children, Education, Lifelong Learning and Skills, Cardiff.

West, M 2000, 'Supporting school improvement: observations on the inside, reflections from the outside', *School Leadership and Management*, vol. 20, no. 1, pp. 43–60.

West-Burnham, J 2010, *Leadership for personalising learning*, National College for Leadership of Schools and Children's Services, Nottingham.

Whelan, F 2009, *Lessons learned: how good policies produce better schools*, Fenton Whelan, London.

Whitby, K & Walker, M with O'Donnell, S 2006, 'Thematic probe: the teaching and learning of skills in primary and secondary education', *International Review of Curriculum and Assessment Frameworks*, NfER & Qualifications and Curriculum Agency, Slough, Berkshire.

Wood, D 1998, *How children think and learn: the social contexts of cognitive development*, Blackwell, Oxford.

Zbar, V 2011, *Leading from the front: turning around an under-performing school. Case studies in principal leadership*, Northern Metropolitan Region, Department of Education and Early Childhood Development, Victoria.

Zbar, V, Kimber, R & Marshall, G 2008, *How our best performing schools come out on top: An examination of eight high performing disadvantaged schools*, report commissioned by the Data and Evaluation Division, Department of Education and Early Childhood Development, East Melbourne.

Index